Prescriptions Without Pills

"Dr. Susan Heitler has done it again! This book is chock-full of life-changing information, practical exercises, and sound advice. A must-read for all: younger, elder, lay people, clergy, and therapists."

—**Chana Levitan, MSc**, author of
I Only Want to Get Married Once and *That's Why I Married You!*

"Dr. Susan Heitler provides constructive solutions for dealing with the emotional distress we all at times experience. Wish I'd read this twenty years ago! A valuable must-have-on-hand book that I am recommending to family and friends."

—**Linda Keller**, author of *Mother* and *You Can Stop Longing*

"This is one of the most comprehensive and at the same time the most practical self-help books I have ever read.

"Dr. Susan Heitler offers 'drug-free' prescriptions in an age of overdependence on medication for managing emotions. From the outset Dr. Heitler empowers her readers with her underlying assumption that we can all learn to manage our emotions in healthier ways.

"As I was reading Dr. Heitler's prescriptions, I immediately began prescribing them to my clients, which demonstrates the usefulness of the book for therapists, including therapists of any theoretical background.

"I am primarily a couples therapist, so I was especially delighted to see the book's integration of individual therapy methods with couple therapy strategies. Readers can learn much from this book about how to better handle emotions in close relationships.

"Dr. Heitler has presented cutting-edge knowledge about managing painful emotions. She is practical in her approach and concisely offers research backing her prescriptions. There are few if any books like this for the general population, or, for that matter, for therapists and for therapy clients."

—**Professor Claire Rabin**, Tel Aviv University, author of
Winnicott and *"Good Enough" Couple Therapy*

"If you would never seek out a therapist, you still may sometimes want a wise friend to talk to when you hit a really rough patch. Dr. Heitler is that wise, comforting person.

"Drawing on research, wisdom literature, her own loving engagement in life, and years of clinical practice, Dr. Heitler brings you vivid insights to keep you on the path to well-being.

"Read this, and smile as you take Dr. Heitler's medicine."

—**Penelope Tzougros, PhD**, author of *Wealthy Choices: The Seven Competencies of Financial Success*

"Susan Heitler's book *Prescriptions Without Pills* is God sent to those suffering from depression, anger, and grief. It is packed full of carefully designed exercises that will bring you back to life and ground you in the knowing that All Is Well!"

—**Eiman Al Zaabi**, United Arab Emirates, author of *The Art of Surrender: A Practical Guide to Enlightened Happiness and Well-Being*

"Difficult emotions are a part of everyone's everyday living. Dr. Susan Heitler explores the reasons for negative feelings and behaviors. She then provides practical and effective pathways that lead to feeling better.

"The writing style is easy to read. The many case examples are compelling and memorable.

"Readers will especially appreciate the exercises and videos illustrating the prescriptions and aiding readers in implementing them that Dr. Heitler has made available on her prescriptionswithoutpills.com website.

"There is a lot of wisdom in this book, and it will be of great benefit to many. This is an invaluable resource for lay readers and therapists alike."

—**Terry Katz, PhD**, co-author of *Solving Sleep Problems in Children with Autism Spectrum Disorders: A Guide for Frazzled Families*

"In her excellent book *Prescriptions Without Pills*, Dr. Susan Heitler provides easy, effective solutions to help us find relief from negative feelings without taking pills. A must-read for all."

—**Valérie Kristiansen**, author of *The Lost Sheep* and *Finding Life Purpose*

"A valuable guide for identifying feelings and finding the path back to feeling good."

—**Laura Doyle**, author of *First, Kill All the Marriage Counselors: Modern-Day Secrets to Being Desired, Cherished, and Adored for Life*

"*Prescriptions Without Pills* is a practical and easy-to-understand guide to resolving personal challenges. This is a good book! I think Dr. Heitler must be a very good therapist."

—**Renée Jones**, author of *Face Your Stuff, Don't Stuff Your Face: Disarming the Triggers of Comfort Eating*

"I would love to live in a world where everyone had read this book.

"We all have negative emotions and need practical tools to ease them. The tools offered here feel like they will work because they're direct and clear, and we can see how they worked for others.

"It's a joy to read this book, which is amazing for a book about negative emotions. It feels great to follow all of the real-life success stories. We also get clear explanations of why our feelings dip and how we can redirect them."

"I especially like the prescription for anger. Dr. Heitler reminds us that anger is appealing because it mobilizes energy. She then explains the many costs of relying on anger as a strength-booster. The book is empowering."

—**Loretta Breuning, PhD**, author of *Habits of a Happy Brain: Retrain Your Brain to Boost Your Serotonin, Dopamine, Oxytocin, & Endorphin Levels*

Prescriptions
Without Pills

For **RELIEF** from
Depression, Anger, Anxiety, and More

SUSAN HEITLER, Ph.D.

New York

Prescriptions Without Pills

For **RELIEF** from Depression, Anger, Anxiety, and More

Published in New York, New York, by Morgan James Publishing. Morgan James and The Entrepreneurial Publisher are trademarks of Morgan James, LLC. www.MorganJamesPublishing.com

The Morgan James Speakers Group can bring authors to your live event. For more information or to book an event visit The Morgan James Speakers Group at www.TheMorganJamesSpeakersGroup.com.

Shelfie

A **free** eBook edition is available with the purchase of this print book.

CLEARLY PRINT YOUR NAME ABOVE IN UPPER CASE

Instructions to claim your free eBook edition:
1. Download the Shelfie app for Android or iOS
2. Write your name in **UPPER CASE** above
3. Use the Shelfie app to submit a photo
4. Download your eBook to any device

ISBN 978-1-63047-810-0 paperback
ISBN 978-1-63047-811-7 eBook
ISBN 978-1-63047-812-4 hardcover
Library of Congress Control Number:
2015915678

Cover Design and graphics by:
John Boak
johnboak@boakart.com

In an effort to support local communities and raise awareness and funds, Morgan James Publishing donates a percentage of all book sales for the life of each book to Habitat for Humanity Peninsula and Greater Williamsburg.

Get involved today, visit
www.MorganJamesBuilds.com

Habitat
for Humanity®
Peninsula and
Greater Williamsburg
Building Partner

I dedicate this book with deepest love to my family:

To my ever-generous parents,
Harold and Mary McCrensky; may they rest in peace.

To Bruce, my life teammate and soul mate.

To our children and their spouses—
Abigail and Adam, Sara and Ken, Shirli and Jesse, and Rachel and Jacob.

And to their children, our grandchildren Elazar, Boaz, Max, Harel, Isaiah, Niva,
Noah, Ezra, Eliana, Yis, Talya, Orly, Sam, and the one who is on her way.

Table of Contents

Acknowledgments

Warmest thank you . . .

To my clients, from whom I have learned so much and whose stories enrich this volume.

To my multi-talented and ever-supportive secretaries, Janet Olson and Teresa Doty.

To my sister Andrea Kremer, whose feedback enabled me to crystallize the title of this book and the content I wanted to convey.

To John Boak, for the brilliant cover design and creative graphics that bring the main concepts to life.

To Yve Ludwig, Lynn Heitler, Gerry of Zichron, and the many other friends and family members whose suggestions have enhanced both the cover and the contents inside.

To Erin Cusick, Margie Rosen, Bruce Heitler, Steve Krauss, and especially to my highly professional primary editor, Amanda Rooker of SplitSeed, all of whom devoted many hours to honing the text.

To my publisher, Morgan James, and especially my acquisitions editor Terry Whalin, my managing editor Margo Toulouse, my book designer Bonnie Bushman, and the many others who are making my author-publisher relationship there so positive.

To readers Chana Levitan, Hanna Orr, Jim Soda, Penelope Tzougros, and Guy Winch, whose insightful comments contributed vital perspectives.

To my grandson Elazar Hirsch for his help with compilation of the endnotes.

To my office partner and long-time friend Barbara Geller and our valued office suite colleagues Peter Berndt, Helen Coons, Heather McQueen, Lynn Paulus, Dale Petterson, Dan Shoenwald, Heather Wedgle, and Mara Yamshon.

To my editor Lybi Ma and blogger friends at psychologytoday.com. The blog posts I have written for my blog there, *Resolution, Not Conflict*, form the core of the prescriptions in this book.

To Steve Harrison, founder of the inspirational book marketing program Quantum Leap, and the many stellar consultants and friends I have met there.

And with profoundest appreciation, I thank my treasured husband, Bruce. Bruce's deep understandings permeate the book. His devoted editing added critical extra assistance, and his patient support over the many hours of my writing and editing enabled me to make it through to the finish line.

Introduction

On Prescriptions, Pills, and How to Use This Book

Who is this book for?

When my grandson Harel was ten years old, he visited me at my therapy office. Testing out one of the bright yellow armchairs, Harel observed, "You just sit here and talk with people? Sounds like your job is offering psychology to people when they need it."

Psychology for People When They Need It could have been the title of this book. If you are someone who feels in need of help to free yourself from a negative emotion, the prescriptions here aim to give you access to much of what you would learn in my psychotherapy office. If you are a therapist, I hope these prescriptions will expand your repertoire of remedies for helping people who suffer from emotional distress.

In my office, large windows invite the bright Denver sunshine to infuse the room with positive energy. This book aims to illuminate and refresh the dark corners in your life. Calmly joyful contemporary art decorates my office walls. May your feelings of distress give way to similarly uplifted energies.

WHY RELIEF FROM NEGATIVE FEELINGS MATTERS

Why is psychotherapy, self-administered with the prescriptions in this book or implemented by a therapy professional, important?

Emotions can hurt. They actually light up the same pain centers of your brain as physical hurts do. Emotional pain and physical pain both serve to alert you when problems need your attention. Yet sometimes the pain messenger becomes as much or more of a problem as the provoking situation.

In addition to causing suffering, emotional distress can substantially impact your physical health. Unhappiness and anxiety increase your susceptibility to diseases from simple colds to cancer. They also retard your body's ability to heal injuries and illnesses.

Fortunately, psychotherapy can make a difference. Psychotherapy improves both physical health and happiness. One major research project found that when patients diagnosed with a mental health disorder received treatment for their emotional distress, their overall medical costs were reduced by 17 percent. By contrast, the medical expenses of those who received no treatment for their mental disorder increased by 12.3 percent.[1]

Can reading a book have similar impacts on your emotional and physical state as in-person psychotherapy? Research suggests that bibliotherapy such as what you are doing by reading this book can offer effective mental health treatment.[2]

At the same time, adding the assistance of a therapist is always an option. Especially if you are suffering severe emotional symptoms, adding a therapist to your self-help treatment plan may be worth considering.

Life need not be an endurance event. Enable yourself to enjoy yours.

THE PRESCRIPTIONS

The prescriptions in this book give you step-by-step instructions for returning to well-being when you feel down, mad, anxious, or stuck in self-harming habits. The prescriptions in the last chapters then add guidance for prevention of further negative emotional episodes.

When my husband, Bruce, and I were still in graduate school, our first baby arrived. We both were relatively clueless about parenting. With great delight, my husband bundled Abigail up, strapped her into a chest-facing carrier so she could snuggle warmly into his chest, and took her for a walk to enjoy together the fresh air on the Connecticut shoreline where we then were living.

As Bruce and infant Abigail were strolling along the beach, clouds blew in. Bruce turned to head homeward as soon as he felt the first drizzle of light rain. By the time we had unwrapped Abigail at home however, the dampness and chill had plugged up her tiny respiratory system with mucus.

To my husband's credit, Bruce never lost his composure.

"Where is that Dr. Spock book?" he asked me calmly. "I think nurses at the hospital packed it in the box of goodies they sent home with us."

I scurried to look. To my relief, I quickly found the still-unpacked book.

"Let's see what the book says if you look in the index under the word *nose*," Bruce suggested. We'd been married less than ten months, but I knew at that moment that Bruce would be a blessedly reliable life partner.

"*Nose*: If a baby's nose is stuffed, use a syringe to remove the mucus."

I retrieved a blue rubber squeeze syringe from the same hospital new parents' gift box. Two squishes later and Abigail was breathing like a normal infant. Phew!

Why do I share that story? I hope you will similarly turn to the prescriptions in this what-to-do book when emotionally challenging situations arise in your life.

Where do these prescriptions come from?

This book prescribes and describes the techniques I would utilize in my office to help you if I was your therapist. During my forty-plus years of clinical practice in my sunny office space, I have continually asked myself a vital question: "Is this therapy technique enabling my client to leave my office feeling better, with no negative side effects, and with long-lasting benefits?" Effectiveness is the ultimate test of psychological theories and techniques. In this regard, I have tested the prescriptions again and again in my clinical practice.

At the same time, *Prescriptions Without Pills* draws also on psychological research. I especially appreciate studies fostered by Martin Seligman and the other psychologists who launched the field of positive psychology. Understanding healthy functioning clarifies how to transition from episodes of emotional distress back to emotional health.

This book does not aim to offer a comprehensive compilation of psychotherapy techniques for removing emotional distress. There are too many to include, and existing books and workbooks already explain most mainstream treatment methods. Rather, I focus on the techniques that I most often rely upon in my clinical practice.

These techniques put me in the category of *integrative* psychologist. Integrative means that I draw from a broad range of conventional to cutting-edge clinical techniques. Each chapter of this book therefore offers prescriptions for five types of interventions. I think of them as the five L's of effective psychotherapy.

- *Label*: Diagnostic clarity is the first step of treatment.
- *Look back*: Clarify and mitigate the impacts of earlier life experiences on your current emotional reactions.
- *Look at current concerns*: Negative emotions disappear as you find solutions to your current dilemmas.
- *Look ahead*: Understand what your current reactions are trying to accomplish; then create better options for getting there.
- *Learn new skills*: Collaborative dialogue and problem-solving skills help you to stay in the realm of well-being.

Where do the case examples come from?

A picture is worth a thousand words. Case examples—the pictures of this book—illustrate each prescription. For these I have drawn from the experiences of clients I have worked with over the years. To protect client confidentiality, I have changed the names and all identifying details such as vocation or number of children. In occasional instances I condense several similar cases into one composite clinical vignette. I sometimes add fictionalized details of who said what to make your reading experience more engaging. Just about all of the cases, however, are based on real people and the real dilemmas they have faced.

There are two exceptions. One is "Billy" in the chapter on anger. Billy is a fictional child. Second, in Chapter 6 two fictional couples illustrate the communication, conflict resolution, and other collaborative skills that sustain well-being. Tim and Tina show what happens when you lack essential skills. Judy and Justin demonstrate the skills that can keep you humming happily.

WHY NOT PILLS?

Medicines can work miracles. I recently suffered an extreme bout of adult-onset asthma. I might now be dead without the potent medication that reduced the inflammation and reopened my airways.

Similarly, medication can work miracles for mental disorders. Psychological drugs are appropriate, even vital, for Attention Deficit Disorder (ADD), for paranoid states, for the mania and severe depressions of bipolar illness, for schizophrenia, and for psychotic disorders whatever the cause. For mental dysfunction and illnesses like these, pills generally are a first and essential step in treatment. While adding talk therapy can further growth and healing, the starting point for treating these physically based emotional states is medication.

My concerns about pills arise when psychological medications are prescribed as a first step in treatment of the mild-to-moderate depression, anger, anxiety and other disorders that this book addresses. For these, talk therapy with a psychologist or other counselor and/or self-help with the prescriptions in this book are likely to be equally or more effective than medication, and without the potential side effects.

In one of the first classes in my clinical psychology graduate school program, my professor quoted his mentor, Harry Stack Sullivan. Sullivan had maintained that most emotional problems arise from "challenges in living." I continue to believe the same.

Why am I reluctant to regard medication as a first line of treatment for the negative emotional states that stem from challenges in living? First, therapy interventions, such as the prescriptions ahead in this book, work. They bring your body chemistry into a feel-good zone without your having to ingest artificial chemicals. Second, pills can cause harm. Here are the downsides that particularly concern me.[3]

Suppression of alerting mechanisms

One theme that I will reiterate often in this book is that bad feelings are there for a purpose. They alert you to problems that need your attention.

When you solve a provoking problem, negative feelings that the problem situation had engendered evaporate. In addition, you feel good about yourself for having sought and found a solution. How's that for a bonus prize? You become a double winner!

Pills for psychological difficulties, by contrast, work by suppressing symptoms. Taking them can be like taking aspirins for chronic headaches instead of seeking to identify and treat the allergy, eyestrain, or, heaven forbid, brain tumor that was causing the pain.

Opportunity costs

Medication may lead you to think you are doing all you can to resolve a problem when adding a psychotherapy treatment component could be more effective. A number of research studies have concluded that for many emotional distress syndromes, medication plus talk therapy combined offer the most effective and longest-lasting improvement.

Either medication or psychotherapy on their own generally can reduce symptoms. Psychotherapy alone, however, produces longer-lasting improvements than the gains from medication treatment alone.[4] Why does psychotherapy create longer-lasting improvement than taking pills?[5] Psychotherapy encourages insights and teaches skills, both of which continue to prove useful long after treatment has ended.[6] Many psychotherapy techniques also remove problems at their roots, making problems less likely to grow back.

Sadly, when pills do not yield emotional relief, their ineffectiveness may create an impression that no treatments will help. In fact, a wide variety of types of therapists now offer an ever-growing cornucopia of highly effective non-medication-based techniques. If you have been taking medication and/ or have been in psychotherapy treatment without seeing clear improvement, shop around.

Inefficacy

For many people, psychological medications produce little or no benefit. Antidepressant medications in particular have low efficacy rates. Some research suggests that these medications, on average, show only mildly stronger effects than placebos. Other research suggests that approximately 60 percent of people who take antidepressant medications find them effective, which means that four out of every ten people—almost half of depressed people—do not benefit from the medication.[7]

Side effects

Even when they do provide real benefits, psychological medications may not give you a free lunch, i.e., a no-risk solution. Antidepressants may, for instance, cause weight gain, which can impact how you feel about yourself and how attractive you appear to others. When one of my clients gained significant weight from an antidepressant, her marriage deteriorated, creating even worse depression and anxiety.

Antidepressants may decrease sexual arousal, to the detriment of interest in sexual connecting. Like weight gain, disinterest in sex is likely to decrease the happiness of an intimate partner and, therefore, the security of that relationship.

Antidepressant medications give some people a spacey, not-fully-present feeling. They may numb out your positive along with your negative emotions. As one woman recently lamented to me, "I lost out on living twelve years of my life from being numbed out on antidepressants." Antidepressants for severe depression also have been reported to double the risk of suicidal thinking.[8]

In sum, while many people find antidepressant medications effective and use them without experiencing significant side effects, others have far less positive experiences.

Drug termination difficulties

Two significant problems can occur when you discontinue use of an antidepressant medication. One is a withdrawal-induced depression. The second is brain zapping.

Pharmaceutical companies describe antidepressant medications as non-addictive. Technically, this claim is correct. Many of these medications do, however, make you "drug dependent." That is, if you stop taking the drug, and particularly if you do so abruptly, cessation of the medication will inadvertently trigger a depressive reaction.[9] Unfortunately, the depression induced by withdrawal of the antidepressant may be worse than the original negative emotional state for which you sought treatment.

Does drug dependency sound to you like addiction? The two are disturbingly similar. The DSM, one of the official manuals for diagnostic criteria, defines addiction as including a craving for the addictive substance when it is no longer available. Because antidepressant withdrawal does not create a craving ("Oh, I can't wait to have my next dose of . . ."), drug companies can say that antidepressant drugs are "non-addictive." However, while craving may not be present, the medication-induced depression that can be triggered by ceasing to take the drugs is a serious consequence. Your body has developed a habit of relying on the chemicals in the pills to function normally and will punish you with bad feelings if you stop providing them. The consequences of rapid discontinuation of antidepressant medications have actually earned a diagnostic label, antidepressant discontinuation syndrome.[10]

If you have been taking an antidepressant medication for a significant length of time, tapering off your dosage slowly over multiple weeks may enable you to avert a drug-termination depression. Or it may not. If you do taper off slowly and nonetheless experience a depression, beware of concluding that your depression means that you really needed the medication. An equally likely explanation is that removal of the medication caused the depression.

The second potential unpleasant aftermath of long-term use of an antidepressant medication is "brain zapping." Buzzing feelings in your brain that feel like brief electric shocks may occur intermittently for years, long after you have stopped taking the pills.

What about anti-anxiety medications? These pills can induce full-fledged addiction. Benzodiazepines, the most common class of anti-anxiety drugs, can become physically addictive within a matter of a few weeks or, at most, months. Benzodiazepines include the following drugs:

- Xanax (alprazolam)
- Klonopin (clonazepam)
- Valium (diazepam)
- Ativan (lorazepam)

If you discontinue anti-anxiety medications too abruptly after having taken them for some time, your body will demand that you resume them. Sudden cessation of anxiety medication causes nauseous feelings, a pounding heart, sweatiness, jitters, upsurges in anxiety, and other unpleasant physical withdrawal reactions. Worse, sudden withdrawal can be lethal.[11] Do seek guidance from a knowledgeable medical professional if you have been taking these pills and want to stop.

Pills and pregnancy

While a recent study of how a pregnant woman's antidepressant medications impact the fetus yielded somewhat inconclusive results,[12] the chemicals in some of these pills do cross the placenta. Recent studies suggest that Zoloft is safe, but Paxil, as well as some other SSRI (selective serotonin reuptake inhibitor) medications, approximately double the risks of birth defects.[13] Pregnant, potentially pregnant, and nursing women need to weigh the risks to a baby from their medications against the risks to themselves of depressed feelings during and after a pregnancy.

The number of people taking these medications

Pill-taking to soothe negative emotional states is reaching epidemic proportions. According to a 2010 study by Medco Health Solutions, a pharmacy benefits management company, one in five women and one in six to seven men were at that time using one or more medications to lessen emotional distress, a significant increase in usage over prior years.[14]

Given the potential downsides of psychotropic medications, that is, pills to ease psychological difficulties, why do medical professionals write so many prescriptions for them?

Think how often you have seen ads on TV for medications that are supposed to help you feel less depressed or anxious. Because drug companies have been investing heavily in advertising, many people who feel somewhat down or nervous believe that pills are the appropriate response to emotional discomfort. They of course then turn to their doctor or other healthcare professional for help.

Medical scheduling does not allow for the longer session times required for psychotherapy. In addition, other than psychiatrists, most medical professionals have not received sufficient training in non-pharmaceutical options to be able to offer talk or other non-drug emotional relief alternatives. As the saying goes, to a man with a hammer, the world is a nail. Writing a prescription for pills is what medical personnel have been trained to do, including for emotional distress.

At the same time, do keep in mind the flip side of the widespread use of psychological medications. Overall, the pharmaceutical industry has been responsible for a positive revolution in our society's ability to help people with serious psychological difficulties. For the many who suffer from true mental illnesses, from ADD, or from severe levels of depression, anger, and anxiety that non-medication options are not adequately reducing, or who lack access to psychotherapy treatment, pills often do succeed in bringing forth the blessing of emotional health. That's a major contribution.

HOW TO USE THIS BOOK

The prescriptions in this book offer understanding and relief from garden variety, happens-to-everyone depression, anger, anxiety, and bad habits—the unpleasant emotional states and habits that stem, as Harry Stack Sullivan and my graduate school professor said, from challenges in living.

Please feel welcome to enjoy the book like a novel, reading it from front to back.

Alternatively, you may prefer to scan the table of contents for a prescription, an Rx, specific to the difficulty that is troubling you. Like Bruce with stuffed-up-nose baby Abigail, you can keep the book on hand to turn to for remedies in times of distress, using it as a first aid manual for the emotional cuts and bruises of everyday life.

Writing your responses to the book's questions, checklists, and charts can make your reading experience a dialogue that more closely simulates the experience of in-person therapy. While you can answer the questions in the spaces provided, treating the book as a workbook, you also can download most of the worksheets from prescriptionswithoutpills.com.

The prescriptionswithoutpills.com website significantly augments what this book offers. Printing the book's exercises from there will be especially important if you have borrowed a copy of the book from a library or a friend. The website offers videos to illustrate many of the prescriptions plus audio podcasts to guide your visualization treatments. Check out also the free bonuses, blogposts, and other helpful resources that I will continue to post for the Prescriptions Without Pills community.

Visualizations

The prescriptions that utilize visualization sequences ask you to close your eyes to watch images from your subconscious on the movie screen in your mind. Accessing images from your subconscious deepens psychotherapy treatments. Visualizations significantly augment the understandings you would get by simply thinking about a dilemma.

The visualizations generally begin by asking you to close your eyes. It is possible to do the visualizations with your eyes open. Some of my clients prefer to pick a spot to stare at. I sometimes do visualizations when I am walking or running. Eyes open, however, may evoke less clarity and have less emotional impact than doing the same exercise with your eyes closed.

Opening your eyes to read each successive instruction can diminish the depth of the trance-like state. Smooth flow without interruptions enables visualizations to work their magic most effectively. To keep your eyes closed so that you can experience maximum impact from visualizations, play the videos I have posted on the book's website. I pause in these to allow time for your responses to emerge.

Alternatively, consider asking a friend or family member to read the questions, one by one, to you. When a live person reads the questions to you, verbalize aloud the images you see. That way your helper can know when you are ready for the next question. Voicing your images also enables the helper to know when to ask you for additional details that would further enhance the visualization. After you have completed the visualization, debrief aloud together to consolidate the changes that the visualization has brought about.

Yet another visualizations option is to ask a therapist, counselor, or coaching professional to guide you. Bring your book or the visualization script to the session. Psychology professionals have been trained to listen openly (without judging or criticizing you) and to respond helpfully even if the specific visualization you are bringing is new for them.

One final word of advice. Visualizations require radical self-acceptance. Consider whatever images come up for you as valid even if they make no logical sense. Some may surprise you. That's part of the fun and the potency of visualization techniques.

Family-of-origin explorations

Prescriptions that help you to explore how your childhood has influenced your current emotional experiences also can be surprisingly high impact. To benefit fully from these explorations, consider discussing the questions with someone who knew you in your growing-up years. Talking about these experiences with your parents, siblings, or an old friend can be enlightening for all of you.

Ready to get started? Ready, set, go!

Chapter 1

How You Feel and Why

E motions come in oodles of flavors. There's disappointed, hurt, furious, wary, delighted, and a dictionary-load more. Why then does this book focus on the particular emotions mentioned in the subtitle?

Like the three primary colors that create all the colors of the rainbow, three primary negative emotions lie at the heart of virtually all emotional distress: *sad, mad,* and *scared*. In psychological lingo these words equate to depression, anger, and anxiety. Disappointed, discouraged, and hurt are subcategories of sad (depression). Irritated, frustrated, annoyed, and furious describe various intensities of mad (anger). Wary and worried are versions of scared (anxiety).

The fourth negative mental health phenomenon in this book, *addictive habits,* is a behavior pattern rather than an emotion. Addictive habits tend to develop to avoid sad, mad, and scared feelings.

Fortunately, in addition to sad, mad, and scared, there is one more primary emotional state. *Glad* is the emotion you feel in a state of well-being.

R̶x 1.1: TREASURE THIS HAND MAP TO GUIDE YOUR WAY.

Well-being is a state of flow, a mode of focus on whatever you are doing without interruption from critical thoughts about yourself, the activity, or others. Paradoxically, the more you are in a state of well-being, the less you are likely to be aware of what you are thinking or feeling. You just are. You are in the moment, and the moment is fine.

Well-being needn't include joy, laughter, enthusiasm, spiritual elevation, passion, or even moral rectitude. While these positive states give your life bonus points, well-being simply describes the self-accepting state of smooth energy flow that enables you to live primarily in a positive energy zone.

Emotional distress, by contrast, signifies that you have hit a bump in the road. The bump could be an upcoming challenge, like a decision you need to make, a current situation that troubles you, or an upsetting event that happened in the recent or even distant past. Whether you stay distressed or return soon to a state of well-being mainly stems from how you respond to the problem.

Three core premises provide the theoretical foundations for this book's prescriptions for obtaining relief from negative emotions:

- Life inevitably, from time to time, presents everyone with challenging situations.
- Ineffective problem-solving patterns lead to the four primary psychopathologies.
- Resolving issues via effective win-win problem-solving reinstates a positive emotional state.

Five potential pathways for responding to problems

Psychologists sometimes refer to fight-or-flight responses. In fact, as the Hand Map below illustrates, there are five options for responding when you face difficulties:

- **Fold.** Feeling powerless or hopeless about getting what you want, you may give up. The Fold Road leads to depression.
- **Fight.** The Fight Road evokes anger. Anger empowers you to become dominant so that you can win what you want by overpowering the opposition.
- **Freeze.** The Freeze Road creates immobilization, sustaining anxiety. Staring at a situation that looks potentially harmful without gathering

further information or creating solutions augments anxiety within you and sustains tension between you and others.

- **Flee.** The Flee Road leads to addictive habits, habits that distract you from a troubling situation though the problem may fester.
- **Find Solutions.** On the Find Solutions Road, you face a problem squarely. You seek out information to more fully understand both your own concerns and others'. As you create solutions that are win-win plans of action, good feelings surge.

The Hand Map | Five Options for Responding to Problems

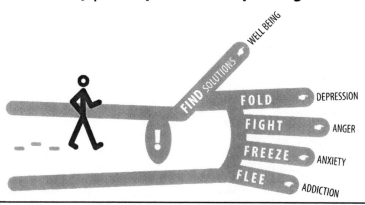

Put your hand out in front of you, palm open; that's your personal and portable version of the Hand Map.

Imagine yourself traveling down the road of life (your arm), journeying merrily along your way until, at your wrist, you hit a difficulty. The dilemma, frustrating situation, choice point, or conflict represented by the bump at your wrist could be a small one. Maybe it has begun to rain and you have no umbrella. Maybe someone said something that hurt your feelings. Or the problem could be a major one like loss of your job, a relationship challenge, or a devastating illness.

From the bump on your wrist—that is, the choice point—you now have five options. The thumb route, Find Solutions, points upwards toward happiness. This route returns you to the land of well-being. Thumbs up! Your four fingers, by contrast, each detour away from well-being. These responses lead you to feeling sad, mad, or scared, or to doing bad, that is, engaging in actions that ultimately hurt you.

Interestingly, humans are not the only ones who rely on at least most of these options. Bears, monkeys, mice, elephants, and other animals large and small all choose from the four nonverbal options whenever they see a potential threat to their safety, survival, source of food and water, or reproductive potential.

Animals, however, lack the ability to talk, denying them the collaborative problem-solving thumb route to well-being. When an animal sees a problem ahead, it can choose only from four options:

- **Fold**, like a smaller elk who defers to a larger elk, giving up on a mate because fighting could result in an injury;
- **Fight**, like a lion who attacks as prey for his dinner a young zebra grazing on the edge of the zebra group;
- **Freeze**, like a deer who suddenly stands still, "like a deer in headlights"; or
- **Flee**, like a rabbit who speeds away to escape you or me if we walk toward him.

Animals often show considerable flexibility in shifting from response to response. A moose, for instance, may Freeze when he first notices you. Then, if you keep walking toward him, he may shift, attacking you with a Fight response. If so, you had better Flee, fast!

People show similar flexibility. Picture, for instance, trying to talk with a friend who is locked in anger at you. If your attempt to discuss the situation collaboratively provokes increasingly angry outpourings, you may try to escalate over your friend with a Fight demand, or decide to Fold, to give up on trying to reach a mutually acceptable solution, at least for the time being. If the anger continues over time, you may eventually decide to Flee. An exit from the relationship may prove preferable to suffering depression or engaging in arguments.

R𝗫 1.2: SELF-DIAGNOSE YOUR NEGATIVE EMOTIONS.

What's in a name? Being able to name something, including feelings, gives you the ability to make choices about it. Naming a feeling begins to give you control over whether you will stay in that emotional state or move forward toward a different one.

Naming feelings launches a good start as well for making your feelings into friends. You probably feel friendlier, for instance, toward someone you vaguely know after you have called him or her by name: "Hello, Joe!" or "Hello, Josephine!" Similarly, giving a name to a negative emotional state shifts it from feeling like a stranger into the realm of potentially becoming an ally.

This friendly attitude, toward even painful emotions, helps you to interact collaboratively with them. No need to fight your feelings, subdue them, chastise them, ignore them, or try to deny them admission into your world. Feelings are your friends. Even the unpleasant ones, you soon will see, are there to help you.

Name that emotional state

Here's a short checklist of indicators that you may be on one of the four distress routes. Checking any symptoms in a category suggests that you may have been experiencing at least some of that type of distress. Multiple checks in a category suggest that attention to that negative emotion is likely to be particularly helpful.

Depression:
- ❑ Feeling down, bluesy, unhappy
- ❑ Feeling hurt, hopeless, or helpless
- ❑ Having frequent negative thoughts about yourself
- ❑ Feeling impatient, easily annoyed
- ❑ Feeling like there's a dark cloud over you
- ❑ Feeling an increased or decreased appetite
- ❑ Oversleeping or awakening in the middle of the night
- ❑ Experiencing self-hatred, extreme hopelessness, or suicidal thoughts

Anger:
- ❑ Irritated, annoyed, frustrated, mad
- ❑ Focusing on what you don't like or on who's to blame
- ❑ Bottling anger within you and later exploding
- ❑ Tempted to say hurtful comments or to strike out physically

Anxiety:
- ❑ Feeling nervous, scared, stressed, or fearful
- ❑ Feeling butterflies in your stomach or a fast-beating heart
- ❑ Tension between you and others (or someone in particular)

❑ Worrying, thinking what if's, envisioning worst-case scenarios

❑ Concerned that others are seeing you negatively

Addictions:

❑ Doing too much of activities that create problems for you

❑ Using excessive alcohol or drugs such as marijuana, narcotics, or cocaine

❑ Compulsively using computers: email checking, Facebooking, games

❑ Exercising, watching TV sports, or working excessively

❑ Gambling or sexual compulsions, including porn watching

❑ Thinking obsessively, including hypochondria or compulsive behaviors

❑ Overeating, under-eating, or binge-purge habits

To what extent are the various types of emotional distress impinging on your life? The chart below can help you clarify their frequency and intensity. There are no right or wrong answers. Fill in the chart with whatever answers come to mind to gain a snapshot of your emotional patterns.

By completing, preferably in writing, your diagnostic self-assessment, you have clarified which specific emotional states you will want to focus on as you read the pages ahead. Note that even mildly negative emotions merit attention. This diagnostic assessment also gives you an initial baseline to which you can return to evaluate your progress.

After you have implemented each chapter of prescriptions, fill in the self-assessment chart a second time. If you find then that you are experiencing fewer and less-intense negative emotions or behaviors, bravo! Hopefully that will be the outcome. At the same time, if too many distressed feelings still trouble you, take them seriously and do consider consulting with a mental health professional.

R_x 1.3: REGARD EMOTIONAL DISTRESS AS HELPFUL.

Emotional distress, like physical pain, indicates you need to pay attention to something. As the Hand Map in Rx 1.1 illustrated, when you are traveling along your road of life and hit a bump, unpleasant emotions tell you, "Something's wrong here! Do something about it!"

Physical pain lets you know when you have an infection, a broken bone, or a malfunctioning body organ. Emotional discomfort lets you know when a situation in your life is problematic.

My Self-Assessment
Download this worksheet at *prescriptionswithoutpills.com*.

	FREQUENCY How often do I feel this feeling? *rarely, daily, all the time*	DURATION How long does it last? *a few minutes, hours, etc.*	INTENSITY How intense is the feeling? *mild, major, overwhelming*
Depression			
Anger			
Anxiety			
Addictions			

Tuning in to even low levels of physical or emotional pain can prove beneficial. Slight feelings of shortness of breath, for instance, could indicate the beginnings of bronchitis, asthma, or pneumonia. Most maladies are easier to treat the earlier you identify them. Similarly, before emotional pain is shouting at you, tune in to the quiet early warning signs of sad, mad, or scared feelings and of potential addictive habits. Taking action in response to nascent distress keeps you in the feel-good zone.

In sum, feelings give you vital information. In this sense, as Rx 1.2 suggested, make friends with your emotions. Know them by name. Pay attention to their messages as you would pay attention to what good friends tell you. While you are unlikely to love emotional pain, you can treasure the information it gives you. Make emotional distress your ally in the project of living in a mode of well-being.

R_X 1.4: CLARIFY THE DILEMMAS IN YOUR LIFE.

Life inevitably presents everyone every day with choice points, that is, situations in which there are a number of alternative ways that you could proceed. Whether consciously or on automatic pilot, at each choice point you are choosing from the five paths clarified by the Hand Map (Rx. 1.1): Fight, Fold, Freeze, Flee, or Find a Solution.

When your alarm clock rings in the morning, you could get mad, feel sad, ignore it while it keeps ringing, turn it off and go back to sleep, or get up with a plan to nap midday. Similarly, if someone criticizes you, your options could include striking back with a return insult, accepting the criticism and feeling hurt, saying nothing but feeling anxious about it, changing the subject to distract yourself, or discussing the criticism collaboratively.

Many synonymous terms describe choice points—for instance, challenges, issues, dilemmas, decisions, conflicts, arguments, problems, and difficulties. In all of these moments, various desires, fears, and preferences may seem to push and pull in contradictory directions. Conflicting pulls indicate that you are facing some kind of conflict, that is, a problem to solve.

People often use the word *conflict* synonymously with the word *fight*. In the way I will be using the term in this book, however, *conflict* is a broader term connoting any choice point. Conflict only creates arguments if one or more of the participants choose to take the Fight Road, that is, to attempt to win by powering over the others. If, by contrast, participants address a conflict by any of the other four routes, arguments do not erupt.

Where do conflicts occur? Three places to look . . .

Conflicts (i.e., dilemmas) emerge in three arenas. They may involve competing preferences within yourself, between you and other people, or between you and external circumstances.

At one point in the writing of this book, I felt a mild sense of depression. What was the conflict I was feeling hopeless about? I had been ill for most of the past week, the week I had taken off from my clinical work to focus on completing the manuscript. My flu overcame my desire to write, leaving me feeling that I was losing my battle with time and also with the manuscript, which seemed unending. Unless I kept writing, I would not be able to complete the manuscript on the timetable I had worked out with my publisher. Still, I felt too tired to keep working.

- **A conflict within yourself**: In the example above, I felt conflict between wanting to take a nap and feeling like I had to stay at my computer to complete the manuscript on time.
- **Conflicts with others**: I had agreed with my publishing company to complete the manuscript by the end of the month. Struggling as I was with my ongoing respiratory illness, I couldn't keep up my end of the

agreement. Publishers set up a production schedule that involves editing, printing, marketing—each of which has time expectations. How would they react to a request to delay the timetable?

- **Conflicts with a situation:** My illness had arrived unwanted. Could I fight it? Should I give in to it? What if it were to linger long term? How and when would I be able to write again?

Fortunately, I was able to address all three conflict arenas.

I asked myself what were my underlying concerns. The main ones were that 1) I was too sleepy to accomplish good writing; 2) my publisher and editors were counting on the timetable we had established; and 3) I saw no way to meet the agreed-upon deadlines.

What might be a win-win solution? Aha! I would contact the various players involved in the publishing project to discuss if I could extend the timetable for an additional month or more. Just thinking about this option immediately lifted my spirits.

Identify conflicts you are facing in each of the three arenas

- **Conflicts within yourself:** In what situation have you felt torn between a *should do* and a *would prefer to do*? Or between competing *want to do*s?

  _____

  Any time you feel caught between differing considerations, between "on the one hand" and "on the other hand," that's a conflict. Difficult decisions are a form of conflict.

- **Conflicts with others:** When has someone recently done something that you have not liked?

  _____

  With whom do you sometimes disagree, feel frustrated, or argue?

  _____

- **Conflicts with a situation:** What circumstances in your life feel undesirable?

  _____

  Problems often induce conflicts in more than one realm, as in the example above of my challenges when I was trying to complete the manuscript for this book. To what extent do the conflict examples you listed above include conflicting considerations in each realm?

R_x 1.5: LOOK FURTHER WHEN EXTERNAL ADVERSITIES APPEAR OVERWHELMING.

Sometimes external circumstances, such as illness, poverty, or political upheaval, leave you few options. When you face extremes of adversity and see no solution options, how do you stay on the road to well-being?

One option is to focus on the elements in your situation that you *can* do something about. Focusing on even the smallest of factors that you can control may foster a mindset of well-being. Natan Sharansky, an impressive man who stands barely five feet tall, focused on details of his interactions with his guards in a Soviet prison to find opportunities to influence them. With his unwavering sense of purpose and powerful intellect, Sharansky conveyed to even the most burly, hostile prison guards that he was the larger man. Sharansky relates this saga in his autobiography, *Fear No Evil*.[15]

Another strategy for coping in adverse circumstances is to focus on gratitude. The more aware you are of your blessings, the less the curses will preoccupy you. Humor also can enable sunshine to penetrate into dark places.

Burt had developed a rare gastrointestinal illness, a painful and debilitating disorder that gave him only brief periods each day of feeling well enough to accomplish work or socialize with friends. Gratitude helped. He appreciated that the medication gave him at least some daily periods of functioning. He appreciated also the Internet where he could connect with sufferers of similar syndromes to share information about their predicament.

Adversity can stir up a potent stew of distress in which all the negative emotions compound each other. Sort out the mixture by focusing on each emotion one by one.

Burt realized that depression would set in if he gave up on finding a cure. Hunting on the Internet for a few minutes each day in hopes of finding a potential medical breakthrough helped him feel that he at least was doing something toward finding a solution.

Lastly, religious faith sustains many people through difficult times. *Waking up* is a Buddhist term for developing an awareness that helps you transcend suffering. Toni Bernhard's *How to Wake Up* explains how to use Buddhist-inspired mindfulness techniques to maintain well-being when you feel bad.[16]

Other religions address this issue as well.

Burt joined a church whose congregation valued offering support to members in need. The new friends boosted his determination to conquer his stomach problem. He began to regard the illness as a blessing that had brought him this loving community.

Onward now to specific prescriptions to help you if you have been heading down one or more of the four detours away from well-being. As you address the adversities that you face, I do hope that you will soon find solutions.

Chapter 2

Depression

Think of a time when you have felt sad, hurt, self-critical, discouraged, or helpless. These feelings all fall into the category of depression, a term that can refer to a broad spectrum of mildly to extremely dark moods.

Carly trudged up the hill on the street that connected her house with her best friend's house. As she slowly plodded upward, her thoughts plunged downward. "Why am I so socially incompetent?" she berated herself. "I hate high school. I feel like such a loser. My friends all have boyfriends. I'm sure no boy ever will want me. How depressing!"

A more severe depression produces intensified versions of these same factors. Self-critical thoughts become self-hating, discouragement becomes hopelessness. In its most extreme forms, depression can become a lethal mental disorder. When depressive symptoms include self-harming or suicidal thoughts, getting professional help is essential. Depression can be fatal.

How long does depression usually last? Like the runny nose of common colds, a wave of mild depression can sweep in causing you to feel "drippy" for a few hours, days, or weeks. Unfortunately, in some cases depression persists for many years.

Carly's depression lifted within a month or two. Her older sister, who attended a college a few towns away, one day invited Carly to go with her to a weekly folk-dancing group on her campus. Carly loved the class. She became a regular. She loved the dancing and especially enjoyed the folk-dance leader, a college freshman named Stan.

Stan and Carly became friends. They started dating. With the blessing of having found a boyfriend, Carly's dark cloud evaporated and her formerly energetic, self-confident emotional state returned in full.

Like Carly, when you are no longer folding, giving up on something important to you, and instead are taking actions that lead to new and better life circumstances, you too are likely soon to feel better.

Rx 2.1: CONSIDER TEN THEORIES TO UNDERSTAND DEPRESSION MORE BROADLY.

The symptoms checklist in Rx 1.2 suggests signs to look for to assess if you or someone you know may be dealing with depression. The following checklist by contrast offers a number of psychological hypotheses about the causes of depression. Each theory clarifies a different aspect of the phenomenon of depressed emotional states.

As you read the list, check the theories that you find especially helpful toward understanding what might have been going on in depressed moods you have felt, now or in the past.

❑ Folding

The core premise of this book is that depression emerges in response to giving up on getting something that you want, to folding in a conflict situation in which what you want meets with opposition. This premise is consistent with all of the following theories.

❑ Lack of purpose

Viktor Frankl, an Austrian psychiatrist and Holocaust survivor who created what he referred to as logotherapy, observed that life always includes some ups and some downs. A sense of purpose or mission can increase your ability to ride your life's roller coaster with resilience. A goal motivates you to keep moving forward without folding in the face of difficulties. Pursuing a mission motivates you to trust that what goes down must eventually come up.

Your mission could be to do good in the world, to raise a family, to care for others, to achieve a work-related or athletic accomplishment, or to pursue any of an infinite number of other potential objectives. Competitive runners, for instance, aim to catch up to the person just ahead of them. Once they have accomplished that goal, they set their next. Successful entrepreneurs similarly harness themselves to goals and press forward, whatever setbacks inevitably occur.

Having a project invigorates you. Notice how children tend to grump and grumble when they feel aimless, then return to good cheer once they have engaged with a toy or embarked on a game. A lack of goals creates what the German sociologist Emile Durkheim called *anomie*, a form of depression. Feeling at a loss as to where you are heading? Hitch your energies to a goal.

Is there a biological basis for the way that goals energize you? Yes, for sure. Movement toward a goal stimulates your body to produce dopamine. Accomplishing the goal, a form of winning, stimulates serotonin production. Both are antidepressant, feel-good chemicals.

Loss of purpose or lack of meaningful goals depletes your stores of dopamine and serotonin. When Olympic athletes, for instance, come home with a gold medal, at first they feel elated. They then may descend into depression. Their initial elation may have depleted their energies for subsequent days. Equally possible, accomplishment of their long-pursued goal may have left them bereft of purpose.

❑ The byproduct of dominant-submissive interactions

Silvano Arieti was a New York psychiatrist born in Italy in 1914. A major contributor to early psychoanalytic thinking and author of the authoritative seven-volume *American Handbook of Psychiatry*,[17] Arieti was the first to note that depression is associated with *dominant-submissive interactions*, that is, with situations in which a person with more power wins and the other, who has less power, loses. This observation comports fully with the idea that depression emerges when you fold, giving up on getting what you want.

❏ Anger turned inward

Another luminary among the early psychoanalytic thinkers, Karl Abraham, explained depression with the short phrase *anger turned inward*. Externalizing, that is, directing your anger outward, only works if you have more power than your adversary. When expressing anger to rectify a situation looks unwise, your anger may seek an alternative target. Anger turned inward, onto yourself, becomes depressive self-criticism.

❏ The negative cognitive triad

One key identifying factor of depressive states is an increase in negative thoughts. Psychologist Aaron Beck coined the term *negative cognitive triad* for the three arenas of negative thinking that typically emerge with depression.[18]

- **Negative thoughts about yourself:** Your inner critic berates you, e.g., "Why did I have to do that?" or "That was a dumb thing to say!"
- **Negative thoughts about others:** "He's so arrogant," or "She sure gets on my nerves."
- **Negative thoughts about the future:** "I'll never earn enough to . . ."

Occasional negative thoughts like these may simply be accurate statements about a current reality. Frequent negative thoughts both indicate and exacerbate depression.

❏ Learned helplessness

In the early 1970s, psychologist Martin Seligman proposed a new way of viewing depression. Depression, he said, could be regarded as *learned helplessness*.

Seligman studied dogs to explore what happened when an animal believed it had no escape or control over a negative event such as receiving a brief electric shock. In situations where animals or people expect that nothing they do will make a difference, they give up on trying.[19]

❏ Negative attributional styles

Seligman later identified three *attributional styles*. This term refers to what you say to yourself about the causes of events in your life. Three kinds of attributions after an event tend to feed depressive reactions:[20]

- **Personal:** Attributing the cause of a negative event to something about you, faulting yourself as opposed to an external cause: "I shouldn't have . . ."
- **Permanent:** Attributing the cause to something you believe you cannot influence or change about yourself. "I'm just not good at math."
- **Pervasive:** Assuming that one bad event represents a broad category of negative events that are, or will be, happening throughout your life: "I always . . ."

When Evan woke up one April morning he discovered that a late spring snowstorm had taken his city by surprise. He was appalled to see that a large snow-laden tree branch had fallen onto his front porch, damaging the porch railing.

"Oh no," Evan sighed to himself.

This situation could have triggered depressive thoughts.

- **Personal:** "It's my fault for having planted a tree so close to my house."
- **Permanent:** "I have bad judgment."
- **Pervasive:** "Bad things always happen to me."

By contrast, Evan, who was not prone to depressive thinking, attributed the porch rail damage to something external, temporary, and specific.

- **External:** "That storm sure was an oddball one. It came so late in the spring. The tree already had big full-grown leaves. The leaves held the heavy wet snow until that huge thick branch eventually snapped."
- **Temporary:** "I'll call a repair service to fix the porch rail and a tree-trimming service. I want to be sure that no more branches will fall on the house just in case we have yet another spring snowstorm."
- **Specific:** "Oh, well. It was just one oddball snowstorm, one fallen branch, one section of the porch rail, and one moment of minor bad luck."

In addition to seeing bad occurrences as external, temporary, and specific singular incidents, people who are not prone to depression react to bad things that have happened by looking for the bright side, counteracting initial dismayed reactions with gratitude.

> "I'm glad that only one branch fell—and on my porch," Evan said to himself. "If the whole tree had fallen, and on the house, it could have knocked a hole in the roof and even injured our baby. He was sleeping in that corner bedroom! Boy, am I feeling lucky!"

Seligman researched how professional athletes reacted to their losses. Sure enough, athletes who described their losses in terms that were personal, permanent, and pervasive had higher odds of losing subsequent athletic events. By contrast, when athletes saw their losses as having been caused by something external, temporary, and specific, e.g., "I wasn't able to sleep well last night and that affected my level of play," they were likely to win in their next event.

Seligman also studied the attributional styles of salespeople. Again, salespeople who blamed periods of low sales on personal, permanent, and pervasive causes tended to give up sooner than those who attributed difficulties making sales to external, temporary, and specific causes. If you are a salesperson who, after you have lost a customer, thinks, "I'm just not good at this," you will feel discouraged. If instead you say to yourself, "That customer looked too distracted when we were talking to be in a buying mode," your morale will stay high.

❑ Depressive collapse

Yet another way to self-diagnose depression is to notice when you feel what I refer to as *depressive collapse*, a feeling of deflation in which:

- The air has gone out of your emotional balloon.
- Your enthusiasm has given way to disinterest or giving up.
- Your desire to get up and go has given way to feeling out of gas.

Self-confidence and tenacity increase your likelihood of success. Anger also pumps up your energies so you feel strong. By contrast, when depression collapses your inner moxie, your ability to sustain a project—for instance, exercise, diet, or launching an entrepreneurial venture—wanes.

In addition to collapsing your enthusiasm, determination, and optimism, depression causes your body's immunological system to weaken. In the Introduction, I mentioned that emotional distress increases medical problems and retards healing. Depression in particular lowers resistance to germs, bacteria, and viruses, making you more susceptible to colds, flu, and other communicable diseases. And as depression retards your body's healing capacity, injuries and illnesses heal more slowly.[21]

> In a study of the impact of depression on wound healing, nurses were each given a minor puncture wound on one arm. Researchers then each day measured the size of the redness around the wounds and had the nurses fill out emotional state questionnaires. When nurses reported feeling depressed, their wounds took longer to shrink, indicating slower healing.[22]

Physical strength also decreases when a person feels depressed.

> To help Raymond, a professional baseball player, understand the concept of depressive collapse, I arm-wrestled with him. Needless to say, Raymond could push my arm down like a reed in the wind.
>
> I then asked Raymond to visualize a situation that had distressed him. Raymond's powerful throwing-arm muscles weakened to such an extent that I was able to match his strength. I am female, and at the time I was already approaching retirement age, so our arm wrestling showed a major drop in power for him.

❑ Grief

The disappointment that you experience after you, or your favorite team, lose in a sporting event is a mini-episode of depression. Losing gives you no option but to fold and give up. In this sense, depression overlaps significantly with grief.

> Raymond mourned, crying profusely, when his dad died. His dad had long been his most ardent supporter and also his main confidant. Grief undermined his ability to function at a professional level on the baseball field until Raymond discovered that he could keep his dad alive in his thoughts

during games. Carrying on an inner dialogue with his dad diminished the sense of loss. "Okay, Dad, I'm going to bat this time for you!"

If a loss also brings up anger at yourself, the sadness may devolve into depression.

Earlier in his career, Raymond had had an opportunity to play in an important baseball exhibition game in Canada. When he arrived at the airport, he was shocked to realize that his passport was outdated. Without a valid passport, Raymond was unable to board the plane. He consequently lost the opportunity to play the exhibition game.

Raymond felt furious at himself. For months afterwards he felt mired in depression. During this period he performed so poorly on the field that his coaches considered dropping him from the team.

❏ Hurt feelings

Young children, and adults as well, often say, "You hurt my feelings!" Hurt feelings indicate a depressive emotional reaction if you feel that the other person has won or at least dominated in your interchange.

Even a faintly negative tone of voice can deflate the receiver. Harsh words worsen the hurtful impacts. Verbally/emotionally abusive behaviors like sarcasm, a contemptuous tone of voice, excessive criticism, and name-calling, even without physical violence, can induce the serious depression that therapists refer to as battered woman (or man, or child) syndrome. For more on this issue, see Rx 3.1.

An exercise

Close your eyes. Allow an image to arise of a time when you have felt depressed.

The situation: _____

Which of the theories above helps you to understand what you experienced in that situation? Odds are, they all apply.

❏ **Heitler:** Did you fold, giving up on getting something of importance to you?

- ❏ **Viktor Frankl:** Did you experience a loss of purpose?
- ❏ **Silvano Arieti:** Were you in a dominant-submissive interaction, that is, folding in response to feeling like the other side had more power?
- ❏ **Karl Abraham:** Did you get mad at yourself (anger turned inward)?
- ❏ **Aaron Beck:** Did you experience the cognitive triad of negative thoughts about yourself, others, and your future?
- ❏ **Martin Seligman:** Did you experience learned helplessness in that situation, feeling that nothing you could do would fix the problem?
- ❏ **Martin Seligman:** To what cause did you attribute the problem? To a factor that was *personal*, that is, your fault? Was this factor a *permanent* feature or a transient factor? Did you feel that the problem indicated not just a one-time situation but rather a *pervasive* negative condition?
- ❏ **Depressive collapse:** Did you experience a sense of energy deflation?
- ❏ **Grief:** Did you experience a loss? Do you still feel the sadness?
- ❏ **Hurt feelings:** Who in your life sometimes does or says things that hurt your feelings?

Your growing understanding of depression can help you to self-diagnose depression as it first is emerging. As with any medical or emotional disorder, the earlier that you diagnose a potential depressive episode, the more effectively you are likely to be able to summon fresh breezes of positive energy to whisk away the depressive cloud and keep the sun shining.

Rx 2.2: APPRECIATE HOW DEPRESSION MAY PROTECT YOU.

Rx 1.3 suggested that negative emotions can be like friends that come forth to help you. How could this idea possibly be true of the demoralizing feeling of depression?

Like joy, anxiety, and anger, depression causes specific biochemical changes in your body. In the case of depression, your levels of serotonin drop. Serotonin is generally a "happy chemical"[23] that makes you feel good. What could be the function of this drop in serotonin?

Serotonin rises when you feel larger or higher in status than others. Serotonin drops when you feel yourself to be smaller, lower in status, or in any way less powerful. The serotonin drop tells you not to try to fight for what you want. It tells you that fighting will likely prove unsuccessful because your opponent is more powerful than you.

Serotonin rises and falls similarly in animals. Animals who face a potential conflict make a lightning-quick assessment of relative power.

> A small baboon senses immediately who is more powerful if a larger baboon makes menacing gestures indicating that he is about to eat the small fellow's recently killed prey. When the small baboon's serotonin drops, it saves him from injury by telling him to slink away.
>
> The small baboon is smart to give up on enjoying his hard-earned lunch. If he and the big baboon were to fight, that could be dangerous. Blood and limb losses pose survival risks. Baboons cannot go to the hospital for help. Better to go hungry than to get gored or wounded. The serotonin drop protected him. A low level of serotonin took away his will to fight.

Many situations in which you have lesser power do not evoke depression. When a kindly parent, teacher, policeman, or employer exerts authority over you, you are likely to feel fine, and maybe even appreciative, in spite of the unequal power relationship. Instead of threatening you, benign authorities help, coach, protect, and, if the authority is your employer, even pay you. Hierarchy yields depression only if a more powerful person threatens to hurt you or blocks you from getting something you want. That's when power asymmetry triggers a drop in serotonin, the impulse to give up, and depression.

A journalist interviewing me on the topic of anger once told me of her tendency to give up in arguments with her husband. "I'd rather be married than right," she admitted. You too may give up on trying to convey your point of view if insisting could cause arguments that might damage a key relationship. Sustaining relationships, like preventing physical injury, can be of higher importance than winning a disagreement.

Meanwhile, when you feel depressed, remind yourself that the powerless, hopeless feeling of depression in some way may be trying to help you.

When has depression enabled you to stay safe? _____

When has depression enabled you to stay in a relationship that you valued?

Better to learn how to have both, how to keep your connections and also have your concerns taken into account. Chapter 6 will explain this skill set, a skill that I call the *Win-Win Waltz*. That's a dance well worth learning.

R$_x$ 2.3: IDENTIFY SITUATIONS IN WHICH YOU HAVE BEEN TEMPTED TO FOLD.

Rx 1.4 familiarized you with the three realms in which conflicts tend to occur: within yourself, between you and others, and between you and an undesirable circumstance. Identify thoughts and feelings in each of these three arenas that might have tempted you to handle conflicts by folding, or giving up on what you want.

Within yourself

- When might you bully yourself, for instance by *should* messages? "I *should* be saving more money"; "I *should* be more outgoing"; "I *should . . .*" List *should* thoughts that sometimes come up in your thinking:

  _____

- While dominating thoughts often take the form of *should* and *have to*, they also may spring from strong fears, desires, or values. What strong fear, desire, or value sometimes controls you excessively?

  _____

- What sometimes helps you to stand up to bullying or dominating thoughts?

  _____

Between you and others

- **At home** (with family and/or a loved one): With whom might you sometimes fold, thinking that this subordination is necessary to stay safe and/or to sustain the relationship?

  _____

- **At work:** With whom might you sometimes give up rather than risk a conflict?

  _____

- **With others:** With whom else do you tend to be reluctant to stand your ground (e.g., with friends, salespeople, a neighbor, community members)?

_____

Between you and difficult circumstances

- What adversities have felt overwhelming to you? Illness? Living in a dangerous neighborhood? Not enough money? Other undesirable life circumstances?

_____

R͓x 2.4: Alleviate depression with a *Three P's* visualization.

Sometimes you may not know what situation has been triggering a depression. Paradoxically, you will be able to see more with your eyes closed. Use the following eyes-closed visualization to identify the cause of the depression so that you then can find new solutions to the triggering problem. With the creation of a satisfying solution option, the depression will lift away like a fog on a bright, summer day.

Please refer to the Introduction for suggestions on how to do the visualization prescriptions. See also prescriptionswithoutpills.com for video examples and downloadable worksheets.

The *Three P's* for Ending Depression

Pinpoint ⇨ Pump-up ⇨ Problem-solve ⇨

Sit in a comfortable chair and close your eyes. As you read or a friend, a family member, my voice (via the website video), or a psychotherapy professional reads the following questions to you, observe the images that appear on your mental screen.

PINPOINT the triggering event.

- **Ask,** if you were to feel irritated or mad at something or someone other than yourself, what image comes up on your visual screen? This question identifies the trigger for your depressive collapse. Adding *other than yourself* prevents you from falling into the depressive trap of self-blaming.
- **Fill in the details** of what is going on in the scene: Who is there? What are they doing, thinking, and feeling? If you are not already in the scene, add yourself. Notice what you do, think, and feel. What do you want in that scene that you have not been getting?

This scene clarifies who or what has been provoking you. The last question clarifies specifically the issue about which you have been giving up.

- **Who appears bigger**, you or the other person or thing? By a little or a lot? By a factor of how much (e.g., slightly bigger, way bigger, about five times larger)?

Physical size in the image equates with your psychological sense of power. Seeing yourself as smaller than the other confirms that the incident you are envisioning is triggering depression. The smaller you are compared to the other, the more powerless you are feeling.

PUMP UP your sense of personal power.

- **Inhale a deep, cleansing breath,** and release it slowly.
- **Visualize yourself becoming bigger** with each subsequent breath, growing larger, and even larger, maybe even HUGE like a cartoon character. Keep growing with each inhalation until you have reached a size that feels satisfying.

- **Pause** after each deep breath to ask what size you are now relative to the other. Does that size feel large enough? If you are not yet as much larger than the other than you would like to feel, take more breaths to invite more growing.

Feeling larger than the person or circumstance you are dealing with enables you to see the situation in a new way. Larger size empowers you to think of new solutions and to be able to take effective action. Some people are satisfied with being just slightly larger. Most people grow to a significantly bigger height.

Remember that height represents power. The relative sizes of the participants represent relative power.

PROBLEM-SOLVE by creating a new solution to the problem.

- **See new factors**. From your new and larger subjective state of power, what data can you see that you hadn't noticed when you were feeling smaller?

  Many people answer, "I see the top of his head!" All answers are right answers. At the same time, continue to ask for more information. "What else do you notice about the situation? What else do you notice now that you couldn't see when you were smaller?"

- **Find new solution options**. With the new information that comes from your re-empowered perspective, what option for solving the dilemma might yield a more gratifying outcome?

- **Visualize implementing this idea**. What would happen next? If the new solution option, for instance, is to step on and squash the other person, ask what would happen next if you were to do that.

- **Stay with this process until you find a solution you might want to implement in reality**. If the answer involves hurting someone or is ineffective in any way, ask what further option comes to mind that would have outcomes that you might like even better. Again, if the outcome looks insufficient, create yet another alternative until a plan of action that looks both realistic and effective has emerged.

The following example illustrates how this series of questions prompted a healing visualization for Barbara, the client I mentioned in the Introduction whose antidepressants had resulted in significant weight gain.

PINPOINT the problem.

- **At whom or what are you angry?** If you were going to be mad at someone or something *other than yourself,* notice what image comes up of whom or what you could be mad at.

  Barbara saw herself playing with her two children outdoors in their sandbox. Her husband, Paul, then entered the scene. Instantly Barbara's happy mood switched to fury at Paul.

- **Fill in the details**.

  The children and Barbara had been chattering together, cheerfully building a sandcastle. When Paul entered, the children leapt up to greet him, knocking over their sandcastle in their enthusiasm to be the first to hug him. Paul loved the children's effusive greetings.

  Barbara felt furious at Paul and abandoned by the children. From her perspective, Paul's arrival had "upset their apple cart," wrecking her lovely interactions with the children and their sandcastle and causing her to feel left out. She wanted Paul to notice her too, not just the children. She wanted him to greet her first.

- **Check relative sizes**. Who appears bigger, you or the other? By a little or a lot?

  Barbara felt small, "the size of a flea." Paul looked huge, "like a joyful giant."

A large size differential like this indicates a severe depressive reaction, which was consistent with the intensity of Barbara's depression.

If there are no size discrepancies, with both people looking equal-sized, the scene probably does not indicate the depression trigger. In this case, ask toward whom or what else are you feeling irritation, frustration, or anger.

Alternatively, equal sizes can indicate that the distressed feeling you had labeled depression is actually another emotion such as anxiety. In this case, the visualization has clarified the diagnosis. In addition, it still can launch useful problem-solving.

PUMP UP your size.

- **Grow.** Take a deep breath. With each breath, feel yourself growing larger. Picture yourself growing tall, like Alice in Wonderland, shooting way up in size.

Barbara had difficultly allowing herself to grow large. Even with encouragement, she initially grew only slightly larger than Paul. I asked if she was satisfied with this size. When she replied no, I encouraged her to take more breaths. Gradually Barbara grew, until eventually she described herself as a giant, taller even than her husband. She smiled, indicating satisfaction with the new proportions.

PROBLEM-SOLVE, looking for new options.

- **Augment your data**. From this new height, this stronger perspective, what can you see now that you may not have noticed before, when you were smaller? About the other person? About yourself? About the situation?

Barbara said, "I see that Paul had no idea that I was in the sandbox. He probably didn't mean to exclude me. He just totally loves when the kids adore him. Maybe I've been taking this scene too personally, as a rejection of me, when it's really all about him. That's Paul; it's 'all about him.' When I see him as doing what he loves—being adored—rather than as intending to exclude me, I feel better."

- **Find new solution options**. Knowing what you now know by seeing the scene from this higher perspective, what are some new ways you might handle the problem that might be more effective in getting you what you want?

"Well, I still don't really enjoy the scene," Barbara mused. "I could get up, though, and go do something I want to do somewhere else when Paul first arrives home. I could take his arrival as an opportunity for me to have some time off. My concern about that solution, though, is whether Paul and I would ever connect. I'd probably feel all the more like an outsider in my own family."

- **Check the outcomes of each option**. If unsatisfactory, seek more options.

"Maybe I could pop up like the kids do and join the race to hug Paul. That feels uncomfortable, though. I would feel like I'm competing with the kids for Paul's attention. Ugh.

"Here's a better idea. Maybe Paul and I could talk. Instead of yelling at him for ignoring me, which is what I've done in the past, I could talk quietly with him one evening after the kids are in bed. I could explain to him how upset I get when I feel left out. I could add that it's not his fault that I feel left out. I often feel that way. Then the odds would go up that he might not get mad at me for having a vulnerable feeling. In that case, we could together re-choreograph a 'hero coming home from the war' routine. He always wants to be greeted as a hero. Maybe he and I could agree that first we'll kiss, and then the kids can get their hugs."

Debrief

Once the visualization has yielded a positive plan of action, open your eyes to discuss what you have discovered. You are likely to feel lighter. You may feel a pleasant sense of personal strength. Impulses to criticize yourself are likely to have dissipated, supplanted by well-being, self-acceptance, and gratitude.

"Yes," Barbara mused. "I feel a pervasive sense of okay-ness. Like, I can do this. And Paul can do this with me. Amazing. I even feel affection toward him—and fortunate to have such a special husband. He really is my hero."

With your eyes closed and the right initial questions (e.g., "Who or what are you mad at?"), the exact triggering problem becomes visible. As you become re-empowered you no longer feel hopeless and helpless. Then you can direct your problem-solving energies at the specific bump on the road that sent you down Depression Road.

As new solution ideas emerge, you may be tempted to wonder why you hadn't thought of that idea earlier. Effective solutions seldom come to mind when you approach a problem from a stance of weakness. A victim rarely can imagine solutions that seem obvious to an equal- or greater-strength person. New solution ideas emerge when you feel strong.

In addition, your depressive collapse may have been protecting you, as suggested in Rx 2.2, from trying to implement solutions from a position of weakness. That may be fortunate if your solutions would have been reactive, like railing in anger. A victim-based action plan might have brought more emotional injuries instead of happiness.

In contradiction to the depressive belief that the situation is hopeless, the *Three P's* visualization protocol assumes that solutions always do exist. Trying out an action plan by visualizing it enables you to see if your plan is insufficient or has potential to be worth giving it a try. Most vitally, once you have visualized yourself being effective, the odds rise that you will in the real world be able to accomplish your goal.

R$_x$ 2.5: RELIEVE CHILDHOOD-BASED DEPRESSION WITH *THAT WAS THEN, THIS IS NOW.*

As many have said, history is not destiny. At the same time, your personal history may give you clues about where the intensity of feelings and the thoughts and habitual actions in some of your responses to a current situation originated. Intense emotional reactions often are fed by feelings that first arose in an experience earlier in your life. Also, earlier life experiences form templates for later life reactions to similar experiences. Seeing the sources of your ineffective reactions frees you up to explore new response strategies.

Exercise: *That Was Then, This Is Now*

Sit in a comfortable chair and close your eyes. Ask, or ask someone else to ask you, the following series of six questions. Pause after each question to let the answers gradually arise to conscious awareness. Verbalizing the answers aloud is preferable.

- **Close your eyes.**
- **Picture, as in the prior exercise,** where the feeling is located in your body and how it feels.
- **Allow an image to appear** on your visual screen of an earlier time when you experienced a similar feeling. How old were you then?
- **What is the same** then and now? Give details.
- **Identify what is different** now that can enable you to feel more safe and to handle the situation with an option available to a grown-up.
- **Older consoler**: Is there an older part of me that can console the younger distressed part of me? If so, let that voice console the younger me.
- **New solution plan:** Given these deeper understandings of myself, what might be more effective ways of handling the present situation?
- **Check again how the feeling looks** and feels in your body. If pieces remain, find solutions for these, perhaps with *Do or Become* (Rx 6.8).

Notice what you feel by the end of the visualization. Notice what you have learned from it. If someone has been reading the questions to you, discuss together your observations and conclusions.

Childhood experiences with depression

Before moving on to learn more about utilizing *That Was Then, This Is Now*, it can be interesting for you to recall examples of depression that you may have observed growing up. Close your eyes and allow scenes from your childhood to come up on your visual screen in response to the following questions.

Did any people close to you experience depression? _____ If so, who?

_____

What do you think you may have learned from this person's example of what depression looks like and what to do when you feel it?

_____

What might you want to do differently when you feel down?

_____

Did either of your parents defer excessively to the other and then pay the price in depressive episodes? _____

Did one of your parents experience a loss such as a financial setback or a death in the family from which recovery proved particularly difficult?

_____

Did anyone in your past experiences expect you to give up on what you wanted and instead respond only to his or her preferences or demands?

_____

Where else, such as with friends or at school, may you have learned to give up on what you want?

_____

As a child, when did you feel powerless, sad, discouraged, or troubled with a feeling that you would now label as depression?

_____

A dramatic instance of suppressed childhood depression

In the following case, Jennifer explored a childhood depression with a variant of *That Was Then, This Is Now*. The format was somewhat simpler, but the content was similar to what she would have discovered with the sequence of questions in the visualization.

I asked Jennifer to close her eyes and allow images to arise of anyone she might have known as a child who might have experienced depression.

Vivid scenes immediately flooded Jennifer's mind. The event that she visualized, which had occurred when she was six years old, had suddenly shattered her happy family.

Jennifer and her toddler-aged sister had been playing on the sidewalk in front of their house. A motorcyclist suddenly sped by, lost control, and skidded straight into her little sister, killing her.

Jennifer's mother never fully recovered from the shock, guilt, and depression of this loss. The result was that Jennifer, though still a young child, essentially took over as the primary parent for her remaining younger siblings.

Jennifer often felt abandoned. Her mother remained trapped in grief for years, and her father, who worked long hours, was seldom present. No adults were there to console her through her own grief over the loss of her sister, to help her with the many tasks of running their household, or to support her through the normal throes of childhood.

If you are prone to experience depression like Jennifer, you also may have experienced an upsetting incident in your earlier years that is relevant to current depressed feelings. Though not necessarily as extreme as what Jennifer experienced, that experience may have yielded a template for depressive reactions in your adult life.

Together in couples therapy, Jennifer and her husband, Peter, both benefitted from understanding the childhood sources of Jennifer's intermittent waves of depression. Peter discovered that if he walked over to Jennifer and hugged her when she looked sad and unapproachable, within minutes she felt better.

If Peter then asked his wife what she had been thinking about, Jennifer's depressive cloud lifted even faster. Jennifer would often note something happening that had some element in common with having felt so profoundly unnoticed as a child. She might, for instance, have wanted to talk with Peter when he was absorbed in reading the newspaper. That desire could easily trigger the six-year-old scared, lonely, and grieving part of her. She then would become mute, sinking into a depressive torpor.

By understanding the link between her present situation and her past, Jennifer could think to herself the mantra *That was then; this is now.*

As Jennifer described it, "Then I just need to say, 'Peter,' and my husband will look up and want to talk with me." Jennifer could then laugh with pleasure. The depressive episode would dissipate. And Peter, who adored Jennifer and loved feeling needed by her, glowed.

Childhood grief

As a child, did you experience any major losses?

_____

If so, your template for early grieving may double as a template for depression. Identifying the reaction can help you to distinguish, as Jennifer does in the example above, what was similar in the earlier experience to the present, and what in the present is different and therefore can free you up to have a different emotional reaction. *Then*, I had a great loss. *Now*, I am just suffering a minor setback.

When have you experienced depressive episodes that felt similar to the grief you felt at the early loss of your loved one?

_____

What was the same in that (recent) incident as during your earlier loss?

_____

And what is different for you now?

_____

In summary

If your answers to any of the above questions indicated vulnerabilities from childhood experiences, your depression risk may be higher than the norm. Current losses and experiences of giving up on something of importance to you may trigger a particularly strong emotional reaction. In addition, recovery may feel more difficult.

Parental depression and also, interestingly, childhood shyness further can indicate a genetic/biological predisposition toward depressive reactions. If so, pay particular attention to the prescription just ahead for strengthening yourself emotionally. These emotionally uplifting activities could make an especially significant difference for you.

Childhood experiences can create templates for depressive reactions later in life. Though initially we may imitate our parents or my learn to give up because of early life losses, learning new patterns and skills is always an option. Conflict resolution patterns mostly are learned, not genetic. The more solidly you learn to do the *Win-Win Waltz* and related skills that you will be learning in Chapter 6, the more consistently you will be able to stay on the thumb route to well-being.

In the meanwhile, any time that depressed feelings come up, asking yourself some or all of the *That Was Then, This Is Now* questions can prove enlightening and hopefully soothing as well.

R_x 2.6: Strengthen yourself with *AGGRESS-N*, eight natural antidepressants.

AGGRESS-N is my acronym for eight factors that can strengthen you emotionally vis-à-vis depression. The same eight factors can also help you to reduce anger, anxiety, and addictive habits. Use them to create a surge of positive energy and, with it, emotional sunshine.

Notice the similarity between the words *aggression* and *AGGRESS-N*. Getting aggressive by taking the anger route to get what you want also can prevent depression. As a young man once said to me, "When I fight, I feel good." If you fight for a positive cause, that kind of fighting can, in fact, give your life meaning, purpose, and an energy boost. Aggression, however, in the usual sense of fighting carries the risk that you may feel better by making the receiver of your angry words and actions feel worse. While that outcome may sometimes feel tempting, hurting others is likely eventually to have unfortunate impacts on everyone involved.

The eight *AGGRESS-N* factors, by contrast, like the other prescriptions in this book, have little to no apparent downside, yet bring many benefits.

AGGRESS-N | 8 Natural Anti-Depressants

Attitude
Gratitude
Giving
Relationships
Exercise
Sleep
Sunshine
Newness

The Eight *AGGRESS-N* Natural Antidepressants

Rate yourself from 0 (not doing this at all) to 10 (totally) on how willing you might be to incorporate this factor into your anti-depression treatment plan.

☐ A—Attitude shift

Switch your view of yourself from seeing yourself as a victim to seeing yourself as a primary actor. A *poor me* victim stance perpetuates depression. "Look what you have done to me!" keeps you feeling powerless. Believing that you are the victim of circumstances, others' misbehaviors, or anything external can leave you waiting helplessly for others to change. Instead, seize control by asking yourself, "What could I do differently to get a better outcome?"

Remember, depression is a disorder of power. Regain your sense of personal empowerment by reminding yourself that there always are actions that you can take to address your problems. Already your depression will begin to lift.

Interestingly, even the simple act of starting your sentences with the word *I* can put you back in the driver's seat of your life. Rx 6.2 will explain this phenomenon more fully, but for now, here's a preview of coming attractions.

"He made me feel . . ." creates feelings of powerlessness. By contrast, "I feel . . .," puts you in control. When you make yourself the subject of your sentence by starting sentences with the pronoun *I*, this small wording change has big impacts. It raises your power level and points you toward problem-solving.

Feel the difference between these two approaches:

- "*He makes me* mad."
- "*I feel mad* when he's late for dinner . . . so I think I'll start aiming for us to eat a half hour after the time we agree on. Then we can sit and enjoy a few quiet minutes together before dinner if he's on time. If he's late, we'll be right on time."

Keeping an empowered attitude can help you in even the most difficult situations. Rx 1.6 introduced this potent secret to emotional resilience. The examples there of the former Soviet political prisoner Natan Sharansky and of my client Burt illustrated staying activated instead of succumbing to believing that you are a helpless victim of external circumstances.

The following case, a Holocaust story, illustrates this principle. Selma died more than a decade ago. This is the only example in this book in which I use the person's actual name. I say Selma's name to honor her memory.

I met Selma over thirty years ago when she attended a lecture on depression that I was giving for the staff at the hospital where my office is located. I still remember Selma clearly because she exemplified so dramatically the refusal to slide into a victim mode.

During the lecture, I suggested a dilemma. What would you do if you stayed late at work and then discovered, as you were ready to leave, that the exit door was jammed? Most people in the group offered a suggestion or two and then gave up, succumbing to a depressive collapse. Selma, by contrast, offered one idea, then another, and another, and then yet another ingenious way to exit the building.

I was impressed. After the session, I asked Selma how or why she had become so inventive, never giving up in a situation that others quickly regarded as hopeless.

"When I was growing up in Eastern Europe in the 1940s, my mother, my sister, and I lived for three years fleeing the Nazis. We hid in forests and barns, moving on each time our hiding places looked at risk. We knew that giving up meant death. Each time we faced a new danger, we found yet another option. That's how we survived, taking care of each other and always thinking of alternatives."

Selma and her family faced life-threatening challenges every day. Their attitude of persistent determination to Find Solutions, even in the most seemingly hopeless circumstances, can inspire us all.

What are the costs of defining yourself as a victim?

_____

When have you been effective at active problem-solving?

_____

❑ G—Gratitude

Remember the old saying about seeing a glass as half empty or half full? Even if you feel understandably depressed about a negative circumstance, somewhere in your life there are elements you can feel grateful for. Gratitude is empowering. Empowerment counters depression.

Burt, in Rx 1.6, accessed gratitude to counter the impulse to give up and sink into depression. So did the couple in the following example.

Dana and his wife, a vibrant newlywed couple, traveled to Hawaii for a vacation. As soon as they arrived at their seaside condo, they headed to the beach where the sparkling surf lured them in for a quick swim. The first wave surprised Dana with its power. The wave pummeled him, head-first, straight into the sand. Dana intuitively protected his head by reaching out with one hand to cushion his fall. As he stood up after the wave had receded Dana realized that the wave that had slammed him down had broken a bone in his arm.

When Dana returned from the hospital with a cast, he and his wife sat on their patio and talked over what had happened.

"At first I was so mad," he told his wife. "I won't be able to play tennis or swim or do any of the sports I had thought we'd be enjoying here. Then I realized how lucky I am. Good thing I've always done so many sports. If I weren't so strong and didn't have such quick reflexes, that wave could have given me a major head injury or even cracked open my skull so I ended up dead. I feel so fortunate!"

If you have been feeling down, how might you shift your focus toward more gratitude?

❑ G—Giving

Most people have heard the saying, "Pick a card, any card." It turns out that if you pick a recipient, any recipient, and give attention, affection, or money—if you give in any positive mode to any person or cause—your body will spurt forth a quick shot of the chemistry of feeling good. Lovingly taking care of a child, elder, pet or even a stranger can help you as much as you help them.

Cole was driving in his car, feeling discouraged about his life. His girlfriend had left him, and now his work situation was showing signs of fraying. While he waited at a traffic light, a disheveled older man standing in the center of the road walked up to his car. "Can you spare some change?" Cole reached into his pocket and pulled out a five-dollar bill.

The old man's pale blue eyes looked straight at Cole. "God bless you, sir. I'm so appreciative," the man said.

Suddenly Cole's spirit perked up. He felt fortunate now. His small act of giving had led to him feeling profoundly blessed.

☐ R—Relationship connections

Feeling depressed often creates an impulse to cocoon at home. Interacting with others can feel like it would take too much energy. Isolating feels safer, less overwhelming.

Contrary to the isolationist impulses you may feel when you feel depressed, talking with others can lift your mood. Even exchanging a few words with someone in the grocery checkout line can grant you a small energy boost. Chatting, receiving smiles, and enjoying shared humor all stimulate positive energy. When you talk with others, your emotional state and theirs eventually will match. Moods are contagious. If yours has been low, others' more positive moods may raise yours.

Social interactions offer opportunity also for fresh perspectives. If you feel flummoxed by a practical problem, discussing it with someone you trust may offer you an alternative way of seeing it. Therapists use the term *reframe* for a new and more positive outlook on a dilemma. A reframe can bring you hope.

Socializing can also have its downsides. While connecting with others re-energizes most people, even those who crave solitude, it can sometimes add to discouragement. Seeing others' apparently comfortable emotional states can heighten your awareness of your own state of discouragement. You do need to protect yourself too from encounters with critical folks. For the most part, though, mingling with almost anyone who is in a normal to happier-than-normal mood can lighten yours.

The following case illustrates the importance of social connection and also several of the remaining *AGGRESS-N* factors: exercise, sleep, and sunshine.

Teresa, an attractive woman in her mid-sixties, suffered one of the most profound depressions I have treated in my clinical practice. She was the only client I have worked with whose depression was so intense that she would curl up in fetal position in my office.

When Roy and Teresa both had retired the prior year, Roy had said that he'd like to move to a larger city in a warmer state. He was bored now that he no longer went each day to work. Especially in the dark, cold, and icy winters he felt housebound and stir-crazy.

Teresa said no. The thought of moving terrified her. She felt safe and loved in her familiar, decades-old friendship group. Moving sounded totally unappealing.

Roy nonetheless scanned the Internet for houses in sunnier cities. When Teresa reiterated her strong desire to stay where they had lived for more than thirty years, Roy replied dismissively, "That's foolish. Living in a city will be fun. You'll make new friends there."

Roy found a house and bought it. Within weeks of their move, Teresa slid into a deep depression. She seldom left their new home and either slept or cried most of every day. Reeling from a decision to move for which her input had not been considered, living in a new city where she had no friends, grieving the loss of her community, and angry at her self-centered husband, Teresa descended into depths of despair.

While Roy's dominant-submissive mode of decision-making plus the loss of her former close-knit friendship group had triggered Teresa's profound depression, the lack of social connections in her new city perpetuated it.

If you have been feeling depressed, how might you increase your social interactions?

❏ E—Exercise

If you are seriously depressed, the last thing you may feel like doing is anything that takes output of energy.

Paradoxically though, pushing yourself to expend energy in physical activity, such as walking, biking, dancing, going to a gym, or doing virtually any sport, will generate more energy. The more you apply energy to moving your body, the more energetic you will feel. Paradoxically too, the harder the workout, the more positive energy you are likely to experience at the end of your workout.

> Living now in the sunshine of Denver, Roy encouraged Teresa to join him in his new morning routine of after-breakfast walks. At first Roy had to reach out and take Teresa's hand to ease her off the sofa. Gradually, exploring their new neighborhood together became a fun activity that helped Teresa begin to re-energize. The more she walked, the more energy Teresa seemed to have to do other activities during the day.

Want to amplify the impact of your exercise on your moods? Exercise with music. Listening to music even without exercise can boost feelings of well-being. Ever noticed that in stores that play upbeat music, your enthusiasm for buying rises? Similarly, listening to music while you exercise makes your mood more upbeat.[24]

Sexual activity, especially in the context of a loving relationship, can prove to be a particularly potently anti-depressive form of physical exercise. In addition to activating your musculature, breathing, and heart rate, sexual arousal impacts your biochemical system by increasing the flow of oxytocin and other feel-good neurochemicals.

The quadruple positive synergies from combining exercise, music, sexual activation, and relationship connection offer especially significant energy enhancement. Of course, like socializing and exercising, starting to engage in sexual activity when you are depressed can feel like it would take too much effort. Still, the payoffs once you get past the starting gate can be high.

What kinds of exercise could you engage in to increase your energy levels if you have been feeling down?

❑ S—Sleep

Sleep rejuvenates your body's energies. Getting adequate sleep therefore merits top priority if you want to sustain your physical and emotional health.

Depression can cause sleep loss. The reverse also is true. Loss of sleep can cause feelings of vulnerability to depression. Beware of a cycle in which insufficient hours of sleep leads to depression, depression blocks adequate sleep, creating more depression, and you get caught in a downward spiral.

For my PhD dissertation, I studied postpartum depression. The single strongest predictor of which of the forty women in the study would fall prey to a depression in the first weeks after a new baby's arrival was insufficient sleep. The single best cure: getting more sleep.

Interestingly, both too little sleep and too much sleep can increase vulnerability to depression. When you feel extremely depressed, you may not want to leave your bed. Excessive sleeping, however, can leave you drowsy instead of more energized.

Teresa had been staying in bed until almost lunchtime. With her agreement with Roy that they would breakfast together then take walks, Teresa found that less sleep time seemed to leave her with more energy.

How might you improve the amount of sleep you get?

_____

❑ S—Sunshine

With the current and well-merited attention to the dangers of sunburn as a precursor to skin cancer, the benefits of sunshine can be overlooked. Yet vitamin D turns out to be a surprisingly strong antidepressant. Absorbing vitamin D straight from the sun boosts your physical health much like vitamin C does, and at the same time boosts your mood.

Sunshine has all the more potent an antidepressant effect if you can access a natural setting. Green grass, leafy trees, and colorful flowers utilize sunshine to grow and then transfer that positive energy into your emotional state.

When natural sunlight is not available, an antidepressant sunlamp can substitute. Seasonal affective disorder (SAD) is a tendency to get depressed in the winter when there is less sunshine. During the months of short, dark days, sit under a lamp while you read, watch TV, or check your favorite websites. You can order lamps for this purpose via the Internet.

Teresa's morning walks outdoors with Roy energized her as much because of the sunshine as because of the exercise and the social interactions. The morning walks improved Roy's mood as well. Relaxing into a happier mode, he became a more enjoyable companion. His better mood increased his openness to listening to his wife's perspectives, adding yet another boost to Teresa's emergence from depression. Walking with Roy each morning, Teresa appreciated the relaxed kindness that had replaced his former grumpiness and do-it-my-way bossiness.

How might you increase your quantity of exposure to sunlight?

❑ N—Newness

New anything tends to be energizing. Are you reluctant to embrace change, fearing it rather than looking forward to it? That tendency could work to your disadvantage. Even small doses of newness can engender an emotional uplift.

Try a new flavor of ice cream or a new restaurant. Go to a neighborhood you haven't been to before in your locale. Take up a new activity, anything from knitting to bowling to volunteer work. Make a new friend by inviting someone different to join you for dinner. Plan a trip and travel.

The move to a new city initially overwhelmed Teresa. Over time, however, she began to enjoy launching new activities and meeting new friends. Bit by bit, her depression lifted.

One morning as Roy and Teresa walked together, Teresa smiled. "Good thing you decided on this move. I would never have made this decision. Now though, I can't imagine being stuck in the dark cold winters we used to suffer through. My new friends are interesting. My study groups and exercise classes here are great. The volunteer work I do at the preschool in the shelter for homeless families feels worthwhile and makes me laugh; the kids are always saying funny things. Life feels more full and more fun. I even enjoy being married to you," she said, teasing Roy affectionately as she squeezed his hand.

How might you add new elements to your life?

R$_X$ 2.7: CHECK FOR RELATIONSHIP FACTORS THAT INDUCE DEPRESSION.

When two people interact as allies, talking together cooperatively, both of them are likely to feel relaxed, interested, and good-humored. The same applies to a group. When work colleagues and also managers, for instance, talk collaboratively, speaking with each other in tones of mutual respect and taking seriously each others' viewpoints, they all feel empowered and valued.

Any of the following warning signs, by contrast, indicate that a key relationship in your life may be putting you or others at risk for depression. When a relationship flips from collaborative to one up and one down, the risks of depression rise.

Relationship interactions that invite depression

Answer the *Yes/No* questions below initially as they pertain to the behaviors of someone of importance to you in your personal, family, work, or friendship world. Then, answer the flip to each question, asking if you yourself sometimes behave in these ways.

> **Y / N Your partner has withdrawn emotionally or sexually.**
> **Y / N You have withdrawn emotionally or sexually.**

Emotional withdrawal by one partner in an ongoing relationship can trigger depression in the other partner. Emotional unavailability—that is, not talking to, smiling at, or showing interest in a partner—signals rejection and abandonment. In addition, any unilateral change in a relationship, a change made without a shared decision, can invite depression. A choice to work longer hours, to train for marathons, or to invest in a risky financial deal that one partner makes without input from the other can trigger depression.

Sex is a sensitive arena in this regard. A marriage commitment generally is assumed to include sexual participation. Withdrawal by one partner from sexual connecting can trigger depression in the other. A marriage without sex is a vulnerable marriage, particularly if one partner still desires a sexual relationship. Similarly, if either you or your partner cease to nourish each other with expressions of affection like smiles, hugs, and appreciation, depression can replace well-being.

Y / N You feel dominated.

Y / N You dominate your partner.

Remember Silvano Arieti's theory (Rx 2.1) that depression emerges in response to dominant-submissive interactions? Any interaction in which one partner assumes a powering-over stance can trigger depression in the lesser-power partner.

As explained in 2.2, some power differences do not create depression. A kindly parent, boss, or teacher can spread goodwill. It's when the stronger person overpowers the weaker, for instance via insistence, anger, or always needing things to be his/her way, that depression is likely to lie ahead.

Y / N Your partner frequently speaks to you in an irritated voice.

Y / N You frequently speak in an irritated voice toward your partner.

Low-intensity anger expressed as frustration or irritation spreads subtle but toxic negative energy. The receiver of toxic energies becomes at risk for depression.

Y / N Your partner speaks to you in a way that sounds critical.

Y / N You speak to your partner in a way that sounds critical.

Feedback is helpful. Criticism, by contrast, is feedback that includes a put-down. Harsh words or an irritated or derogatory tone of voice sting.

Contempt goes a step further, communicating disgust. In his writings, Robert C. Solomon, a professor of philosophy at the University of Texas in Austin, places contempt on the same continuum as resentment and anger. Clarifying the differences between the three, Solomon explains that resentment is directed toward a higher-status individual, anger is directed toward an equal-status individual, and contempt is directed toward a lower-status individual.[25]

In contrast to criticism and contempt, any form of appreciation adds to good feelings. It's pretty simple. Put-downs yield emotional downs; positive comments yield emotional uplifts.

Y / N Your partner often argues with you.

Y / N You often argue with you partner.

Anger and arguments signal that depression may be just around the corner. As anger rises, odds go up that disagreements will be settled with a winner and a loser. The person who is more determined, persistent, or overpowering will win. The one who gives up becomes at risk for depression. If the fight ends in a draw, both partners lose. Both then become at risk for depression.

According to a literature review by B. Fink and A. Shapiro in *Couple & Family Psychology*, individuals in high-tension marriages are ten to twenty-five times more likely to experience depression than people who are unmarried or in collaborative relationships.[26]

Y / N Your partner expresses anger too often or too intensely.
Y / N You express anger too often or too intensely.

Feeling anger is normal; speaking in anger is not. If you or your partner speak to each other in critical or angry voice tones on a daily, weekly, or even monthly basis, your irritability is probably unnecessary and too much. Pay particular attention in this case to the upcoming chapter's prescriptions for relief from anger.

Y / N Your partner often tells you what to do.
Y / N You too often tell your partner what to do.

Bossy attitudes are demoralizing. Even a seemingly benign order like, "Go get the paper for me please, honey," is likely to trigger either irritation or depression in the receiver. No one likes being told what to do. Spouses are people, not puppets.

Frequent controlling behavior can indicate an abusive relationship. Attempts to control time, finances, friendship choices, or family relationships are particularly likely to invite feelings of depression in a partner. Depression is a disorder of power. If one of you often tells the other what to do, violates the other's right to make personal decisions, or refuses to allow input from both of you toward decisions that involve both of you, this habit could be the tip of an iceberg of a larger pattern of abuse. Abusive relationships pose an especially serious depression risk.

In contrast to issuing orders and demands, respectfully asked requests include a question, a *quest*, giving you the option of responding either yes or no. Requests enhance the recipient's sense of personal autonomy instead of engendering depression.

"Could you get me the paper please, honey?"

"Sorry, not now. I'm frying eggs at the stove."

"Okay. I'll get it myself. While I'm up, would you like me to set the table?"

"That would be great. Thanks!"

Y / N Your partner doesn't listen to you.

Y / N You don't listen to your partner.

If you or your partner typically brush aside differing perspectives, that dismissiveness can initiate a depressive collapse.

Some partners have an especially hard time hearing others' feelings. When they hear "I feel overwhelmed" they may personalize the message, respond with something like "Stop criticizing me for not doing enough to help you!"

Y / N Your partner always needs to be right.

Y / N You are the one who is always right.

When one partner has to be right all the time, making the other person wrong, problems lie ahead. Conversations that take the form of "I'm right, you're wrong" demoralize the loser.

In a healthy relationship, both participants' viewpoints count. The consensus that emerges from discussions includes points made by both of you. Similarly, if either you or your partner cannot admit mistakes, beware. The potential for demoralization rises when apologies for mistakes are not forthcoming.

Y / N Your partner is depressed.

Y / N You are depressed.

Depression is contagious. Remember the cognitive triad of negative thoughts about self, others, and the future (Rx 2.1)? A depressed partner sees the world through dark glasses, flooding your shared space with negative energy and gloomy pessimism about the future. Both of you can become at risk for sinking emotionally in a double drowning.

Y / N Your partner doesn't do his/her responsibilities in the partnership.
Y / N You don't do your responsibilities in the partnership.

Marital partners share responsibility for the business of living. When he scrambles eggs for the two of you in the morning or she scurries around with a quick cleanup before his mother comes to visit, mutually pitching in builds goodwill. By contrast, shirking the shared work required to sustain life can engender either anger or depression in your mate. If either you or your partner seems to be doing less than a fair share in your household, find out why. Then decide together what to do about the asymmetry.

Joyce felt annoyed when Charlie would come home from work and plop into the armchair in front of the TV. Joyce worked during the day at a job out of the home. By evening she too was exhausted. Yet someone needed to make dinner, interact lovingly with their two young children, make lunches for the next morning, do bedtimes, and more. Did everything in their household have to be her responsibility?

When Charlie responded to Joyce's question about why he wasn't pitching in, Joyce's frustration melted into a mix of compassion, appreciation, and love.

"My foot, from my accident as a kid, begins hurting at work by lunchtime," Charlie said. "I hang in there and force myself to keep working. We need the money. By the time I get home I can't stand the pain any longer. I just want to get off my foot and tune out, at least until the throbbing stops. I'm really sorry that I haven't explained this to you. Silent suffering was probably a bad idea. Since I was young, I've always been reluctant to say anything to anyone about my pain. I never want to come across as complaining."

Y / N Your partner has submissive habits and beliefs.
Y / N You have submissive habits and beliefs.

To what extent does your partner, or do you, subconsciously assume a submissive role, inviting dominance from the other? For instance, do you speak up about your concerns and preferences or expect your partner to "just know" them?

> Colette wanted to talk over differences as they arose with her husband. Lance, however, had grown up in a family where differences were unsafe to discuss. He, of course, sometimes disliked things that Collette did. For instance, he bristled when she talked in a loud voice, but he said nothing.
>
> Suppressing his reactions took a toll. When Collette started having long friendly chats with their next-door bachelor neighbor, rather than speak up about his concerns, Lance sank into a deep depressive torpor.

Submissive beliefs as well as submissive habits can undermine healthy partnership. Beware if you, perhaps subconsciously, fall prey to beliefs such as I'm not lovable, I don't deserve to be treated respectfully, or I'm a loser. Beliefs such as these can invite excessive toleration of a partner's mistaken behaviors. If so, rethinking these beliefs may help. While it is not your job to change your partner, it is your job to give feedback. "When your voice gets loud, I stop listening." It is your job to express your concerns instead of building up internal resentment and depression.

In summary

If the checklist above has yielded any *Yes* answers, be sure to keep reading. The prescriptions in Chapter 6 will spell out skills you can develop to prevent depression-inducing relationship dangers. As I will keep repeating, *mistakes are for learning*. Awareness is the first step in the learning process.

R$_X$ 2.8: CHOOSE COUPLES COUNSELING FOR THERAPY IF YOU ARE MARRIED.

Depression is highly treatable. Because most depression is either caused or exacerbated by interactions with loved ones, both partners generally need to participate in the treatment. If you are in a committed or married relationship, couples therapy is preferable to having one or more individual therapists. That way both of you can learn and grow. That way your growth will bring you closer, not split you apart.

Unfortunately, depressed individuals who seek counseling often end up in individual therapy. Depression feels like a problem within a person, so involving your spouse or significant other may seem irrelevant. In addition, if you ask friends or a doctor for a recommendation of a mental health professional, odds are that the therapist who has been recommended will be trained primarily in individual treatment methods.

Most therapist training programs mainly teach skills for one-on-one treatment. Because few programs other than explicitly marriage and family therapy training programs spend adequate time teaching the additional skill sets needed for effective marriage counseling, most therapists just work with one individual at a time.

Couples therapists do exist. You just may have to hunt and google to find them.

Therapy for just one partner in a couple may help

Individual therapy for a married depressed person sometimes does suffice. Depression after losing a job, for instance, or from interactions with a toxic boss, a critical parent, or a hostile friend may respond well to individual treatment methods. When a depression is a response to something other than interactions between the couple, clearing up the depression will be likely to help the marriage. As the saying goes, happy wife, happy life. A happier husband also can make the relationship more positive for both partners, though women sometimes, at least for a short while, may experience at least some emotional satisfaction from being able to nurture a depressed spouse.[27]

Sometimes, too, one partner is not willing to participate in couple-format counseling. Then individual therapy may be the only option.

Fortunately, individual therapy can lead to improvement in the marriage for both partners if the therapist helps you to identify what you could do differently to improve the situation.

For decades, Albert had believed his wife when she would angrily blame him for her frequent hurt feelings. As Paulette's angry outbursts became, over the years, more frequent and vitriolic, Albert felt increasingly depressed. His wife was unwilling to go to couples counseling with him, so he went to therapy on his own.

Albert gradually began to accept what a part of him had always suspected, namely that Paulette's anger was excessive. Albert had been naïve about phenomena such as emotional abuse, narcissism, bipolar disorder and borderline functioning. As he started doing computer searches to learn more about these diagnoses, he began to realize that his wife's anger stemmed from dysfunctional reactions rather than his having, yet again, done something wrong. With this realization, his depression began to lift.

Albert learned two other empowering understandings in his individual treatment sessions. First, he learned about *projection*. Understanding that his wife often projected her inner state onto him, accusing him of what she herself was doing, thinking, or feeling, enabled Albert to translate her accusations. When Paulette accused Albert of being selfish, that meant that she herself was being selfish. With this new translation capacity, Albert no longer found his wife's accusations upsetting. Instead, he treasured these windows into what Paulette was experiencing. See Rx 3.3 for more on projection.

Second, Albert learned to exit the room at the first signs that his wife was potentially heading for an angry outburst. With her husband no longer in front of her to serve as a recipient for her anger, Paulette's anger explosions fizzled. Within days, her anger outbursts ceased.

Beware!

Psychotherapy for depression without both partners present tends to be structurally problematic irrespective of how competent a therapist may be. For starters, in order for a therapist to clarify the factors contributing to a depression, he or she needs to observe the couple talking together. Descriptions in individual therapy from the perspective of the depressed partner of what has been going on at home seldom paint as accurate a picture as what a therapist sees when partners interact in a therapy session.

For instance, does the depressed partner speak up about concerns or suppress them? Suppressed disgruntlement tends to smolder into depression. Does the depressed partner make tactful requests or issue complaints and criticism? Do the partners listen to each other? To clarify these patterns, and all the more to remedy them, couples therapy is preferable.

Cordelia, who had been feeling vaguely depressed for months, called my office to schedule an appointment for therapy. My secretary asked if she was single or in a relationship, explaining my policy of seeing all married clients in a couples-therapy format, at least for the first session.

When I met Cordelia and her husband, Ken, in the waiting room, Cordelia seemed to be a spunky and fun middle-aged woman. Yet when Cordelia and Ken entered my treatment office and began to discuss together why they had come to see me, Cordelia went silent.

Ken quickly took over the dialogue, dominating the airtime with long monologues. I asked if the couple shared their airtime with similar asymmetry when they talked together at home. Ken and Cordelia both readily agreed. Yes, their conversations were almost always lopsided. Ken was the talker, the one around whom all the family revolved. "I'm a narcissist," he said proudly.

Cordelia added that if she interrupted her husband's monologues, and all the more if she expressed viewpoints that differed from his, he became irritated. Letting him do all the talking seemed safer. Ken agreed.

Until that session, Cordelia had not realized the connection between her depression and her self-muting. Giving up on having opinions in order to avoid Ken's anger had been emotionally costly for her.

Ken showed zero interest in changing. Yet Cordelia's understanding of why she had long gone mute at home relieved her depression. Now that she saw her husband's domineering behavior as a sign of his social handicaps, she no longer felt dominated. In spite of Ken's significantly greater height, Cordelia now felt like the bigger person, viewing her husband's social skills deficits with compassion.

No longer depressed, Cordelia happily stayed in her marriage. With multiple loving adult children who lived close by, grandchildren, and many close friends, her relationship needs felt satisfied. She appreciated that in spite of her husband's limitations, her marriage to him gave her a large and joyful intact family, financial security, and status in her community. Well-being returned.

In addition to providing insufficient diagnostic data, individual depression therapy raises multiple further treatment risks for couples:

- Therapy with one half of a couple guides just one partner's growth, unbalancing their long-term unequal but stable arrangement.
- Therapy with one partner alone does not fix the other's problematic behaviors.
- The burden of fixing the relationship falls solely on the depressed spouse, who already feels relatively powerless.
- The depressed spouse may attempt to take on a dual role, adding the role of therapist in charge of relationship repair to the role of spouse. This dual role is likely to backfire, provoking defensiveness in the other spouse instead of growth.
- Growth in therapy by one partner may appear threatening to the other, exacerbating anger and/or withdrawal.

What is a likely outcome, therefore, if you decide to seek out individual depression treatment when much of your distress stems from your relationship? Your depression may or may not decrease, but your marriage is likely to be stressed. You then may surmise that the problem is partner choice, that is, that you have picked a hopelessly flawed or mismatched partner. Now divorce may seem like the only remedy. Individual therapy in this way can split the two of you apart instead of healing the depression and, along with it, the marriage.

The term *iatrogenic* (doctor-induced) damage sums up the danger. Individual therapy for a depressed married person, or, for that matter, for any emotional difficulty being experienced by someone who is married, can aggravate underlying marital difficulties. Two individual therapists, one for each spouse, is likely to make the situation even worse, almost guaranteeing an outcome of divorce. Individual treatment for depression can be like a surgery that saves the heart but kills the person. A divorce is a death of a marriage.

By contrast, when therapy for someone who is married includes both partners, both learn and grow simultaneously. As you learn to speak up openly and yet tactfully about your concerns, your loved one is learning listening skills so that what you say is more likely to be heard receptively. And vice versa. The odds then rise that eventually both of you will enjoy a depression-free relationship.

In this regard, if you are married or in a committed relationship, do consider inviting your partner to read this book. If you alone are reading it, the impacts may be problematic as well as helpful, like the impacts on a relationship of individual treatment for depression. I would hope not, because the emphasis in this book is on what you yourself can do differently that will help you both. Still, participation by both of you increases your success odds.

If your partner is not likely to read along with you, maybe you can share aloud the specific prescriptions that feel most relevant, or at least show your spouse the graphics. The goal is for everyone to gain: you, your partner, and also your children. Even your dog will be happier in brighter emotional sunshine.

R_x 2.9: HANDLE GRIEF AND RELATIONSHIP ENDINGS WITHOUT DEPRESSION.

Relationship endings from death, or from the departure of one party, can trigger sadness, grief, anger, and also depression. Negative feelings arise less if you have initiated the disengagement. They arise more strongly if you are the one who has been left.

Grieving helps you heal from a loss. Whether you lose a game, a job, a love relationship, or a person who has died, loss to some extent gives you no choice but to fold, that is, to give up on being able to have what you want. Grief facilitates the flow outward of sad feelings. Mourning, the talking part of the grief process, enables you to package up memories of what was lost, put them away for safe storage, and move on.

Verbalizing to others or journaling your thoughts and feelings facilitates gradual movement from initial shock and denial, through bargaining, anger, and sadness, to the fifth and final stage of grieving, acceptance. According to Elisabeth Kubler-Ross, who identified these five phases of grieving, allowing the flow of this natural healing sequence enables you eventually to return to normal functioning.[28]

At the same time, grief generally proceeds in waves. At first the waves, like waves in an ocean storm, may feel so frequent and strong that they seem continuous. Gradually, the waves feel further apart and less strong. Increased distance between the waves and decreases in the waves' strength indicate that that the mourning process is moving forward in an emotionally healthy manner.

Protracted grief and the *Best Possible Light* question

Protracted grieving can indicate a depressive collapse. If you feel stuck in grief with intense waves of anger or sadness that show no signs of abating, ask yourself, *If I look at my protracted bereavement in the best possible light, what is it intended to accomplish?*

Some thirty-plus years ago, I needed to ask myself that question. I was mired in darkness after the shocking sudden murder of a young man who had been my tennis coach.

Seeing how immobilized I had become, my husband asked me, "If you look at your overwhelming grief in the best possible light, what is it intended to accomplish?"

I closed my eyes to see or hear what answer my subconscious would deliver. The image and words that came to my mind surprised me. I was staying devastated, unable to concentrate on my work or to experience emotions other than deep sadness, to show my coach how important he had been to me.

With that answer, I then began looking for an alternative way to show my lost young friend's soul how important his life had been. Just days before his death, I had taken a photo of him with a group of his younger tennis students crowding affectionately around him. I made the photo into a wall plaque in his honor. The photo hangs prominently on a public wall in his tennis center to this day.

Life is for the living. If grief continues to waylay you, do consider speaking with a professional grief counselor or therapist. The goal of grief and mourning, remember, is to return to living your life. It is not to lock you into a permanent state of sadness or a depressive collapse.

When someone ends a relationship with you

The manner in which a breakup ends can play a major role in determining if the ending will yield relief, simple sadness, or full-fledged depression. In the emotionally healthiest endings, both of you participate with input into the decision. Then even if ending the relationship was not your first choice, the odds go up that you will move forward without depression. You may grieve the ending with relief or with sadness, but without depression. What invites depression is powerlessness, that is, feeling that the ending was done *to* you instead of *with* you.

One solution to depression induced by a unilateral ending to a relationship can be for the two people to talk together one additional time. A last opportunity to digest what worked and what didn't in the relationship and then to express affection and best wishes for the future can give both participants closure in a way that feels mutual. Having requested the meeting and then shared your perspective, now you can experience the ending as a decision you made together.

Be careful, however, about how you give your input. Pass up the temptation to blame or criticize. Instead, talk about yourself, about what you have appreciated and what you would do differently if you had a second chance. The more positivity and insight that you convey, the more re-empowered you will feel at the conversation's end.

Because searching for the other is a normal part of grieving, you may feel tempted to initiate repeated attempts to re-contact an ex. That is likely to be a mistake. Refusal to let go of a relationship after your partner has left emotionally will extend your distress. Grieve and move on.

Removing from view, giving away, or throwing out physical reminders of an ex who has left or a loved one who has died can help you to stay empowered. Say to yourself, "Okay, I'm ending that era of my life and readying myself to go on to something new. I'm taking charge now. I'm in the driver's seat."

At that point, utilize the seven *AGGRESS-N* options (Rx 2.6). Take action instead of adopting a victim stance. Focus on gratitude for the benefits you gained from your time in the relationship and for the good that still remains in your life. Give to others. Socialize. Exercise, get plenty of sunshine, and sleep. Build new friendships and experiment with new activities. Get a puppy or take a trip to explore new places. Re-enter the stream of life.

Loss can be hard, even devastating. At the same time, new beginnings can be invigorating, heralding a better future.

R$_x$ 2.10: CONSIDER RIGHT-LEFT PREFRONTAL LOBE ENERGY-SHIFTING.

Begin by watching the video *Rapid Relief of Depression* that I have posted on the prescriptionswithoutpills.com website. Seeing can be a helpful first step toward believing. For this prescription, that saying is especially likely to be true. The technique of frontal lobe energy-shifting is totally unlike most therapy treatments.

Several years ago my colleague Dale Petterson and I stumbled on neuroimaging studies of depression and the brain. Dale, a highly talented energy therapist, noticed that studies with MRI scans reported that when a person is depressed the brain has more energy in the right than in the left prefrontal lobe. With happiness, the left prefrontal lobe shows more energy. Elkhonon Goldberg's book *The Wisdom Paradox*, among others, describes these interesting findings.[29]

"Hmmm," Dale thought. "If I ask a depressed person's subconscious to shift some of the prefrontal lobe energy from the right lobe over to the left, would anything change?"

The answer turned out to be yes.

Dale and I first tried the technique with Marty, a troubled man in his late twenties with whom I had been working in marriage therapy. Marty had been depressed since childhood. Within minutes after the treatment, which took less than five minutes, Marty's face began to brighten. He was feeling lighter than he had for years.

Had Dale stumbled on a remarkably potent new depression treatment option? Marty's case and the many that have followed indicate that the treatment at least merits serious further attention.

What are the relative amounts of energy in each prefrontal lobe?

Muscle kinesiology, the technique also known as muscle testing that I explained initially in Rx 6.2, gives a voice to the subconscious. Muscle testing offers Dale and I a way to ask an unusual question. We use it to ask our clients to assess the relative amounts of energy activation in their two prefrontal lobes.

Our muscle-testing findings have been consistent with our clients' self-reports of how much, if any, depression they feel. Ratios up to fourteen times more energy in the right than the left correlate with mildly dark moods.

Moderately depressed clients typically test as having twenty to forty times more energy in the right than the left prefrontal lobe. More than forty times more energy in the right seems to be associated with severe depression levels. Fifty or more times higher energy in the right prefrontal lobe correlates with suicidal levels of depression.

Correspondingly, people in a state of well-being typically test as having about twenty-seven to thirty-seven times more energy in their *left* prefrontal lobe.

Outcomes

At this point Dale and I have used prefrontal lobe energy-shifting with several dozen clients. The results in most of these cases have been encouraging. The procedure itself takes less than ten minutes. Some clients, like Marty, feel a major emotional shift almost immediately. Others stay the same or maybe even feel slightly worse for a day or two and then realize, "Hmm. I no longer feel depressed!" One or two clients have reported that they experienced no change.

What drawbacks keep such a simple, rapid, low-tech, inexpensive, and seemingly harmless intervention as frontal lobe energy-shifting from becoming broadly available?

Research

This technique has not yet been validated with rigorous clinical trials because my office is not set up to conduct scientific research. Carefully controlled studies with large numbers of cases and a variety of therapists eventually, I hope, will legitimize this promising technique as an evidence-based treatment. If a psychotherapy researcher were to contact me about interest in conducting clinical trials, I would welcome this next step.

Meanwhile, the appreciative reaction of clients who report feeling markedly less depressed after the energy-shifting procedure has definitely impressed us.

Muscle kinesiology takes practice

To conduct prefrontal lobe energy-shifting, whether as a lay person or as a therapist, you need to be able to do muscle testing. Although increasing numbers of alternative treatment psychotherapists are beginning to utilize muscle testing, the technique is not yet a standard part of psychotherapists' training. Therein lies the rub.

Muscle testing looks easy as you will see if you watch the explanatory video on prescriptionswithoutpills.com. In fact, the technique takes significant practice. Dale himself says that when he first set out to learn the technique, he was unable to do it. He practiced again and again with friends and relatives, getting increasingly discouraged. Then one day, suddenly, the technique clicked in. He could do it!

I mention this personal story about Dale in hopes that if you yourself decide to take on the challenge of learning to do muscle testing, you will keep at it—even if at first, second, and far more times you don't succeed.

To a traditional therapist like myself . . .

Energy therapy procedures yield impressive psychological improvements that make no "scientific" sense. However, I have watched Dale do these interventions for more than three years. The promising results I have seen compel me to mention the technique here in hopes that others will pick up the ball and carry it further down the field.

What are your options if you would like to utilize this prescription?

As far as I know, Dale Petterson and I as a team, plus one of the other therapists in our office suite, are the only therapists who utilize this new antidepressant technique. At the same time, the technique is quite simple. A therapist or alternative health care provider in your local area whose treatment techniques already include muscle testing (muscle kinesiology) could easily learn and implement it. Ask such a provider if s/he would be willing to experiment with the prefrontal lobe energy-shifting procedure modeled in the video on this book's website, prescriptionswithoutpills.com.

The only technically difficult part of this treatment is the muscle testing. A therapist who has this skill is likely to be able to follow the script from the video. In addition, there is one physical tool. The Magboy magnet that Dale Petterson uses can be purchased on the Internet.

The initial relief from this procedure may last from several days to several weeks. The procedure then needs to be repeated. Over time the results hold for increasingly longer periods before a repeat is necessary. Eventually, well-being becomes the norm.

Will prefrontal lobe energy-shifting make other depression treatments obsolete?

No. To end depressive tendencies, you still need to address the multiple facets of depressive vulnerabilities. Even if prefrontal lobe energy-shifting, like medication, does release dark feelings at least temporarily, readdressing the situation that triggered the depressive reaction is an important component of an ultimately effective solution.

Energy-shifting is one of the pieces of a full package of approaches to ending depression. Even if energy-shifting successfully buoys your mood, you still are likely to benefit from addressing long-ago emotional injuries that have continued to leave depressive aftershocks. You may need to rethink habitual thoughts and actions that invite and sustain depression. You are likely to need to strengthen your collaborative dialogue and conflict resolution skills detailed in Chapter 6 so that when future conflicts arise you can deal with them without either folding or fighting.

So if you have been working with a traditional psychotherapist, do continue that relationship. Energy therapy treatments such as this one augment, rather than replace, traditional psychotherapy.

When energy-shifting does produce rapid mood change, standard talk therapy afterwards consolidates the results of the energy-shifting. For this reason, when Dale and I use these procedures, I follow up in the next session with debriefing and more conventional talk therapy methods. You can do the same by including this chapter's full set of anti-depressant interventions rather than just energy-shifting into your self-treatment plan.

Getting depressed about feeling depressed would be a shame. Better to keep exploring than to give up. Stay mobilized. Keep looking for new solutions.

Chapter 3

Anger

Anger mobilizes your energy resources for a fight, preparing you to protect yourself and to force those who oppose your will to do what you want. At the same time, anger clearly can wreak havoc in your life. As early as two thousand years ago, the Roman philosopher Seneca wrote that anger is "the canker of human nature" and "the most outrageous, brutal, dangerous, and intractable of all passions . . . and the subduing of this monster will do a great deal toward the establishment of human peace."[30] Jewish Talmudic scholars and also Christian religious thinkers such as Augustine and Peter Abelard similarly place anger as a primary cause of discord.

Yet anger earns no diagnostic code in *The Diagnostic and Statistical Manual of Mental Disorders* (DSM) or in the ICDM, the manuals therapists use to diagnose emotional and psychiatric syndromes. Unlike depression, anxiety, and addictions, which these manuals do classify as mental health issues, anger evades notice.

Do you, like the treatment manuals' authors, turn a blind eye to the possibility that your anger is a mental health problem? No one likes when others talk irritably to them. Yet you may regard your own moments of frustration, irritation, and even outright angry outbursts as legitimate responses because "You made me mad!" If you do regard anger as wrong when others express it but justified when you express it, maybe now would be a good time to reconsider the role of anger in your life.

If your anger outbursts are ego-syntonic, that is, if you regard your anger outbursts as legitimate, your motivation to rid yourself of impulsive anger reactions is likely to be low. That would be unfortunate—both for you and for those with whom you live and work.

How would you feel about learning to step back for a few calming moments instead of attacking when you feel angry?

> *I am always amazed when my reaction to situations is the same as it was when I was fifteen years old. Hard to admit it, but the city kid in me sometimes automatically responds, "Push me, and I'll push you right back!"*
>
> *Yet, I have learned that there can be a secondary response to situations which is far healthier and much more productive. I have referred to this as the principle of the second response. We need not always respond impulsively, with our first response reaction, to how we feel.*
>
> Author, storyteller, and former Catholic priest Salvatore Tagliareni[31]

R̽ 3.1: CLARIFY SIXTEEN COSTS OF ANGER AND ONE CORE REMEDY.

Anger, like all negative emotions, can serve positive purposes. Anger alerts you to threats and readies you to respond with counter-aggression. Without anger, you would be at risk for under-responding to dangerous situations.

When you feel anger or fear, adrenaline, a hormone and neurotransmitter produced in your adrenal glands, surges to prepare you for action. Adrenaline raises your heart and breathing rates so you can run, bite, punch, or kick with sufficient blood, oxygen, and glucose supplies for the battle. Adrenaline dilates your pupils, widening your band of vision for gathering data about danger and giving you a wide-eyed look to scare off predators.

Unfortunately, the same anger that pumps you up for physical aggression is likely to cost you in other ways. Here's a checklist of many of anger's downsides.

Checklist: Sixteen costs of anger

Check which of the following anger downsides may be proving costly to you.

❑ 1. Anger blocks listening, that is, information uptake.

As a friend of mine once aptly said, "When you are mad, what you want appears to be holy. What others want becomes a mere whisper." Others' concerns become "a mere whisper" because anger closes down your brain's ability to uptake and process new data. This temporary deafness makes you momentarily selfish, even if in general you are a caring, generous person.

Information is power. Blocked uptake of new data and resultant misinterpretations of situations disempower you, making you less able to find solutions to the problem that provoked your anger.

Bradley felt a sense of urgency about re-reading the contract for the new insurance policy he and his wife wanted to purchase. He asked Sharon to email him the document right away. Sharon wrote Bradley a lovely email about how appreciative she was that he had spent so much time investigating and deciding on the right policy for them.

When Bradley saw his wife's email, however, he erupted in fury. The documents he needed were not there.

Bradley immediately phoned Sharon. In his angry state, instead of asking for information about where the document was and listening to Sharon's answer, Bradley raged about how he never could depend on her.

Sharon thought she had sent the documents to her husband. Angered by Bradley's raging, she slammed down the phone. At home that evening she continued to feel too angry to listen when Bradley tried to talk more calmly with her.

Several days later, with the insurance documents still unsigned, both Bradley and Sharon had recovered enough that they now were able to broach the subject again.

They began by together checking Sharon's email. The email did not have the attachment. Sharon had inadvertently clicked Send before attaching the document.

Bradley's anger and then Sharon's angry reaction in return had ballooned a common technical error into a major blockage of information flow. When anger starts, listening stops.

❑ 2. Anger halts problem-solving.

The angrier you feel, the less effective you become at finding solutions to the problem that triggered your upset. Anger decreases ability to think. It minimizes ability to consider more than one factor or to creatively design a plan of action.

> In a business school class studying how emotional tone impacts thinking ability, college students were paired into two-person teams and given a complex business problem to solve. Each team was instructed to talk cooperatively, role-playing businesspeople who want to optimize a deal to give both of them the highest possible individual and aggregate profits.
>
> Half of the student pairs did the exercise right away. The other half were told, "We've had a delay. Would you mind taking this joke book and reading the jokes to each other while we finish getting ready to give you the business problem?"
>
> Sure enough, the pairs who first read a joke book together earned significantly higher scores. The jokes had induced a relaxed, good-humored emotional tone in both participants, enabling them to think more creatively and to co-create more effective solutions.

Relaxation enables a brain to perform optimally. Intense emotions cause information-processing as well as information uptake to shut down.

❑ 3. Anger damages your health and the health of your spouse.

Anger raises your blood pressure.[32] Anger stresses your adrenal glands and stores toxins in your liver. Anger can induce headaches. In addition, researchers have found links between anger and a wide range of medical problems including digestion difficulties, abdominal pain, pancreas dysfunction, insomnia, high blood pressure, skin problems such as eczema, stroke, and more.[33]

Does getting mad impact your heart? At Washington State University, a team of researchers headed by Bruce Wright, MD, focused on adults fifty and older to study if anger impacts heart health. They found that anger outbursts increased the likelihood of arterial calcium deposits, deposits that elevate heart attack risk. Stress hormones that surge when you become angry injure your blood vessel linings, another risk factor for heart problems.[34]

Would you be better off bottling up your anger instead of expressing it? A Dutch research team led by Dr. Johan Denollet found that suppressing anger triples your risk of heart attack.[35] Another Dutch team also found that suppressing anger leads to an increase in medical problems both for the person suppressing the anger and for the partner.[36] The bottom line is that heart attack vulnerability increases with anger whether you suppress the anger—most likely creating depression, which also tends to have physical health consequences—or express it.

Anger increases other medical problems for recipients of vitriol as well.

Researchers led by Jing Liao at University College London[37] tracked older couples for ten years, measuring the extent to which a partner expressed anger at his or her spouse. Their results clarified that adults who live with a partner prone to irritability, criticism, demands, or anger outbursts succumb to earlier and more significant dementia than those who live with more consistently positive partners.

Pretty much everyone knows that it's important to eat your vegetables, maintain a moderate body weight, exercise daily, refrain from smoking, and wear a seat belt if you want to stay physically healthy. Reacting with calm information-gathering and problem-solving to seemingly provocative situations instead of reacting with agitation and anger is equally impactful.

❏ 4. Anger induces feelings of power, to your detriment.

Anger pumps you up physiologically to feel large, strong, and dominant. Feeling powerful so you can go for the kill is great if you are an animal that needs to fight to get what you want. If you are a person though, the deceptive self-inflation from anger can lead you to engage in self-defeating bullying. Bullying wins the battle and loses the war. Over the long term, cooperation gains you more, especially with those with whom you have ongoing interactions.[38]

> Clara distrusted her neighbor. When her neighbor had a plumbing backup that might affect her plumbing as well, Clara reacted angrily. She immediately called her lawyer, demanding that he file a lawsuit against her neighbor.
>
> Eventually Clara realized that the lawsuit had no legal basis. In the meantime, however, she had spent thousands of dollars on needless legal fees.

The pumping-up effects of anger deplete your future energy reserves. After the anger has run its course, you are likely to crash, feeling exhausted and even depressed. Abusive people, for instance, typically experience emotional depletion along with shame and guilt after verbal or physical rampages.

Ironically, while anger may cause you to feel powerful in the moment, it makes you look childlike. Young children get mad on an almost daily basis. Emotionally mature adults seldom interact with others from an angry, much less raging, stance. Mature adults rarely speak with irritable or contemptuous voices, issue threats, or speak angrily to dominate. They discuss differences calmly and collaboratively.

❑ **5. Anger turns others against you.**
Most people immediately dislike anyone who speaks to them in a critical tone of voice or with harsh words. Even children dislike irritable peers and quick-to-anger adults. This point should be obvious. Yet it amazes me how often parents and also athletic coaches address children with needlessly critical voices.

> Polly and her friends were playing happily on the beach during a family summer vacation. Aunt Elizabeth, concerned that the children would brush sand onto her beach towel, harshly told them to move.
>
> For decades after that one incident, Polly avoided all contact with her aunt.

Especially when you are tired, hungry, or rushed, do you let your voice take on an angry edge? If so, when?

❑ **6. Anger stresses bystanders.**
Anger has a negative impact on onlookers, even if they are not directly involved in the interaction.

> Catherine told her husband, Sam, that she was considering divorcing him. Sam was stunned. He thought he'd always been a fine husband. Not quite, Catherine said.

Though Sam had always treated Catherine well, his political rants felt toxic to her. Catherine was no longer willing to allow her personal space to be contaminated by Sam's venomous retorts to television political pundits. She was no longer willing to have her dinnertimes, evenings, and weekend hours spoiled by Sam's angry political fixations.

At work, a negative atmosphere generated by even one or two irritable colleagues or managers creates an unpleasant workplace. A friendly environment that feels emotionally safe, by contrast, invites creativity, productivity, and company loyalty.

At home, parents' arguments distress children. When parents bicker, the children are the grand losers. Want to undermine your children's foundation for adulthood? Vent your anger. Even moderate amounts of anger, belittling interactions, and tensions between parents can stunt children's intellectual development.[39]

Argumentative parents undermine their children's emotional well-being even if they divorce. As difficult as divorce can be, children generally fare better living in two separated but calm households than one anger-ridden home. Separation into two households with continuation of hostility, emotional storms, or court battles between their parents is an equally bad—and maybe even worse—option.

A climate of emotional storminess damages children. Children who live in emotional sunshine thrive.

❑ 7. Anger invites divorce.

Affection strengthens marital bonds, Irritability, snide comments, judgmental reactions, contempt, and overt hostility all snip away at the ties that bind, raising the likelihood that at some point the bond will snap and one of you will issue divorce papers.

❑ 8. Angry parenting is destructive parenting.

Do you often speak to your children in an irritated or outright angry voice? If so, you are teaching your children to be afraid of you, to resent you, and to dislike themselves as well. Because children interpret a parent's angry tirades as meaning that they themselves are bad and unlovable, your negativity undermines your children's confidence in themselves. They are likely to hear the "You're not okay" message implicit in an angry voice more strongly than any message you intended to convey about what specifically they should or should not have done. Better to quietly explain the child's mistake and how to fix it.

❏ 9. Anger can become abusive.

Anger expressed frequently and harshly in criticism, sarcasm, name-calling, humiliating or demeaning comments, threats, demands, or accusations is verbal and emotional abuse. Anger expressed by throwing things, pushing, hitting, and any similar actions that could cause damage to things or people constitutes physical abuse.

The time to stop abusive patterns is now. If your anger escalates to the level of either emotional or physical abusiveness described above, consider finding an anger management program or professional, or use the exercises on my poweroftwomarriage.com website to augment what you are learning in the prescriptions in this book.

The loud volume, insults, and demanding words of abusive anger aim to establish power and control and to induce submission. The term *battered woman syndrome*, coined some years ago by psychologist Lenore Walker,[40] describes a wife's potential depressive reaction to a husband's excessive anger. The term, now extended to *battered (or abused) partner syndrome*, applies equally to men whose loved ones dominate them via anger, to unmarried as well as to married loved ones, and to abused children.

If you have been abusive or abused, or if you have loved ones who are abusive or have been abused, take action. Contact an abuse hotline, program, or mental health professional.

Abused children especially deserve help. When a parent relieves internal anger buildups by venting on a child, the child typically has little or no power to change the situation without third-party intervention. Even simply befriending such a child is a good start. Explain to the child that he or she is not causing the parent's anger. Explain that excessive parental anger stems from an emotional disorder within the parent, not from what the child is or isn't doing. Your kindness, expressed even just once, can potentially mitigate the long-term damage.

❏ **10. Anger attacks people instead of attacking the problem.**
Anger tends to lead to pointing fingers instead of to seeking out solutions. As Roger Fisher and William Ury, authors of *Getting to Yes*,[41] first put it, "Separate the people from the problem."

"Billy, you spilled your milk again! You do that too often!" attacks the person with criticism. By contrast, attacking the problem by looking for solutions leads to fixing the problem. "Whoops. Let's get a sponge."

❏ **11. Anger exaggerates how bad a problem is.**
Anger makes frustrating situations appear more consequential than they really are. When you feel angry, minor incidents appear to be catastrophes. Psychologists and especially cognitive therapists refer to this mental error as *catastrophizing*.

"That spilled milk is totally wrecking the morning. Now I'll be late for work, and my whole day will be ruined."

❏ **12. Anger blocks awareness of what you like in the person you are mad at.**
By hyperfocusing you on what you dislike, anger can cause you to lose awareness of what you *do* like in the person or situation.

Confirmatory bias is the psychological term for receptivity only to information that confirms what you already believe. Anger increases confirmatory bias. Repeated angry statements reinforce negative beliefs and block uptake of new, more positive and in this sense contradictory data.

When Billy's mother erupts in anger about spilled milk, she becomes at risk for ignoring her child's generosity, cleverness, playfulness, and other positive qualities. The more she angrily repeats to herself negative words about her child, the more she may begin attending only to what she does not like, thereby confirming her belief about how bad a person Billy is. How sad.

The same pattern can occur between adults, which is one way that positive relationships deteriorate over time. Angry thoughts like "My boss is so inconsiderate" can lead to ignoring when your boss acts generously or takes the organization in creative directions.

❑ 13. Anger fosters overgeneralizations.

Overgeneralizing expands a reaction to a specific action that you don't like to the creation of a broader belief about that person.

A parent may expand her angry observation to her child—"You spilled your milk again!"—to an overgeneralization about her child's character, such as "You're so clumsy!" The negative label of a broader trait then becomes part of the child's self-image, inviting self-fulfilling prophesies.

Psychologist Haim Ginott, in his 1956 parenting classic, *Between Parent and Child*,[42] wrote that "Constructive criticism confines itself to pointing out how to do what has to be done, entirely omitting negative remarks about the personality of the child." Elicit the child's help in cleaning up the spilled milk. But do not label him or her with pejorative character terms such as lazy, careless, or clumsy—unless the word you are using characterizes the kind of person you want your child to become.

With adults, if anger that your spouse forgot your birthday expands into "He doesn't love me" or "He's so selfish," the full relationship can get needlessly soured.

❑ 14. Anger invites personalizing.

Beware of assuming that problems that occur are directed at you personally. Personalizing assumes "it's all about me." If you then feel guilt, shame, or defensiveness, you may strike back with angry blaming. "You spilled your milk? How could you do this to me when you know we're already late this morning!"

❑ 15. Anger focuses your attention excessively outward.

By focusing exclusively on whomever "made you mad," you block thinking about what you yourself could have done differently and could do differently in the future to prevent repeat upsets.

Note the difference if you say, "You spilled your milk yesterday, and now look—you've done it again!" versus "I can see that I need to get you a shorter, wider cup. This tall skinny glass is too tippy."

❑ 16. Anger invites backward-looking thoughts.

"Why did you do that?" stays locked in the past. By contrast, constructive thinking in response to an upsetting situation looks ahead, first at how to fix the problem and then at how to handle similar situations differently in the future.

For example, "I'll get two sponges so we can wipe up the milk together. And see this spot above your plate? Let's make that spot the special parking place for glasses so they won't tip over onto the floor so easily. *Mistakes are for learning.* Let's practice putting your cup in its new parking place."

A review exercise

In the following short example, how many costly impacts of anger can you identify?

> Jerry often pitched in to help his mom. He cleaned the kitchen without being asked and often put his little brother to bed in the evenings so his mother could have some alone time to relax. One day, however, Jerry forgot to return early from sports practice to babysit for his little brother so his mother could attend a community meeting.
>
> "This was a disaster!" his mom angrily shouted. "I had to bring the baby with me to the meeting, and he fussed. You're so thoughtless. You should have remembered your responsibility!"

Check to be sure you found each of the following cognitive distortions commonly induced by anger:

- ❑ Attacking the person instead of the problem
- ❑ Over-generalizing from a specific mistake to a character flaw
- ❑ Exaggerating how bad the offense was by catastrophizing
- ❑ Losing awareness of her son's many virtues
- ❑ Blaming instead of seeking to identify her own role in the upset
- ❑ Personalizing
- ❑ Inducing guilt instead of assuming that mistakes are for learning
- ❑ Looking backward instead of looking ahead to figure out how to prevent repeats in the future
- ❑ Over-generalizing from a specific mistake to a character flaw

Having been accused of being inconsiderate too often, Jerry felt increasingly frustrated. Without consciously making a choice, he did, in fact, become less considerate of his mother's needs. He began staying away from home as late as possible after school and on the weekends. He switched to doing as little as possible to help out at home.

The remedy

If you pause and remove yourself from the topic or situation that felt provocative, even for just a few minutes, you can let your anger cool. From a calmer state you are likely to be able to address almost any problem more effectively.

Jerry's mother felt furious yet again when she poked her head in his bedroom. Instead of angrily lecturing him about the mess however, this time she paused for a few minutes to calm down. Once she could think about how to handle the situation effectively, she decided to use the *Safe Sentence Starters* that you will learn in Rx 6.3.

"*I feel* overwhelmed when your clothes get scattered around the bedroom. *I would love to* resign from the job of dirty clothes collector. *How would you feel about* either hanging up your clothes or tossing them in the laundry basket instead of dropping them on the floor? I'll get you a wide laundry basket so it will be easy for you to toss them in from wherever you are standing in the room."

The choice to calm down before talking to Jerry paid off.

Jerry responded, "My teacher in kindergarten used to say, 'The last phase of any project is cleaning up.' Maybe I could apply that rule. I'll probably keep dropping whatever I take off, but I would be willing to do a pickup before I climb into bed. And I like the idea of using the laundry basket like a basketball net for shooting my clothes into!"

Jerry's mother, surprised by such an insightful and creative response, gushed appreciatively, hugging her son. "Wow, Jerry. I'm so glad you like the basketball idea. You've always been good at shooting hoops."

Save your anger outbursts for life-or-death situations. The rest of the time, like Jerry's mother, appreciate angry feelings as helpful alerts to a problem that needs your attention. Pause to calm down. Then think creatively about how to fix the problem situation, for now and for future occurrences.

In sum, pause or exit, self-calm, and then think of effective solutions. This trio, a three-part remedy that will be reiterated multiple times in the prescriptions ahead, constitutes the core prescription for avoiding the costs of anger. Utilize this prescription virtually every time you feel any irritation or anger and your life will flow smoothly, remarkably free of fighting.

R_x 3.2: RATE YOUR AMYGDALA REACTIVITY.

To understand anger, think about cavemen. Cartoon images of cavemen typically picture a short fellow with a sloped forehead who carries a big stick. The stick indicates a propensity for fighting. What does the caveman's sloped forehead suggest?

The part of your brain responsible for thinking with words lies in the frontal lobes, the area under your forehead, which is the area that cavemen lacked. Without much room for thinking matter in the frontal lobes, odds are that cavemen acted with what Daniel Kahneman, in his book Thinking Fast and Slow, refers to as fast thinking, that is, impulsive responses as opposed to the slower-thinking, frontal lobe process of gathering information and evaluating options.[43]

Early cavemen probably relied mainly on fast thinking for quick self-defense to apparent threats. The caveman's stick helped him to implement instantly his brain's "Attack!" messages.

What triggers inner-caveman, overly emotional, and impulsive responses in you? Your amygdala, or more accurately, your two amygdalae. Amygdalae are small, almond-shaped organs hidden deep in the back and more primitive part of your brain. The subcortical amygdala, situated beneath the outer layers of your brain, is referred to as "primitive" because it's an organ that even reptiles have. When a lizard sees a shadow move across the rock where it has been sunning, its amygdala triggers an instant response. The lizard darts away. Waiting to see if the shadow had correctly signaled a predator would be dangerous.

Your amygdala similarly (the two together are most commonly referred to as one organ) scouts for danger. Its job is to keep you safe. When it spots something that could portend trouble, the amygdala's rapid messaging service sends out an anxiety alarm to mobilize you with anger to fuel immediate action.

A caveman may have a small head, limiting his language and analytical thinking abilities, but his amygdala is highly developed. His amygdala works long hours, remaining on duty all the time that he is awake, lest animals or other cavemen steal his food, his cave, his wife, or his children.

What would happen if you had no amygdala? Without an amygdala, a reptile, a caveman, and even you would have trouble surviving.

> In a 2010 study of a woman who had empty space where the amygdala should be, scientists found that the woman lacked ability to perceive potential danger. She also did not learn from experiences that had induced negative emotions.
>
> Justin Feinstein, the University of Iowa clinical neuropsychologist who was the study's lead author, reported that the woman went walking at night in an obviously unsafe park. She did not appropriately anticipate danger and, in fact, was assaulted. Then the next night she walked again in the same park.[44]

What if your amygdala is running the show?

When you feel threatened and get mad, odds are that you "go back brain"—that is, your amygdala takes charge. By contrast with reptiles, you do have information-gathering and language-capable frontal lobes in addition to your amygdala. Frontal lobe brain parts accomplish the "slow thinking" of data collection and solution creation that is unique to humans. Frontal lobe thinking gets shunted aside, however, when threats appear. You go back brain if your amygdala has taken charge. Your brain's frontal cortex gives up its say over your actions, letting the more primitive parts of your brain take over, so that impulsive behavior can speed up your reaction times.

The amygdala of people who get mad often and with excessive intensity is hyper-reactive. They too quickly "go back brain" because their amygdala overreacts in two ways: it sees danger where there is none, and it overrates the degree of threat. Like a smoke alarm that goes off in response to a harmless match flame, a hyper-reactive amygdala gives false positives, screaming "Danger!" when the trigger does not merit such a strong response.

In informal research that my colleague, energy therapist Dale Petterson, and I have done in our offices, an amygdala setting of 4 on a scale from 1 to 10 feels optimal to most people. Some prefer slightly lower or higher, at 3 if they want to feel especially mellow, or 5 if, like a writer or artist, they can manage and benefit from somewhat higher than average sensitivity.

Rate Your Amygdala's Emotional Reactivity

Is your amygdala set at an appropriate level of reactivity? Or does it mislead you to become angry too often and too intensely? Use the following scale to rate your emotional reactivity.

0	I have no emotional reactions. I am like a robot.
1-2	I am slow to react with fear or anger. I live my life in a friendly mellow mode and probably underreact to actual dangers.
3-5	I react with appropriate concern when I see a danger in my world.
6-7	I seem to be more emotional, anxious, or quick to get mad than most people. I often feel stressed. My emotional reactivity bothers my family members and sometimes embarrasses me.
8-10	I'm emotionally super-intense. My emotions make my life difficult. I feel agitated often and intensely. I may not show my emotional reactions publicly, but my emotions sometimes do cause me to misinterpret benign situations as threatening, to strike out with aggressive actions, and to say harsh words that that I later regret. My frequent anger interferes with being able to enjoy close, smooth, long-term relationships.

I would rate my amygdala's reactivity level at _____.

If your amygdala's reactivity hovers at 6 or 7 or above, your inner caveman probably adds to your stress as much or more than it protects you. If you rated your amygdala's setting at 8 to 10, your amygdala is in serious need of a reset if you want to enjoy a life—and want your family to enjoy a life—in which well-being prevails.

Resetting your amygdala's sensitivity level

In addition to assessing amygdala reactivity, Dale Petterson and I have experimented with techniques for adjusting emotional reactivity. Our technique for this challenge is similar to the energy-shifting technique we use to treat depression (Rx 2.10) in that it utilizes muscle kinesiology plus engagement of the body's subconscious knowledge of what it needs to do to heal. To view this potential amygdala reset option, check out the video example on prescriptionswithoutpills.com. Anyone, therapist or otherwise, who has learned how to do muscle testing (muscle kinesiology) could potentially do amygdala resetting. See prescriptionswithoutpills.com for instructions both for how to do muscle testing and for amygdala resetting.

Dale and I would welcome researchers who might want to research amygdala resetting. At this point, as I explained about our prefrontal lobe energy-shifting treatment for depression, our office does not have research capability for doing clinical trials ourselves. We do, however, hope that neuropsychologists and other researchers will soon begin to explore the potential of this and related techniques.

R_X 3.3: CHECK FOR FACTORS THAT FUEL ANGER.

The following vignette illustrates a situation that ignited anger in a man who was not particularly anger prone, yet, in this instance, did get mad.

Jim and his wife Elsie were visiting New York. When they left their hotel one evening to meet for dinner with new friends whom they were looking forward to getting to know, they realized they were running later than they had planned.

Because it was Saturday evening, many people were trying to flag down taxis, and too few cabs were driving by. Jim and Elsie both felt frustrated. Jim began to steam internally. He was annoyed that his wife had not planned for them to leave earlier. He strongly did not want to be late for the dinner date, yet hailing a cab was proving to be a much slower process than he or Elsie had anticipated.

"Let's head down the block," Jim said. "There's too many people competing for cabs here in front of our building."

Elsie joined Jim in heading that way. Elsie then noticed that several taxis seemed to be passing along a side street. "Let's go around that corner," she suggested to Jim.

"Stop telling me what to do!" Jim snapped.

Trusting her hunch nonetheless, Elsie rounded the corner herself, convinced that the side street would be more likely to yield an empty cab. Sure enough, she immediately spotted one. The driver stopped for her to get in. Meanwhile, drivers of cars behind him honked impatiently for her taxi to move on.

"Here's a cab!" Elsie shouted, in hopes that Jim, who had not followed her around the corner, would hear her voice above the din of the honking horns. Jim looked up, but instead of walking quickly toward her, he seemed to be slowing down. Elsie shouted again with increased urgency, "Hurry, the cab driver is blocking the cars behind him!"

When Jim did arrive and climbed into the cab, he was clearly angry. "You're always telling me what to do!" he seethed at Elsie. "You have no right to yell at me to hurry! I hate when you criticize me and boss me around!"

The following eleven factors often fuel anger. How many of these may have factored in to Jim's flare-up at Elsie? Check the ones that you guess might have fueled Jim's strong anger reaction.

Anger Fuels List
Download this worksheet at *prescriptionswithoutpills.com*.

❏   **Rushing**

❏   **Importance** when a situation feels like it has significant consequences

❏   **Frustration** from inability to accomplish something that's important to you

❏   **Hunger**

❏   **Fatigue** or **debilitation** from physical pain or illness

❏   **Overwhelmed by complexity** from too much happening at once or excessive background noise

❏   **Personalizing** from interpreting as directed at you personally something someone is saying or doing for other reasons. See Rx 3.1 and also 3.9 for more on personalizing.

❏   **Should thoughts**, as in "He should have..." or "She shouldn't have..."

❏   **Externalizing**, which is blaming someone or something outside of yourself instead of seeing your role in the situation. Externalizers believe "If I feel bad, it must be your fault."

❏   **Misplaced focus** when anger focuses you on what you want others to do instead of on being in charge of yourself

❏   **Projection,** which is accusing others of doing, feeling, or thinking what you yourself are doing, feeling, or thinking. See 2.8 and 4.7 for more on projection.

❏   **Feeling threatened or injured, emotionally or physically** so you defend yourself or counterattack to protect yourself

How many of the anger factors above were fueling Jim's irritated response? All of them!

The first several are fairly self-explanatory. Jim and Elsie both were understandably *tired*, *hungry*, and *frustrated* with respect to getting to an *important* destination. They were late, stressed about the fact that they were making their friends wait for them, and *rushing*. With so much New York evening traffic going this way and that, horns honking, darkness of night, bright lights from the cars, and crowds of people pushing here and there, the *complexity* of the environment further heightened their stress.

Externalizing involves attributing the problem to something wrong with a person or factor other than yourself. "She should have planned for us to leave earlier." And later, "I'm only mad because *you* were telling me to hurry!"

Jim *personalized* in interpreting his wife as berating him. She had shouted to him in order to be heard above the din of honking horns. He personalized also when he interpreted his wife's comment that their cab was blocking other cars as implying that the blockage was his fault or that he was too slow.

Jim's *misplaced focus* also was typical of what happens when an excessively stressful situation shifts someone into anger mode. Instead of being able to say, "I found that situation of having to hail a cab here in NYC at night totally overwhelming," Jim focused on what Elsie had or had not done, blaming her for his stress. Misplaced focus causes externalizing, blame and also controlling habits that come out as bossiness.

Projection works like a movie projector, projecting onto the screen of the other person the movie that is in the speaker's projector. When Jim criticized Elsie, saying, "You're always telling me what to do!" Jim was accusing Elsie of what he himself was prone to do.

Use the Anger Fuels checklist to understand what fuels your fires

Now use the checklist above to understand what might have fueled your fires in a recent anger episode that you may have experienced.

- Write out all the details you can recall about an annoying situation you have faced. Include what you did, felt, thought, and said.
- Then circle back to assess the incident with your Anger Fuels checklist. Were you or others feeling rushed, urgent, or hungry? Were you personalizing or projecting? Continue down the full list of anger fuels.

R$_x$ 3.4: EXPLORE YOUR ANGER TRIGGERS AND MODELS, THEN FIND BETTER SOLUTIONS.

Are you a hot reactor or someone who tends to stay cool in challenging situations? And even if you are slow to anger, what triggers set you off? Self-awareness offers a springboard for change. This prescription starts therefore with charting your anger patterns. It then suggests a visualization exercise for exchanging needless angers for healthier interactions.

When, about What, and How intensely do you get angry?

To answer these questions, become a scientist studying your anger. Keep a list for one week of all the times you feel, suppress, or express any angry feelings or actions. List every anger moment. Include those incidents that stir up tiny traces of irritation, full-blown anger storms, and everything in between. You may be surprised at what you find.

To fill in the anger log below, plumb your vocabulary for anger words or use the list below. Anger words that clarify the quality and intensity of your feelings can help you to realize that some of the interactions you have been considering normal in fact convey needless anger to others.

Annoyed	Miffed	Chastising
Irritated	Snippy	Judgmental
Frustrated	Indignant	Blaming
Agitated	Insistent	Frantic
Displeased	Galled	Mad
Impatient	Huffy	Outraged
Hurried	Appalled	Furious
Piqued	Exasperated	Storming
Pissed	Resentful	Raging

After you have kept the chart for some time, preferably for a week or more, look back to identify patterns. Are you more prone to anger at certain times of day? At transition times, like getting children out the door for school? In other repeatedly occurring situations? Toward particular people? What particular triggering thoughts or concerns come to mind?

My Anger Log
Download this worksheet at *prescriptionswithoutpills.com.*

DAY	TIME	TRIGGER	MY FEELING	FUELS	I HAD WANTED
Mon	7:30 am	Kids still in bed	Annoyance	Rushing	Kids catch bus

---

Toni thought of herself as someone who rarely gets mad. When she kept an anger log, however, she was struck by the number of times she snipped sarcastically at her husband or spoke in a frustrated tone of voice to her children.

If you keep your anger log for a full week, you may gain a surprising bonus. Keeping track of your anger gradually gives you more control over it. Are your anger episodes decreasing as the week goes on? If so, consider keeping the log for a second week or more.

Day and time

Irritability before breakfast (or dinner) can be a sign that low blood sugar, i.e., hypoglycemia, may be a risk factor for you. If so, consider keeping a chunk of cheese or other protein handy. Similarly, are you prone to anger in the evenings when you get tired? If you have an alcoholic drink?

Triggers

Most people repeatedly get angry in a small number of recurring situations. I learned this principle from Mrs. Bales, my violin teacher. Mrs. Bales taught me that if I make a mistake when I am playing a music piece, I am likely to make the same mistake in the same place in that piece the next time I play it. By circling on the sheet music the specific passages where I had flubbed, I could see where to concentrate my practice in the week ahead to eliminate the trouble spots. The strategy of keeping an anger log is similar. Note your trouble spots. As you then find new solutions to replace anger in these repeat situations, your anger outbursts may virtually cease.

> Kevin realized that he and his son Bobby frequently fought about what time to leave for soccer practices. Because Kevin coached the team, he liked to arrive at the field a half hour early to set up and to talk to parents who might have questions. Bobby liked staying home as long as possible and would drag his feet until Kevin shouted at him.
>
> As he looked closely at these arguments, Kevin realized that neither he nor Bobby had been listening to the other's concerns. Kevin really did need to arrive a half hour early before practices. Bobby wanted to stay at home to enjoy computer time. By telling Bobby that he would be allowed to bring his small portable computer with him to use while he waited for practices to start, Kevin brought the arguments about departures totally to a halt.

In the *Best Possible Light* . . . ?

Circle back over the items in your chart to ask yourself the *Best Possible Light* question, a technique I first explained in Rx 2.9 for understanding and ending protracted grief reactions. *If I look at my anger in the best possible light, what is it intended to accomplish?*

This question is nearly magical with regard to the extent to which it can bring you clarity. Once you understand the well-intended goal of a habit, you can then create an alternative, more effective, and less costly strategy for accomplishing the same objectives.

> Kevin asked himself, "If I look at my anger in those fights with Bobby in the best possible light, what was it intended to accomplish?"
>
> His answer was clear. "I want him to do what I want just because I said so."
>
> Hearing his revelation, Kevin groaned. "Oh no," he said to himself. "That's just what my dad used to expect that I hated so much growing up. He didn't get it that I also had concerns, just like I've been dismissive of Bobby's."

Sometimes answering that question—*If I look at my anger in the best possible light, what is the anger intended to accomplish?*—can be deeply enlightening. Anger causes your eyes to point outward. If your focus has been fixed on others—that is, on what *others* are doing or not doing—asking yourself the *Best Possible Light* question can refocus your thinking on yourself.

> Kevin then had a further thought. "Looking at my anger in the *best possible light*, I see now another reason why I get so mad at Bobby. I'm trying to be a more-than-perfect coach, and Bobby's thwarting that.
>
> "I've been putting too much pressure on myself. If I arrived sometimes just ten minutes ahead of the practices, I'd still be a plenty good coach.
>
> "As I think about it, I see now that I'm doing the same thing at work, which is why I've been feeling so stressed. Aiming to excel so far beyond the job requirements probably isn't necessary there either. Wow."

Where did you learn your anger patterns?

Before leaving the subject of anger patterns, a quick look back to your personal history may prove useful. Your mother and father were your first models for how men and women are supposed to treat each other and their children. You then learned also from peers at school and in the neighborhood, especially if you experienced a bully, or if your neighborhood was one where violence was the norm. These experiences may have influenced your adult ideas of when and how to deal with angry feelings.

Close your eyes. Allow images to come up of people in your younger years expressing anger. Who do you see? _____

What are they doing? _____

What, as a child, was your emotional reaction to these scenes?

_____

What did you do in response? _____

If your parents frequently spoke to each other or to their children in anger, that puts you at increased risk for doing the same. The *content* of your parents' arguments is likely to become your own as well as the style of their anger habits. List the issues that you can recall your parents bickering or battling over.

_____

To what extent do these same issues trigger anger in you?

_____

Roger's dad used to become irritable each time the family needed to leave to go somewhere together. Departures seemed to him to involve excessive waiting for his wife. No doubt this was true, given that the family included five children, all of whom needed to be readied at every transition, a role that belonged to his mom.

When Roger himself married and became a dad, he saw himself repeating his dad's irritability at departure times.

How did your parents react when you expressed anger toward them?

_____

Some parents become intimidated by their children's anger. Instead of retaining a sense of parental authority, they feel helpless vis-à-vis their children's outbursts. Did your parents give you your way if you became angry enough? _____ If so, their inability to stand up to your anger could leave you vulnerable today to using anger to get your way.

Larry recalled his parents telling him that even as an infant he had overwhelmed them with his strong personality. He always seemed to know exactly what he wanted. He didn't just cry. He shrieked until he got it. Then as a teenager, he shouted intimidatingly at his parents until they caved in to his demands.

Larry's parents both had grown up with abusive fathers. In addition, because they both worked stressful full-time jobs, they were too weary after work and on the weekends to stand up to their strong-willed young son. Instead, they slipped into the template of appeasement they each had learned as children for dealing with an angry parent—except that, alas, the "parent" now was their young son.

By the time he was a teenager, Larry had become as cruel a tyrant over his parents as his parents' fathers had been. Larry had learned from his interactions with his parents that he was entitled to get anything he wanted. Now Larry was on his way to becoming an abusive spouse.

Some children interact collaboratively with their parents until their teenage years. They discover then that they can use anger outbursts to control Mom and Dad. That was the case for Margaret.

When she was in her elementary school years, Margaret's parents had adopted a child who turned out to have severe biologically based behavior problems. Overwhelmed by trying to keep him safe and themselves sane, Margaret's parents had ceased to notice that Margaret was feeling increasingly neglected.

In her teen years, Margaret finally found a solution. If she raged, her parents would pay attention to her. As an adult, when she wanted attention from her husband, what did she do? Rage.

Find new solutions

The ultimate goal of the exercise of noting the times and triggers for your anger is to figure out new systems for handling these repeated situations. Assume in every case where you have been getting angry that a new system for managing that kind of situation could prevent the old trigger and, therefore, the anger, from occurring. The key to being able to design a new system is to ask the *Best Possible Light* question.

Anger trigger #1

Brent felt angry when his wife, Kate, would tell her mother about their marital problems. Kate in this case asked the *Best Possible Light* question. Kate discovered that she felt helpless vis-à-vis her mother's intrusiveness into her personal world.

Kate surprised Brent when she told him that her mother's involvement in the intimate details of their married life felt as uncomfortable to her as it did to him. Her dilemma was that when her mother would ask questions, she felt caught like a fish on a hook. She squirmed but couldn't get away.

Kate realized, "I love my mom. But if I don't talk with her about my problems, I don't know what we would do when we have coffee together in the mornings."

New solution: Kate would invite her mom to start going to an exercise class with her in the mornings during what used to be their coffee times. That way they could enjoy exercising together instead of talking about Brent and Kate's marriage.

Anger trigger #2

Janice gets mad when her boyfriend, Geoffrey, flirts with women at social gatherings. Janice's *Best Possible Light* discovery was that she wanted to do all she could to prevent marrying someone who would be unfaithful to her the way her father had cheated on her mother.

New solution: Janice and Geoffrey sat down to talk realistically, without rancor, about Geoff's flirting. The outcome surprised them both. "I'm just not the marrying kind," Geoffrey admitted. "I'm always on the prowl for the next partner, and I like that part of me."

Geoffrey's self-description came as a relief to Janice. Now she could stop beating herself up for not being "good enough" as a girlfriend. In addition, the information enabled her to admit that she herself definitely *was* "the marrying kind."

Janice and Geoff mutually decided to end the relationship, affectionately, and with no feelings of rejection on either side. Within months, Janice met a man whose companionship she enjoyed as much or more than Geoffrey's and whose mindset, like hers, included eagerness to commit wholeheartedly to monogamy, to marry, and to start a family.

Anger trigger #3

Steven gets mad when his wife, Joy, has said she'll pay their energy bill, yet they then receive a notice that the bill has not been paid. Steven's *Best Possible Light* question helped him to realize that being responsible held high value for him. Overdue bill notices did not fit with that self-image.

New solution: Steve and Joy agreed that their current bill-paying system was unreliable because, with a full-time job plus three children, Joy had too much on her plate. They decided to look on the Web for a "personal assistant." They would find someone they could pay for several hours on the fifteenth of each month to do bill paying at their home.

Once the assistant had begun paying the bills, Steve and Joy realized that while she was at their house for the evening she also could babysit their sleeping young children. They took the opportunity to slip out of the house for a movie date night. With the new routine, the bills got paid, the fights went away, and Steve and Joy could revel in a monthly bonus evening out together.

Anger as a motivator

Besides regarding anger as a means to identification of problems, how else can you use anger as a valuable asset? Because anger energizes you, it can motivate you to accomplish positive goals such as athletic, scholastic, or financial achievement. Sill, beware. Like fire, which can be used to heat homes or to burn them down, anger can help you or can become self-destructive.

> Victoria had been determined to win the race. As she entered the final stretch, two women remained ahead of her.
>
> "I'm mad!" she thought to herself. "I've worked so hard, and now I'll come in at third place. That's not good enough. I'm mad at how sluggish my start was. I shouldn't have slowed down midway. That was dumb. How could I have messed up so much! I'm furious at myself!"

Victoria's self-defeating series of anger-turned-inward thoughts resulted in her falling even further behind. Notice the change after Victoria had learned to use her anger constructively.

> Victoria, in a later race, again was determined to win. Again, two women remained ahead of her.

"I'm mad!" Victoria thought to herself. "I'm mad that those women are ahead of me. I can run better than them. They don't deserve to beat me. I'm going to overtake the one just ahead. NOW. Go, Vicky! Kick butt!"

Within minutes, the fire within her had powered Victoria's quickened pace enough to overtake the woman just ahead of her.

"Now I'm mad at that other gal. She beat me two years ago. Once was enough. I'm going to pass her and stay on fire until I've passed the finish line. Go! Show them who's best! Go! Go! Go, girl, go!"

What did Victoria do differently in the second version of her race? In the winning version, she focused her anger externally, not on herself. At the same time, the anger did not control her. Rather, she harnessed her anger in a way that allowed her to keep control of the reins. And yes, Victoria won.

R_X 3.5: REGARD ANGER AS A STOP SIGN.

If your pot has a tendency to boil over, you probably still have within you a small voice that whispers *Getting mad will not be the best way to handle this problem.*

Chuck had been waiting too long in the ticket line. He was worried that he would miss his plane. When he finally reached the front of the line, he hissed at the ticket agent, "What's wrong with this airline? These long waits are inexcusable!"

Instead of speeding up, the ticket agent walked away. She paused to chat with another agent. She clearly had not liked feeling lectured.

For Chuck, listening to his quiet voice would have been helpful. The mantra *Anger is a stop sign* would have been helpful as well. What do you do at a stop sign? Everyone knows the answer to that. You do not pick up the stop sign and clobber oncoming cars with it. No. You Stop, Look, and Listen.

A vital prescription for relief from anger, therefore, is to think of anger as a stop sign. That is, any time you become aware of feeling angry, resist the impulse to cudgel people with your anger. Resist the impulse, too, to ignore your anger until suddenly, seemingly out of the blue, you explode. Instead, remind yourself that *Anger is a stop sign. What do you do at a stop sign? Stop, Look, and Listen.*

Anger Is a Stop Sign

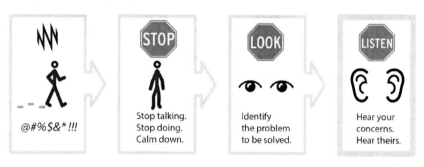

	STOP	LOOK	LISTEN
@#%$&*!!!	Stop talking. Stop doing. Calm down.	Identify the problem to be solved.	Hear your concerns. Hear theirs.

Stop

As soon as you realize that you are beginning to heat up, stop your participation in the current interaction. Stop talking. Stop doing. Stop to take a moment for calming distraction. Pleasantly turn to another topic: "Oh, by the way, did you notice that the crocuses are coming up in our garden? I love springtime . . . " Or turn physically to leave the situation that is triggering you.

> Ellie, just six years old, was in the family room, trying to learn to throw darts. The more she practiced, the fewer darts hit the dartboard. She felt more and more frustrated, then angry.
>
> Suddenly Ellie turned around and ran into her mother's in-home office. She picked up a book, curled up in the corner of the sofa, read until she felt calmer, and then went back to the dartboard to try again.

Look

Once you have paused long enough to allow your adrenaline to drain down, long enough that you feel back to your calm self, look about you for relevant information about the problem situation.

A helpful starter question is, "What biological factors may be making me anger prone at this moment? Am I tired? Hungry? Getting sick? Feeling anxious or overloaded?" Conditions that create emotional brittleness and excessive amygdala reactivity could be causing you to interpret a minor problem as a major catastrophe.

Next, take a fresh look at the provocative situation. Pinpoint the specific trigger that ignited your anger. The trigger could have been external, like something someone said or did. It could have been a thought within you. As soon as you identify it, pause again, lest you reignite.

Once you are sure that you are still emotionally in the calm zone, ask yourself, "What do I want?" This question focuses you internally, that is, on what you want rather than on what others are doing.

The magic question from Rx 2.9 and 3.4 also works: "If I look at my anger in the best possible light, what was I trying to accomplish?" The questions "What do I want?" and "What do I want to accomplish?" focus your attention ahead as well as within. Refocusing forward, on where you are trying to go, prepares you to find a successful strategy for getting there. They redirect you to the Find Solutions Road to well-being.

Lastly, query yourself, "What might I do differently to more effectively get what I want?" Now you are solidly on the road to finding solutions.

Beware, though, of two technical errors to avoid. First, avoid the negative *don't want* version of the *what do I want* question. Asking yourself what you *don't want* would give you little to no guidance as to what you *do want* to accomplish. If you know you *do not want to* go to Houston, you may end up in Miami. If you know that you *want to* go to New York, the odds zoom up that you will find a route there.

Second, avoid the trap of misplaced focus. Anger draws your focus externally, to what you want others to do differently. Ruminating on others' mistaken actions and what they "should" do differently, however, will just escalate both their irritation and yours. Others want to direct their own lives. It is not your job to write their script for them.

Instead of asking yourself, "What do I want *you/him/her* to do differently?" your job is to figure out what *you* can do differently. This distinction will be further explained in Rx 6.2 and 6.6, prescriptions that clarify the skills that sustain collaborative relationships.

Avoiding the misplaced focus trap by focusing on what you yourself can do differently can be challenging. This re-direction takes a conscious decision. You are likely to need to put your mind on manual control until the new habit becomes automatic.

Anger | What to Look For after I Have Calmed Down

Was I
Hungry?
Tired?
Rushed?
Getting sick?
Overwhelmed?

What
was the
trigger?

STAY
CALM

Think:
**What do
I want?**

Smarter ways
to get
what I want?

Listen

Here comes the hardest part of using anger as a stop sign. In response to a stop sign on a road, everyone knows to look both ways before proceeding forward. Use this principle in response to anger as well. Let the stop sign, when you feel angry, remind you to look in two directions. Look first within yourself to listen to your own concerns. Then look to listen to clarify what others want.

How do you find out the concerns of others involved in a problem situation? Ask open-ended *how* or *what* questions. Listen then to their concerns with an ear to understanding what makes sense about what you are hearing, not to criticize their answer.

"I'm furious!" Andrew exploded. "How could you buy a new car without including me in the decision? We always buy big-ticket items together. Why didn't you invite me to go with you to the car dealer?"

Aria paused a moment to calm her impulse to react defensively. She then responded calmly, "I noticed a car that I really liked in the used car lot I pass on the way home. I tried to phone you, but your cell phone must have been off.

"The salesman offered a great price. I knew it was good because we've looked together at so many cars of that type. As the salesman and I were talking, someone else came over and said he wanted to buy the car so I spoke up right away, 'I'm sorry, sir; I've already decided to buy it.'"

Andrew, who had been reminding himself to listen openly and not to reject what he was hearing, replied appreciatively, "Oh . . . I get it now. Now I'm glad that you took immediate action. Good thing we've gone together so many times to look at cars. And great that you had the guts to just buy it without me. I picked a winner when I married you!"

Fortunately, if you do remind yourself to ask about others' concerns, and then listen openly to understand and take seriously their responses, your odds of getting what you want will zoom upward. Sound paradoxical that listening to others' concerns helps you to get what you want? It is, and it's real.

Ask any skillful salesperson. The more a salesperson understands a customer's concerns, the more likely that the two of them will reach an agreement. The more you understand the concerns of a person you're angry with, the more likely you will succeed in finding solutions—solutions that will work for both of you.

> Jordan, a single father, had set up an appointment several months prior for dental surgery for his teenage daughter, Amy. When Jordan, who had taken the day off from work without pay, picked up his daughter to take her to the surgery, Amy announced that she had decided she didn't want to go.
>
> Remembering that Amy never wanted to go to dentists, Jordan at first tried cajoling her. When Amy still said no, Jordan began thinking about getting billed for very expensive dental procedures that his daughter was unwilling now to receive, not to mention the lost day of income. He felt his anger rising. How could his daughter, who had been complaining so much about her teeth hurting her, be so unappreciative of his attempt to help?
>
> Before letting himself explode in anger to force Amy out the door and into the car, Jordan quieted himself. "*Stop* to calm down; *Look* to clarify what I want; and *Listen* to Amy's concerns as well as to my own," he reminded herself.
>
> Jordan paused. He chatted with Amy for a few minutes about her cute new haircut. Feeling calmer, Jordan then asked himself what he wanted and how better to get it.
>
> *I want Amy's teeth to stop hurting her. I hate seeing her suffer. And I want to do it without unnecessary further expenses or having to take more time off from work,* he said to himself. Pausing for a moment, Jordan then switched his focus to Amy. *Actually,* Jordan realized, *I have no idea about Amy's concerns.*
>
> Determined to listen with open ears to his daughter's concerns, Jordan asked Amy what was holding her back from wanting to fix her teeth. The answer transformed Jordan's anger immediately into empathy.

"I'm afraid you'll be mad if I tell you," Amy said.

"No, I promise I won't. I really want to understand," Jordan replied.

"You're sure?" Amy asked again.

"Yes, I'm sure," Jordan said, noting that Amy sounded ominously fearful.

"A week ago I had a terrible experience. I was out running in the park, like you've always told me I shouldn't do alone at night. Someone attacked me. He tried to rape me, and it hurt a lot. Ever since then, I've been bleeding and throwing up in disgust. By now I just feel too weak for dental surgery."

"Oh, horrors, Amy! I love you so much. Thank you so much for telling me! Forget the dentist. Let's go to a doctor—and to the police. My poor baby!"

In sum, for reliable anger control when you see red, remind yourself, *Anger is a stop sign. What do you do at a stop sign? Stop, Look, and Listen.*

R̽ 3.6: DESIGN EXIT/RE-ENTRY PLANS TO PREVENT ARGUMENTS.

Anger is to emotions what speeding is to driving your car. The odds of dangerous injuries zoom upward as your anger-ometer begins to spike. If you or someone you are interacting with is exhibiting even low-level anger, the risk that you will collide increases. Faster or louder emotions exacerbate the danger.

Keep in mind that anger is contagious. If you do not feel angry but the person you are speaking with is beginning to sound inflamed, that too signals that a stop would be helpful for both of you. Fatal accidents with major injuries in both cars often start with just one person who is speeding dangerously.

How can you implement the rule that anger is a stop sign if a brief pause does not suffice? Look for an off-ramp. If you feel anger rising within you, or if you sense it rising in the person you are talking with, exit the conversation. Exit the room. Exit the house if need be. Or, in extreme cases, exit the relationship.

In my first job after earning a master's degree, I worked as an English teacher in a drug treatment program. The director of the program, Mr. Lancet, was a handsome, youngish fellow, so I was flattered when I received a message asking me to come to his office.

I had no sooner sat down in the upright office chair across from his large desk when Mr. Lancet began berating me. I felt stunned. The tongue-lashing seemed to come out of the blue.

Within seconds, I instinctively stood up. "I don't do anger," I said from the heart as I turned and walked out of the room.

Mr. Lancet never bothered me again.

Implement graceful exits to eliminate arguments. It works with just about any and everyone, including a salesperson, work colleagues, your boss, friends, parents, children, a spouse—yes, anyone. There's no need to say why you are leaving. Gracefully excuse yourself, for instance with the words, "Excuse me, please. I need to get a drink of water."

Exits implement the "one hand clapping" principle. What happens if one hand tries to clap and the other refuses to join in? No clapping will occur. If, when someone speaks to you in an unpleasantly irritated tone, you leave the conversation for a few minutes to go get a drink of water, no fighting will ensue. Exits ensure fight-free environments.

Plan ahead, preferably together

In part, the power of an exit comes from the fact that only one person needs to know what to do to implement it. If you or someone you live or work with sometimes has anger management difficulties, there's no need to change anyone. You just need to exit when anger begins to brew.

At the same time, for ongoing and especially for intimate relationships, design your anger exit plan together to launch a new fight-free era. Co-planning mutual exit-reentry routines prevents either of you from feeling that an exit means that one of you is walking out on the other. Your exits are more likely to feel mutual if together you plan dual choreography. That is, agree that as soon as either of you initiates an exit, the other will simultaneously exit in a different direction. No door-slamming, and NEVER follow after someone as they exit.

Design your exit and reentry routines with the questions below or write it out on the form you can download from prescriptionswithoutpills.com. Well-being and goodwill thrive in an atmosphere of consistently collaborative interactions, unmarred by intermittent anger.

How will I know when I need to initiate an exit?

Early exits are preferable. Pay attention to even subtle indications that either you or the person you are talking with is heating up—sounding frustrated, irritated or defensive, talking louder or faster, criticizing, accusing, sounding contemptuous, or listening dismissively. Note also small inflammatory words like an accusatory *you*, a dismissive *but*, or a demoralizing *not* (Rx 6.2). These words raise the danger levels.

As soon as you notice any departures from calm dialogue, take an off-ramp. Continuing to talk once one either of you is becoming angry is likely to prove more costly than productive.

What I will notice that indicates time for an exit:

_____

What my partner will notice:

_____

How will I initiate the exit?

If you have noted anger rising early enough that your exit requires just a change of topic, use distraction. Reset the emotional tone by chatting about something safe like the weather or what to eat at your next meal. If, however, a physical exit looks necessary, start with your legs. Stand up and start walking, saying calmly as you move forward, "Excuse me. I need to get a drink of water." Or together, in your planning session, pick an easy-to-remember code word or phrase to indicate an exit moment.

> I once explained exit routines to a young adult woman, Jill. We were preparing for a session which would include her parents and the sister toward whom she had a long history of erupting into angry rages. We practiced her exits several times so that Jill would be able to accomplish them smoothly.
>
> Less than five minutes into the hour of the subsequent family session, Jill stood up and started walking toward the door saying, "I need a drink of water. Be right back."
>
> Jill subsequently left the room several more times, executing her exits so gracefully that I had been wondering if her frequent thirst indicated diabetes. It was not until her third departure for water that, even though I had taught her the exit technique, I realized that Jill was using her exit routine.

Pay attention to which body part to use to start your exit. Remember to begin with your legs, not your mouth. Talking about whether or not to exit is seldom helpful, nor is asking for permission. Just quietly stand up, start walking, and leave the room saying only one brief, pre-planned exit sentence or code word.

My part of the plan:

_____

My partner's part of the plan:

_____

What will my partner do when I exit?

When you first try exit-reentry routines, you or your partner may think, "Don't turn your back on me!" No one wants his/her partner to walk out on him/her.

To prevent abandonment feelings, practice the choreography when you both are feeling fine. Agree that as soon as either of you initiates an exit, the other will exit as well, with both of you heading toward pre-designated areas. Practice simultaneously turning your backs on each other.

In addition, agree to guidelines including no door slamming, no hostile parting comments, and NO following after each other. Agree that if either of you is unable to follow the mutual exit plan, one or both of you will immediately leave the building. If your relationship is volatile, keep your keys, wallet, and cell phone by the door.

Increase the odds that both of you will remember your new routines by repeatedly practicing them, like actors would practice their movements and lines in a play or like students would practice a fire drill. Be certain that both of you can exit safely.

My part of the plan:

_____

My partner's part of the plan:

_____

Where will I go?

Go to separate rooms. Designate a Quiet Chair in your respective rooms for each of you. A Quiet Chair is a pre-designated place where you can sit comfortably, undisturbed, until you have returned to feeling calm. Arrange distraction materials like music, magazines, books, knitting, or a computer within reach of your chair to busy your mind with pleasant activities.

If arguments begin in a car, exit the conversation by turning on a radio. Anger in cars can be particularly dangerous. Exit early.

My part of the plan:

_____

My partner's part of the plan:

_____

How will I calm myself?

Sip a cooling glass of water and take a few minutes to enjoy yourself in your Quiet Chair. Or turn to distractions, like watering plants, working out, listening to music, or playing with children. Check your email and favorite websites, take a walk outdoors and focus on what you see there, or make a phone call. Do activities that keep your thoughts on pleasant topics.

My part of the plan:

_____

My partner's part of the plan:

_____

What will I not do?

The most common exit mistake is to take your anger partner with you in your head. Tempting as it may be, do not continue to think about him or her. Ruminating on "What he did" or "She had no right to . . ." will keep fanning the anger flames, preventing a successful cooldown. To relieve anger, remove your thoughts from the situation that troubled you.

Telling yourself, "Don't think about . . ." will not suffice. That would be like telling yourself, "Don't think about pink elephants." All you will see is more pink elephants. Instead, put your thoughts elsewhere. Distract yourself with an alternative activity, a book, etc.

For a particularly fun exercise on this vital point, see the anger section of my website poweroftwomarriage.com.

My part of the plan:

_____

My partner's part of the plan:

_____

When and how will we reengage?

As you become skillful at cooling down, you are likely to be able to return to the prior conversation within five to ten minutes. However, because people vary significantly in how long they take to self-calm, develop realistic expectations.

When you have both returned to your pre-designated re-engagement room, begin reconnecting with easy chitchat. There's always the weather, sports, or similarly benign topics about which you can talk cooperatively.

My part of the plan:

_____

My partner's part of the plan:

_____

How can you be sure that you will readdress the issue cooperatively?

Once you feel confident that both of you have successfully self-soothed, gently readdress the sensitive topic. Utilize the prescriptions in Chapter 6, especially the following, to keep the dialogue productive and safe:

- Rx 6.2 on *Word Patrol*
- Rx 6.3 on *Six Safe Sentence Starters*
- Rx 6.6 for the *Win-Win Waltz*
- Rx 6.9 on healing after upsetting incidents

My part of the plan:

_____

My partner's part of the plan:

_____

Consider printing out the worksheets for guiding these skills that you can download from prescriptionswithoutpills.com. Use them to insure that your discussion will stay calm and constructive.

And for children . . .

Mutually designed exit plans work for angry children as well as for overheating adults. Encourage the child to choose and set up a Quiet Chair to have a safe and comforting place to go to for anger cool-downs. Select a few favorite toys and books to keep nearby. Even young children can learn to treat anger as a stop sign.

For sibling squabbles, establish a "peace table," a place where children who have been fighting and then calmed down in their Quiet Chairs can go to sit and talk for the re-entry part of their exit/re-entry routines. Even young children, after they have calmed down, often can be surprisingly collaborative, insightful, generous, and creative about solving the problem that triggered their upset. Sometimes children (and adults as well) also need food, a nap, or an engaging activity if the fighting came from being hungry, tired, or bored.

Building exit, calm-down, Quiet Chair, and Peace Table routines with children teaches them that talking, not angry flailing, gets them what they want. By teaching your children that raging is out of bounds, you also are minimizing the risk that when your children become adults they will choose an anger-prone life partner.

One additional technique for insuring that your home stays fight-free is vital. Answer your children only when they talk to you in normal voice tones. If your children whine or rant, explain, "I only understand what people say when they talk quietly." Be consistent in responding only when they are in talk, not agitated, mode. Similarly, make an agreement with your spouse that the two of you will talk together only in comfortable voices.

R̫ 3.7: DEFUSE ANGER WITH *THAT WAS THEN, THIS IS NOW*.

A decision that you will no longer interact with others when either you or they are angry launches change. Anger may still boil up within you from time to time. Even if you succeed in taking the pot off the stove by removing yourself quickly from situations that are getting too hot, you may find that specific triggers repeatedly foment anger within you. *That Was Then, This Is Now*, a visualization strategy prescribed earlier for depression (Rx 2.5), can help you to recognize and deactivate anger triggers that are holdovers from earlier life experiences.

Here are again the questions that guide this visualization, questions that, as I mentioned in Rx 2.5, I read aloud for you on prescriptionswithoutpills.com:

- **Close your eyes.**
- **Picture, as in the prior exercise,** where the feeling is located in your body and how it feels.

- **Allow an image to appear** on your visual screen of an earlier time when you experienced a similar feeling. How old were you then?
- **What is the same** then and now? Give details.
- **Identify what is different** now that can enable you to feel more safe and to handle the situation with an option available to a grown-up.
- **Older consoler**: Is there an older part of me that can console the younger part of me that feels distressed? If so, let that voice console the younger me.
- **New solution plan:** Given these deeper understandings of myself, what might be more effective ways of handling the present situation?
- **Check again how the feeling looks** and feels in your body. If pieces remain, find solutions for these, perhaps with *Do or Become (Rx 6.8)*.

The prescription works by unlinking current anger escalations from the specific childhood experience that formed that particular anger template.

When Paul returned home from work that evening, Anita didn't even look up when he entered. She didn't come over to kiss him and welcome him home. Instead, she stayed absorbed in the magazine article that she was reading. "I don't matter to her!" Paul thought, feeling anger rising quickly within him.

Paul was tempted to walk straight over to Anita and demand that she greet him. Fortunately, he realized that angrily forcing her to do what he wanted would be counterproductive. Instead he implemented his exit routine, turning away from Anita and heading for the kitchen.

Paul also knew to use distraction so that his exit would include a change in his internal thoughts, so he focused on pouring and then sipping a cooling glass of lemonade from the refrigerator. Spotting the newspaper on the kitchen table, he read the sports pages, becoming absorbed in the recent travails of his favorite team.

As his mind began to gravitate again back to angry thoughts of how his wife had ignored him, Paul returned to reading the newspaper to ease his again-rising distress. He had learned that he sometimes needed repeated gentle reminders to himself to keep his mind on pleasant topics.

Unaware that Paul had taken an anger exit, Anita came into the kitchen. "Paul! Welcome home! I'm so glad to see you! Sorry that I barely noticed when you came in the door. I was totally absorbed in the article I was reading about problems in the banking system. How did your meeting today with the bank about our mortgage go?"

Later Paul asked himself why he had felt so upset when Anita didn't greet him immediately. "I don't matter to her," he had quickly concluded. Realizing that fear of not mattering to his wife was a hot button for him, he decided to use a *That Was Then, This Is Now* visualization.

Would closing his eyes enable scenes to come to his mind of an earlier time in his life when he had experienced similar hurt, scared, frustrated, and angry feelings?

Paul closed his eyes and focused initially on where in his body he felt anger. It was a tennis-ball-sized hot ball of fire in his chest.

He then accelerated his access to the linked memory by asking himself, "How old do I feel now?" That question can facilitate identifying the specific experience from younger days that set the template for a current anger reaction.

"How old do I feel when I think that I don't matter to my wife?" To his surprise, the answer was clear and immediate. He felt seven years old. Why that age?

Paul recalled an incident at age seven in which he had desperately wanted his mother's attention. He had been playing outside when his foot became wedged between the spokes of his bike. He couldn't pull it free and suddenly felt terrified. Yet his mother, who was standing across the street, was too engaged in talking with a neighbor to hear his cries for help.

"I don't matter to her!" had been Paul's conclusion, the same thought that had accompanied his anger when Anita seemed to be ignoring his arrival at home.

As soon as he realized this connection, Paul felt relief. He immediately became aware of what now was different from when he was seven. "I'm a grown-up now. And the grown-up part of me knows that Anita does love and care about me. Phew."

The goal of *That Was Then, This Is Now*

Use any surprising upsurge of anger to think about what may have amplified your emotional reaction. Was your response because you were tired, hungry, or overloaded? Is there a situation for which you need better routines, a better system? Could there be an earlier-in-your-life sensitivity source?

If the answer to this last question is yes, find the link, the element that is the same in the earlier and current events. Then clarify what now, fortunately, is different. Seeing what is different re-empowers you. With this data, you can plan a new way to handle the situation that before had troubled you.

R_x 3.8: IDENTIFY WHAT YOU DO THAT INVITES ANGER IN OTHERS.

You are innocent, right? You certainly are not purposely inviting others to become angry toward you. How could anything you do be provocative? Well, here's how.

Out-of-bounds behaviors such as affairs and/or addictions clearly invite others' anger. So do actions that are inconsiderate, selfish, hurtful, dishonest, or irresponsible. Any of the above provoke ire in others because they are inherently injurious.

At the same time, the most common inadvertently provocative triggers tend to emerge in language patterns. Here are some examples. Check any that sound like part of your verbal repertoire. Even when these kinds of comments are well intentioned and spoken in a respectful, non-irritated voice, they are likely to provoke irritation or anger in others.

❑ **Criticizing, evident in *You*-messages**
   "You didn't look in the refrigerator to check if we have enough milk!"
   "You shouldn't stay up so late at night."

❑ **Complaining**
   "Why am I the only one who does the grocery shopping? I have a job too, you know!"

❑ **Controlling, that is, telling others what to do.**
In the language of my earlier book *The Power of Two*, I refer to violations of others' personal space as *crossovers* because they cross over the psychological boundaries between your personal space and others'.[45]

Telling others what to do and what not to do invites boundary-protection responses because you are violating their autonomy. You are responsible for governing your own behavior, not others'. You may be the boss at work. Telling employees there what to do may be appropriate. If, however, you tell friends or loved ones at home what you think they should be doing, you are switching from collaborative interactions to an invasive or controlling mode.

- "You need to . . ."
- "You should have . . ."
- "Why don't you just . . ."

Telling a spouse what to do is likely to trigger a spouse's sensitivities to being treated like a child, provoking a "Don't tell me what to do!" reaction.

"Be sure to stop for milk on the way home from work today."

"Don't treat me like a child. Of course I'll remember to pick up the milk! You're not my mother!"

Parents of course do sometimes need to tell children what to do. Even then, phrasing matters. If you were a child, which would you rather hear? "Tie your shoe." Or, "Shoelace alert!" The first sounds bossy. The second sounds like a game.

❏ Negating with *no, not, n't,* or *but*

Negations make the following dialogue frustrating to both participants. See Rx 6.2 for more on this provocative verbal pattern.

"I'll pick up milk on my way to Joey's daycare drop-off."

"*No,* I do*n't* think you should do that. You wo*n't* get Joey to daycare on time."

"Joey will cry if he has*n't* had his milk before he gets dropped off after daycare."

"We do*n't* need to cater to everything he wants. We can say *no* to him."

"I like being responsive when he tells us he wants something."

"*But* that will just make him spoiled."

❏ Ignoring or listening dismissively

"I'll be late tonight because I have our annual meeting at work."

"Have you seen my boots? It's muddy out."

"I said I have a meeting tonight."

"So what's new? You're always going to meetings."

❑ **Negative labeling and other attempts to humiliate or induce guilt**

"You're lazy. Just because you're sick doesn't mean you can't help."

❑ **Insisting *I'm right, you're wrong***

"It might snow today."

"*No*, it won't. I'm sure."

"I heard on the radio that there's a 30 percent chance of a snowstorm."

"I told you, *you're wrong*. I can tell by our barometer."

"Look outside. It's snowing now."

❑ **Getting agitated; raising your voice**

"I just hate it when the house gets messy!"

"Yeah, right," spoken sarcastically.

Do any of the above patterns of talk sound like you?____ If so, pay particular attention to the prescriptions ahead in Chapter 6. These prescriptions clarify the communication and conflict resolution patterns that sustain collaborative relationships. Whereas the patterns above invite anger from others, collaborative verbal patterns create goodwill.

R$_X$ 3.9: RELEASE RESENTMENTS ABOUT THE PAST.

While anger often arises to force others to give you something you want, anger also can be backwards looking. Angry grudges and resentments over past events, like embers from a campfire insufficiently extinguished, keep the fire danger high. They can easily re-ignite. As psychologist Stephen A. Diamond points out in his book *Anger, Madness, and the Daimonic*, anger that smolders becomes resentment; resentment can consolidate into bitterness; and bitterness can harden into hatred.[46]

Trade in guilt, regret, resentment, and revenge impulses for recovery

Do you repeatedly chastise yourself for your mistakes? _____ Do you often stir your anger pot by reminding yourself of actions by others that left you feeling hurt and angry? _____ Repetitive thoughts about what you have done that was mistaken will produce chronic guilt and regret. Repetitive thoughts about how someone else has hurt you will perpetuate angry resentment.

Continually feeding yourself with negative thoughts about your or others' mistakes usually stems from the belief that sustaining anger can protect you against repeats of the damaging incidents. In fact, angry ruminating produces more anger—and less safety. Sustained anger against others feeds resentment and against yourself invites depression.

> Lois berated herself for not having sold the large family home. She had received an offer from a buyer two years prior. Since that time, the real estate market had turned. The money she would receive for a sale now, money she was depending on for her retirement, would be considerably less than what she would have received by accepting that earlier offer.
>
> Lois was especially mad at herself for having caved in to fears of moving on to something new. She hammered herself into ever-increasing depression with the thought that opportunity doesn't knock twice. Feeling depressed made her even less able to make decisions or face changes.

Sustaining resentment in a relationship can inadvertently push away the very person you most want to draw closer to you.

> Howard had made a major mistake. On a business trip, he got drunk with a female work colleague, then invited her to his hotel room. Afterwards, Howard told his wife of his mistake and apologized profusely, overcome with shame.
>
> Howard's wife, Hannah, believed that the only way she would be able to protect herself from being hurt in this way again would be to punish him by holding on to a permanent state of resentment.
>
> In fact, Hannah's chronic resentment created a permanent wall between herself and Howard that never came down. Several years later, they agreed to divorce.

You may also use resentment to justify impulses to strike back. "I'm a victim, so I have the right to victimize you" invites a life mired in negative emotions. While striking back may even the score from your perspective, the wounds in the receiver invite a next round of retribution.

Belief in the need to sustain resentment to prevent further hurts or to get back at those who have hurt you invite unending trips down Fight Road. Retribution leads away from, not toward, well-being and secure relationships. Cultures of vengeance that lack healing mechanisms can stay on anger and hatred routes for centuries.

What is a better alternative? Recovery.

A patch of fire had erupted a week after lightning struck a tree near one of my favorite mountain walking pathways. The fire had been smoldering in the tree's roots since the lightning strike. Fortunately, a neighbor spotted smoke. The volunteer fire department at Timberline Fire Station quickly hiked up to the spot, calling in helicopters with water to help them put out the blaze.

Now, several years later, the spot that had burned has become one of the most florally exuberant on the hillside.

When old angers no longer smolder, forgiveness can blossom. Upsetting events that have healed can bring a re-flourishing of goodwill and affection.

The following set of twelve mantras and strategies that facilitate recovery from regrets and resentments gives you a variety of options. Use them for soothing anger at yourself and also for ending anger at others. Experiment with them. Different options and combinations of options work for different people and in different situations.

Mistakes are for learning

Instead of holding on to negative feelings after you or others have made mistakes, repeat the post-mistake self-talk mantra *Mistakes are for learning*. With this perspective, there is no such thing as failure. Situations that work out disappointingly are just learning opportunities. *Mistakes are for learning*.

Look back to learn

Look back to learn twins with *Mistakes are for learning*. Learn, and then move on. Whereas reactions of shame, blame, or failure lead to feeling worse and worse, looking back to learn leaves you feeling that you gained something from the mistake.

Robert, in the early years of his marriage, had succumbed to a narcotics addiction. "I can never forgive myself for all the damage I did to my wife and kids during that time." The result was a chronic cloud of regret that blocked him from being able to fully enjoy his life. His cloud of regret blocked him also from fully absorbing the affection of the many friends and family members who adored him.

At some point, Robert realized that he had not yet looked back to learn from his addiction years. "I can see that when I was addicted, I was either too drugged up or too preoccupied with when and how I would get my next fix to be there for my wife or children. The lesson I've learned is that for the rest of my life, starting now, I want to be actively involved in a loving way with all of them. That would be much better for me, and for them as well, than staying locked in regret. Regret has isolated me almost the same as the addiction did."

Business errors as well as personal mistakes offer opportunities to *look back to learn.*

Joshua's startup business venture sputtered and then crashed. Without the necessary capital to hire employees, he couldn't continue to try to launch the business. The substantial money he had invested so far, his life savings, now was gone.

"That was my business school," Joshua said to himself. "Now I understand what the word undercapitalized means. Next entrepreneurial idea I get, I'll make sure that I have or can get investors to lend me enough money to sustain the company until the business takes off. It takes a lot of initial cash to fuel a trip down the runway. Next time I'll know."

Professional athletes debrief by looking back to learn after their sporting events. In tennis, skillful professionals may debrief and reprogram themselves after many, or even every, mistake.

"I over-hit that shot. I need to stay relaxed when I go for a winner." The player then, ideally, would picture himself hitting with relaxed strength to consolidate the correction.

As the tennis example above illustrates, when you look back to learn, include two parts in the looking. First, figure out what went wrong. Second, feel or visualize yourself implementing a solution that will right the problem from that point forward.

> When Margery, who was in her seventies, glanced at herself in a full-length mirror at the clothing store, she realized that her body was tilting forward.
>
> "Oh, no!" Margery gasped. "I've been hunching over like my mother used to. How will I get myself to stand straight? I have an idea. When I stand, I'll remind myself to stand like I'm in a ballet class. And when I walk, I'll pretend I'm a model." Standing tall, she could feel the difference immediately.

Mistakes happen

Too much looking back to learn can become problematic, especially if the learning does not lead to reprogramming. *Could've*, *would've*, and *should've* responses then just prolong distress. As President Lyndon Johnson once said, "Yesterday is not ours to recover, but tomorrow is ours to win or lose."[47]

The famed American rapper, songwriter, actor Tupac Shakur, also known by his stage names 2Pac and (briefly) Makaveli, amplified this idea: "You can spend minutes, hours, days, weeks, or even months over-analyzing a situation, trying to put the pieces together, justifying what could've, would've happened . . . or you can just leave the pieces on the floor and move the f--k on."[48]

> Sophia spent a half hour driving to the license renewal office. She waited for a frustrating hour and a half to get to the front of the line. The renewal person looked at her license. "Did you know that you are two years early?" In looking at the renewal date, Sophia had misread the small numbers with the renewal year.
>
> On the way home, Sophia thought back on the wasted morning. "I can see I need to pay more attention to reading the fine print before I make decisions to take action," she said to herself, realizing that glancing at the renewal date instead of reading it carefully had caused her error. After this brief *look back to learn* she released her frustration with a sigh. "*Mistakes happen*," she soothed herself, and then turned on the radio and enjoyed the drive back to her office.

Understand others' concerns to convert anger to compassion

Developing an empathic understanding of people toward whom you have felt angry transforms anger to gentler feelings. Understanding others' perspectives can replace anger with compassion and sometimes even with affection.

Corinne had long harbored resentment at her father for his frequent anger outbursts. He usually directed his anger at her mother, whom Corinne viewed as sweet, vulnerable, and undeserving of the criticism. At one point when Corinne and her adult siblings were talking about their shared love for their mother, Corinne asked if her siblings had any ideas about why their father so often spoke angrily to such a special spouse.

Together Corinne and her siblings came to a new realization. Their father suffered from intense anxiety about the potential loss of his job, which was in a field that the Internet revolution was marginalizing. Worrying about how he would provide for his family kept his emotions on heightened alert, like dry tinder. Though their dad seldom voiced his anxiety, his chronic nervousness kept him jittery, short-tempered, and prone to angry outbursts. He tried to be on best behavior with his children. That left just their mother for him to yell at.

Seeing her father in this new light released Corinne's long-held animosity toward him. Instead of harboring resentment, she now felt waves of compassion and even affection for this hardworking, longsuffering, and dedicated family man.

End personalizing by seeking more information

Personalizing, first introduced in Rx 3.1, occurs if you interpret someone's actions as having been directed at you when, in fact, they had an altogether different intent. Personalizing breeds hurt and anger.

Claudia was furious, wounded, and insulted by the fact that her husband Darren's family hadn't invited them to their recent dinner party. Worse, her in-laws had tried to keep the party a secret from them.

Darren fumed as well. "How could they do this to us?" he complained to Claudia. "We are so generous with them. We invite them whenever we have a gathering with other family members. How mean to us!"

Claudia agreed, continuing to personalize. "We've been married less than a year. I feel like they don't want me to join the family."

Defensive on behalf of his wife, Darren wanted to get even, to find a way to get back at his parents. He weighed various revenge options. They could stop attending family functions. They could refuse to answer his family's phone calls. Or should they call his parents and read them the riot act?

Claudia and Darren had interpreted their exclusion from Darren's parents' dinner party as an intentional insult. They assumed that Darren's family had wanted to hurt them.

The first key word in this definition is *assumed*. With insufficient information, Claudia had connected the dots with an immediate, though ultimately wrong, assumption about her in-laws' intentions toward her. Leaping to a quick conclusion based on hurt feelings inflames anger.

The second key word is *intentionally*. When you apologize, you probably say, "I'm sorry for having . . ." and then right away add, "I didn't mean to . . ." Assuming intentionality makes injuries sting all the more.

How can you prevent personalizing? As earlier prescriptions in this chapter have explained, once you have become emotionally inflamed, new information is unlikely to penetrate your angry beliefs, so the first step is to pause to calm yourself.

Then, instead of leaping to negative interpretations, ask questions. Let information-gathering replace your initial quick assumptions.

Darren decided to ask his sister what the dinner party exclusion had been about. Leaving Darren and Claudia off the guest list had, his sister said, been intentional, but with the intention of protecting, not hurting, them.

Uncle Jerry, Darren's dad's brother, was going to be in town for the weekend. Jerry and Darren's dad had grown up together on an isolated farm where they mainly had just each other as friends. Unfortunately, though, in his adult years, Uncle Jerry had become an alcoholic.

Jerry would be sure to bring a whiskey bottle in his pocket for swigging. With liquor, Jerry often turned ugly. At any excuse, he would start to rage. The victim was usually someone who might be vulnerable. With Claudia new to the family, she could be a prime target.

Was it a mistake by Darren's family to try to keep the dinner secret? Maybe. The decision, with long roots in hiding the realities of their family's alcoholic member, certainly had yielded unintended negative consequences. Was hurting Darren and Claudia's feelings intentional? Absolutely not.

So how do you prevent personalizing? Pause to calm down. Then ask questions instead of assuming hurtful intentions. Ask what motivated the behavior that at first glance seemed to you intended to hurt your feelings. The outcome? You are likely to get even—that is, to get even happier.

If it's in the past it's for the good

This antidote to allowing upsetting events in your past to brew ongoing resentment in your present and future involves making an active decision. Use this mantra to remind yourself to decide to discover how the past mistake or upsetting event can lead to a better tomorrow.

Jeremiah was elated when he received an attractive job offer from a growing real estate sales firm—until two weeks later when he failed the realtor licensing exam. Now he felt totally distraught. "*If it's in the past it's for the good*," he reminded himself, "but how could failing that test ever possibly turn out to be for my good?"

At first Jeremiah could think of no ways the curse could possibly hold within it the gems of a blessing. He felt angry at himself for failing the test and angry also at the realtor training course for not having taught an adequate curriculum. He thought about suing the prep course owners for its subpar teaching.

Instead, however, Jeremiah decided to launch, albeit skeptically, the "For the Good" guideline for looking at past events. To his surprise, two helpful thoughts emerged.

"I can see that I didn't take seriously enough the number of hours I'd have to put into studying. I failed because I needed to learn the material in much more careful detail than I had realized. Next time I take a licensing exam, I'll study much more thoroughly.

"And what's even more valuable to me is that I can see now that my heart wasn't in learning to be a real estate broker. I would rather invest my energies in a different career direction. Really, if I'm honest with myself, I would love to follow up my military experience by looking toward a career in police work. Good thing I didn't pass the realtor test!"

If it's in the past, it's for the good.

An unpleasant event will initially create negative feelings. The mantra *If it's in the past it's for the good* does not deny initial disappointment, hurt, or anger. Rather, the goal is to transform your distress into acceptance and even gratitude by finding the hidden treasure. Decide that *If it's in the past, it's for the good*, and then search until you discover how.

It was late afternoon, and Julie's three hungry children in the backseat had begun to squabble. Suddenly Julie felt flooded with frightening thoughts. "Oh, no! I've taken a wrong turn, and now I have zero idea of where I am. I have no idea where to go from here. My GPS is not working. The battery is dead on my cell phone. I don't see any restaurants where my hungry kids can eat. I'm totally lost. I'm scared and mad."

Julie felt especially angry toward her husband. The mistaken driving directions he had given her had led her into a run-down warehouse area of downtown. She then remembered, "*If it's in the past, it's for the good.* I've gotten lost. That's happened already, so now it's in the past. So where's the good?"

Looking out her car window with determination to find something of good, Julie noticed among the warehouses one with a small store window in the front. The window displayed a charming loveseat.

"Oh, my goodness! That's just the kind of cozy blue loveseat I've been trying for months to find for our family room!"

Julie parked in front of the warehouse entrance, announcing, "Undo your seatbelts, kids. We're here!"

The children followed her reluctantly into the dingy warehouse showroom, still bickering with each other. A kindly elderly saleslady greeted them. To everyone's delight, the saleslady immediately offered them milk and cookies.

"How fun!" the saleslady enthused. "I almost never get to see children in this store, only interior designers and architects."

Meanwhile, Julie took a closer look at the small sofa. She sat on it, breathed a happy sigh, and told the saleslady, "I love it! Can I buy two?"

"Hmm," Julie thought. "*If it's in the past, it's for the good* really worked. I just had to decide to lift up my eyes to search for how."

Put Your Past in the Past

The following visualization can help you when distress over past events is preventing you from moving forward toward well-being.

- Close your eyes.
- Picture your past. Is it in front of you or behind you?
- If your past is in front of you, visualize yourself packaging the past into a container or box. Notice the type of box you use: large or small, its color, the details on it, whether you can close it, what you like about it.
- Then put that container somewhere behind you. Put it someplace behind you so that past memories no longer impede your movement forward.

Richard harbored negative feelings toward Thomas, his son-in-law, for the hurtful words Thomas had said to his daughter Carrie during the years when he had had a major drinking problem.

For many months now, Thomas had stayed clear of alcohol, returning again to being the loving husband Carrie had married. Richard, nonetheless, remained too haunted by the stories Carrie had told him of Thomas's drunken rages to be able to accept him again.

Richard closed his eyes and visualized his past. Thomas's mean words were in front of him like floating sparks that never dimmed. To package the sparks into a container, Thomas envisioned a small, steel box. It was airtight, so that once he had enclosed the sparks in the box, they would gradually snuff out.

Visualizing placing this steel box onto a shelf behind him, one of the storage shelves in his garage, Richard felt a sense of relief.

When Richard opened his eyes after his visualization exercise, he felt a sense of calm. From that point forward, his past stayed in the past. Richard now could sit again with Thomas on the rockers on his front porch, sipping fresh-made lemonade and talking and laughing together.

Ask yourself the *Best Possible Light* question

A further way to loosen the hold of past hurts and angers on the present is to ask yourself the *Best Possible Light* question from earlier prescriptions (Rx 2.9, 3.4 and 3.5). *If I look at my continuing to hold on to resentment about that past incident in the best possible light, what is my staying angry meant to accomplish?*

> Zeke for years had been unable to forgive his wife, Savannah, for an affair she had had thirty years earlier. When he looked in the *best possible light* at his chronically smoldering how-could-you-have-done-this-to-me anger, Zeke realized that the goal was to give himself the right to have affairs as well, which he had been doing.

Look back with gratitude

Looking back with anger at an old, upsetting moment? Look back instead by asking yourself what, in that situation, you can feel grateful for.

> Norma, now in her late twenties, had long resented the teachers in her school years who had treated her as unable to learn. Norma loved music, so she especially resented the singing teacher who had told her she had no musical talent and the piano teacher who said she would never be chosen for the group of children who were being given piano lessons.
>
> Eventually, Norma stumbled on an abandoned drum set. Her family could afford no music or drum lessons, yet by the time she was in high school, she was already sitting in for drummers in established rock bands. A few years later and her all-girl rock band was playing professionally to large crowds across the nation.
>
> Encouraged to look back with gratitude on the teachers toward whom she had so long harbored resentment, Norma smiled. "Drums are my thing," she said. "I'm so thankful that those teachers didn't get me distracted with singing or piano. Someone up there must have been watching over me, blinding those teachers so they couldn't see my musical talent. Drums have given me a great life."

Focus on your blessings instead of on others' shortcomings

When other people have done things that annoy you, notice what happens if you focus on the blessings you have been given.

Tara, a high school senior, was totally annoyed. After every Frisbee team practice, she came home grumpy and upset. The other girls on her team were so inept. Their aim was poor. They couldn't throw far enough. They ran too slowly. Their catching skills were inconsistent.

One evening after practice when Tara yet again was complaining to her mother, the two of them had an astounding insight. Instead of feeling annoyed at her teammates' inadequacies, Tara could appreciate herself.

"My Frisbee skills are way ahead of the other girls' skills on my team. I have been incredibly fortunate. I learned to throw and catch a Frisbee with Petra (her older sister) when I was just a little kid. She needed someone to practice with, so I practiced with her for hours every day. I loved it. I don't think I ever realized what a blessing that was. Maybe it's not that the other girls on the high school team are so bad. It's that with all the practice I've been given, I've been able to become really good!"

Fix the system

Cynthia was furious at herself. A real estate agent, for a third time she had missed an important phone call because her cell phone was of juice.

Cynthia realized then that instead of using her energies to berate herself she would be better off figuring out how to *fix the system*. Her system of trying to remember to recharge the phone every few days clearly was insufficient.

The new system? Whenever she entered her apartment she would immediately put her cell phone on the small table by the front door. Plugging in her phone to the connecting cord she would keep there meant that she would be able to hear the phone from anywhere in the apartment and at the same time that the phone would daily become fully recharged.

Each of the recovery options above can release anger about something you or someone else has done that had been problematic. Harboring old angers generally hurts you. Fortunately, there are many roads to recovery.

R$_X$ 3.10: RECOGNIZE NARCISSISTIC, BORDERLINE, PARANOID, AND BIPOLAR ANGER.

A friend recently said to me that it was difficult for her to know when her anger stemmed from over-reacting. It was hard for her also to be clear when someone else's anger was an appropriate response to a genuine problem and when it indicated that the person had an anger problem. Recognizing when anger gives you good guidance about a problem and when it signals an emotional disorder can be helpful.

Freud, the father of much of modern psychological thinking, aptly described mental health as the ability to love and work. When anger interferes with effective functioning in either or both of these realms, the anger signifies psychopathology.

The Diagnostic Manuals mentioned at the outset of this chapter that do not include excessive anger as a primary pathological emotional state do list four syndromes in which anger is a prominent feature. These four patterns, described below, are not mutually exclusive. Many individuals exhibit features of several or even all of these syndromes. Also, the patterns ebb and flow. Under stress, anger habits tend to become more pronounced.

Narcissism

Narcissism is a mentality of "it's all about me." Anger fosters narcissism, and narcissism fosters anger. As mentioned earlier (Rx 3.1), when you feel angry, you experience what you want as paramount and what others want as minuscule in importance. Even without a personality disorder, the angrier you feel, the more narcissistically you are likely to act. At the same time, the more you operate from a narcissistic perspective—listening only to your own concerns and ignoring others'—the more you will find yourself anger prone. Likewise, if you have to interact with someone who operates narcissistically, dismissing whatever you say, the more you are likely to find yourself anger prone.

While narcissism has many facets, in my view narcissism is primarily a disorder of listening, that is, of the ability to hear others' perspectives. If your ears close off to hearing others' points of view, you are likely to believe that your way is the only or best way. The way you see things is all that matters. What you want is all that matters. [49]

This assumption increases your risk for angrily trying to coerce others into doing what you want. Narcissism, therefore, often results in using anger to overpower others so they will do what you believe they "should."

When narcissism combines with cruelty, creating a tyrannical personal style, the diagnosis may be malignant narcissism. Beware of on-going interactions with a malignant narcissist, that is, someone who is purposely hurtful to others and obsessed with exerting control over them. Hitler, Stalin, and Saddam Hussein offer extreme examples of malignant narcissism. Malignant narcissists raise the thought, "That person is evil!" Hopefully you will never have to deal with this kind of person.

What can you do to combat garden-variety narcissistic tendencies, especially those within yourself? If you often feel irritated at others, ask yourself, "What are their concerns?" and then, "What makes sense about their concerns?" As you listen to others' concerns with an ear toward taking them seriously instead of dismissing them as unimportant or wrong, your anger is likely to dissolve.

If you are dealing with someone else's narcissistic tendency to ignore, minimize, denigrate, or dismiss what you say, you may still get your point through if you patiently hang in there. Agree with and validate that person's ideas. Then, add yours. If you keep at it until your perspectives have been taken seriously, you may, but may not, succeed.

A person with narcissistic tendencies will be most able to hear you if you stay relaxed and good-humored. Appreciation and flattery also open the ears of people with narcissistic non-listening. In some situations though, becoming quietly stern works more effectively. Narcissistic people do listen to people whom they regard as of higher status.

Borderline disorders

The term *borderline* first emerged in 1890 when an individual named J. C. Rosse labeled excessive emotional intensity as "borderline insanity." Now the term *borderline* is used to describe a syndrome in which the primary feature is intense emotions, and especially anger storms. The anger storms create chaotic, "high-maintenance" relationships.

Researchers now regard the underlying problem in borderline syndromes as stemming at least in part from a too-sensitive amygdala (see Rx 3.2). Amygdala oversensitivity may be a consequence of emotionally overwhelming experiences from, for instance, childhood abuse or military traumas. In this regard, borderline dysfunction may be a form of Post-Traumatic Stress Disorder (PTSD). In other instances however, the source of borderline hyper-reactivity is unclear. It can be present from birth and tends to be associated with family systems with collapsed hierarchy, that is, where the angry child controls the parents.

People with borderline personality disorder usually target their anger at family members, though their anger may also emerge in work and other situations. Women with borderline anger generally express their rages verbally, though they may become physically abusive as well, especially toward children. Men who rage are more at risk for using physical force.

Angry men diagnosed as abusive, bipolar, and/or narcissistic may actually be suffering from a borderline disorder. Diagnosis of anger disorders in this regard seems to be influenced by gender biases. Angry women generally get diagnosed as borderline. Few men receive that diagnosis.

Perhaps because of their emotional hyper-reactivity, people with borderline personality patterns are prone to misinterpret benign situations as hurtful. This phenomenon may account for another tell-tale sign of borderline functioning. When borderline individuals recount an event that bothered them, their narrative may sound significantly more negative than the descriptions of others who observed the same situation. For instance, a borderline individual who felt angry at a friend might later describe her friend's kitchen as "filthy." Others who were there would have described the kitchen as having a few dishes from last night's dinner neatly rinsed and stacked on the countertop.

High-intensity emotional reactions create all-or-nothing thinking. Individuals with overly intense emotions consequently tend to either love or hate, adore or despise, elevate others on a pedestal or else deprecate them in the extreme. As a consequence, in groups individuals with borderline personality disorders create "splitting," another hallmark of the borderline syndrome. They gather allies for their side against whomever they have defined as an enemy. Splitting can divide what had been a cohesive family, office, community group, or country into hostile camps: *us* against *them*. Cultures with a borderline cultural style get into frequent hostilities both within their country and with other countries.

Lorna, a new hire who turned out to have borderline tendencies, decided that her boss, Marissa, a well-liked manager who had worked in the company for many years, was treating her unfairly. Lorna complained bitterly about Marissa to her fellow employees, to Marissa's fellow managers, and to their supervisor.

Over a period of several months, the office that for decades had been pleasantly harmonious split into those who continued to support Marissa versus those who sided with Lorna.

Marissa was stunned to see how many of her colleagues sided with Lorna against her, believing Lorna's inaccurate, accusatory accounts of how Marissa had victimized her. Many naïve individuals support without further investigation anyone who claims to be a victim.

Fortunately for Marissa, Lorna eventually was fired for incompetence. Unfortunately, by the time Lorna left the organization, Lorna had sowed enough dissension that several long-loyal employees already had left for jobs elsewhere to escape the negative energy.

When borderline individuals like Lorna claim to be victims, their victimhood status is often based on misinterpretations and exaggerations of others' actions. These misinterpretations may stem, in part, from an excessive sense of entitlement. When people wrongly believe that they are entitled to receive special privileges, they feel angry when they do not receive them. Sometimes, however, the accusations are outright fictions, which then cause them to be described as manipulative.

The borderline individual who claims victimhood usually victimizes others, believing, "I am a victim, so I have the right to victimize you."

Lorna's family had owned a large piece of land. After her parents both had died, her older brother Barnett was in charge of distributing the inheritance. Anticipating that Lorna would believe she was entitled to more than her fair share and, therefore, would feel taken advantage of in the division of assets, Barnett tried to prevent dissension by giving Lorna an extra-generous distribution.

Lorna still reacted with anger. She distrusted any division of the family assets that did not give her a vastly disproportionate share. When her siblings tried to explain the extra advantages that Barnett had given her, Lorna was too agitated to understand their explanations. Instead of trying to listen, she brought an expensive lawsuit against her siblings, victimizing them.

Borderline dysfunction can be confusing to recognize, especially when the borderline individual's anger episodes at home alternate with attractive and competent-appearing public functioning. These alternations are reminiscent of the nineteenth century nursery rhyme by famed New England poet Henry Wadsworth Longfellow who wrote about a little girl with a little curl in the middle of her forehead:

"When she was good,

She was very good indeed,

But when she was bad she was horrid."

While individuals with borderline personality features cause major emotional stress for others, they themselves also suffer greatly. Their hyper-intense emotions can brutally buffet them as much as they do others. People with borderline anger may feel as unable to control their rages as someone with epilepsy is unable to control a seizure.

They also typically suffer from intense fears of abandonment. These fears may be realistic. Others may leave them to escape the anger volcanoes.

One physician who suffers from borderline phenomena wrote to me describing her tendency to rage at others and her parallel tendency to rage at herself:

As a borderline personality disorder sufferer myself, I want you to know that we are not bad or manipulative people. We are desperate. Our uncontrollable and horrible emotions deprive us of ability to think and control our behavior. Our behaviors are not meant to harm, at least not mine. Rather, they are an expression of desperation.

Having a borderline personality disorder means suffering which I can only compare to terminal cancer. If you saw a cancer patient howling with pain, you would have compassion. The world does not have compassion toward us, even though we howl with pain, because our efforts to escape unbearable pain cause behaviors that antagonize people.

Please believe me, the depression and dysphoria of BPD is the most horrible feeling. Sometimes I would prefer to have cancer instead. At least then the whole world would not blame me for my desperate efforts to blunt the pain brought about by my biological vulnerability plus the abuse I suffered as a child. [50]

When people with borderline tendencies recognize that they have a problem and reach out for professional help, they can grow and change. The prognosis is less promising for those with entrenched borderline patterns who recoil from insight, insisting instead that their anger is always other people's fault. "I'm only mad because *you* . . ." signals an especially serious anger problem. Blaming blocks changing.

Fortunately, therapists have been discovering effective treatments for borderline personality patterns. Dialectical Behavior Therapy (DBT), created by psychologist Martha Linehan, earns particularly high marks in clinical outcome studies.

In addition, as I mentioned earlier in this chapter (Rx 3.2), my colleague Dale Petterson and I have been experimenting with a brief intervention that resets the amygdala so that excessive emotional storms cease to occur. Another therapist in my office suite, psychologist Heather McQueen, utilizes a further set of techniques that seem to help, a treatment strategy from Australia called Body Talk. While this treatment is not well known and has not been extensively studied in the United States, Dr. McQueen's clients report that it quiets their emotional hyper-reactivity so that they become far less prone to anger.

Paranoia

Anger and blame can indicate a paranoid style of coping with problems. Feeling hurt or anxious is uncomfortable. By contrast, blaming your problems on someone or something outside of yourself mobilizes your fighting spirit and at the same time frees you of anxiety about any role you may have played in your problems.

It may seem paradoxical that feeling like a victim of external forces creates strength. In fact, blaming inflates your self-esteem with self-righteous anger, so concocting an explanation for difficulties that blames someone else can be tempting. Look at how many politicians rely on this strategy, blaming a scapegoat instead of problem-solving.

At the same time, life is not a football game. The best defense is not necessarily a good offense, especially if your goal is to fix problems that interfere with your ability to enjoy personal well-being and positive relationships.

Once you have begun to utilize a blaming way of connecting the dots in your life situation, your ideas may rigidify into a "fixed belief system." As mentioned earlier in this chapter, a mistaken idea or belief solidifies when contradictory information is brushed aside, blocked by a wall that allows only confirmatory data to enter your data bank. Without uptake of disconfirmatory data, new data cannot modify initial ideas. In the extreme, the result can become fixed paranoid delusions.

> George struggled to perform work responsibilities for which he lacked the requisite training. Rather than acknowledge that he needed help, he blamed his colleague for his failing.
>
> "I'm not doing well at work because Mark withholds information from me about what to do," George told his boss. When his boss responded that he had a lot of respect for Mark's work, George insisted, "No, Mark is the problem."

A paranoid belief can be difficult to identify when it sounds plausible. Identification of delusional beliefs is easier if they are overtly delusional as in "I'm not doing well at work because invaders from Mars sneak in through my office window, riffle through my drawers, mess up my computer, and scramble my brain."

Bizarre fixed beliefs like this one would indicate psychotic levels of paranoia. Psychiatric consultation and medication are essential treatments in that case. Bizarre paranoid delusions are one of the mental disorders for which medications can be a great blessing.

Projection

Rx 2.8 and Rx 3.3 introduced the concept of projection. There will be more on projection in Rx 4.7, which is about worrying. Meanwhile, what does projection have to do with paranoia? In fact, projection is one of the hallmarks of paranoid functioning. When anger gets expressed in angry accusations, the accusations predictably come from within the accuser. Paranoid people generally express traits characteristic of the blamer, not of the recipient of the accusations. The pattern of externalizing what is internal tends to be true of others who rage as well as of people with paranoid habits.

> "You're off your rocker!" George insisted to his boss. "Mark is confused and lying to you!"

George, without realizing it, was describing himself with the words he used to describe his boss and Mark. George accused his boss of being "off his rocker." He accused Mark of being "confused and lying." In fact, these words described George.

Another way of understanding the concept of projection is that George is like a movie projector. He projects the film that is within him onto the screen of others.

Paranoia connotes suspiciousness. Angry, paranoid people are suspicious of others because they project onto others the hostility that they have within themselves. Suspiciousness can be a healthy response to a dangerous situation. With clinical paranoia, by contrast, the suspiciousness stems from projection.

If you need to deal with a paranoid or other often-angry individual, understanding the nature of projection can give you access to valuable data. Instead of becoming defensive when you feel wrongly accused, listen closely to the specifics of what the angry person is saying. Accusatory words give you a window into the angry person's own thoughts, feelings, and behaviors.

Bipolar illness

What used to be called manic-depressive disorder has in recent years been relabeled *bipolar illness*. *Bipolar* describes a tendency toward emotional extremes. In the manic mode, dysfunctionally high energy creates pressured speech, inability to listen to others, and unrealistically positive thinking that leads sufferers to think they can do what they in fact cannot. Excessively intense delight and overblown positive self-regard can lead to shopping sprees, hypersexualized adventures, and bad business decisions. The high energy also creates quickness to raging anger. In the depressive mode bipolar individuals become intensely angry at themselves, berating themselves with harsh self-criticism.

The trigger for manic and/or depressive episodes, including for people with a biological predisposition to bipolar disorders, is almost always a specific, real-life challenge. The ending of a relationship or a job loss, for instance, can overwhelm their ability to remain in a functional emotional zone. Body chemistry is one part of the picture. Challenging situations are the other half. For this reason, medication is generally essential. Augmentation of treatment with psychotherapy also is essential, including family therapy so that family members can work out the issues that come up for them in dealing with the bipolar family member.

The bottom line with regard to anger

My view is that arguments are virtually all out-of-bounds and unproductive. Just as you would expect play to stop on the basketball court if the ball has gone out of bounds, stop talking as soon as one, never mind both, of you is getting emotionally out-of-bounds. Take the prescription to regard anger as a stop sign totally to heart.

The triggers for extreme as well as milder anger outbursts are almost always situations that require you to find a solution, not to engage in a fight. Aim to pause, withdraw temporarily if need be, self-soothe, and then return to address the problem calmly, cooperatively, and productively.

Chapter 4

Anxiety

What signs indicate that you are taking the Freeze Road to anxiety in response to a challenging situation? You first may note the physical indicators: jittery "butterflies" in your stomach, tightness in your chest, a racing heart or skipped heartbeat, a breathless or nauseous feeling. You might also note that worries and fears permeate your thinking. Labels that you then use for these feelings and thoughts could be anxious, scared, wary, tense, stressed, fearful, panicked, nervous, worried, or phobic. In some geographic areas in the United States, folks say, "It's my nerves."

As Rx 1.3 explained, unpleasant feelings serve a purpose. Although anxiety can arrive mysteriously, like a sudden fog on a clear day, it usually is triggered by a specific thought or situation. Anxiety arises to warn you when something ahead looks threatening. Freezing then aims to keep you safe.

A deer stays still when movement would attract the attention of predators (see Rx 1.1). Moments of stillness may similarly keep you safe, at least temporarily. While the saying "strike while the iron is hot" sometimes proves to give good guidance, sometimes doing nothing is preferable to impulsively doing something that would worsen the situation.

At the same time, lack of movement toward a solution perpetuates fearful feelings. Anxiety will continue to hover until you move forward. Action toward gathering information and Finding a Solution to the provoking problem bring relief.

> Calvin was scheduled for surgery to repair a long-standing difficulty with his eyes. He was quite confident that the surgical procedure would heal the problem. At the same time, he felt a nagging anxiety.
>
> Focusing on the thought triggering this nervous feeling, Calvin realized that the surgeon's arrogantly non-communicative personality style concerned him. The doctor was reputed to be an outstanding surgeon. Still, his impatience when Calvin asked him questions left Calvin wary.
>
> Once he realized what had triggered his nagging nervousness about the surgery, Calvin reconsidered his choice of surgeons. "I chose this surgeon because he has done this procedure over a thousand times. Still, my number two choice of doctors—though he's done the procedure fewer times—left me feeling more comfortable and optimistic when I talked with him. If anything should go wrong, I want a physician who will answer my questions and offer emotional support. I'm switching!"

Unpleasant as anxious feelings can be, anxiety is like a good angel that visits to help you. It arrives to give you a message about where your problem-solving attentions are needed. Address this problem and decide on a solution. The anxiety, like a good angel, will have accomplished its mission and will disappear of its own accord.

R_X 4.1: RECOGNIZE ANXIETY, THEN TAKE THREE STEPS TO ALLEVIATE IT.

When anxious feelings arise in response to a frightening-looking circumstance ahead, the anxiety impacts your ways of seeing. Anxiety can broaden your attention like fog headlights that spread light over a wide area. Anxiety also can narrow your vision so that you hyperfocus like a laser beam on one detail. Both expanded and narrowed vision interfere with the ability to grasp a full picture of a dilemma. Both, therefore, can keep you immobilized.

How, in these circumstances, can you move from immobilization to finding solutions? Take the following three steps.

Three Steps to Alleviate Anxiety

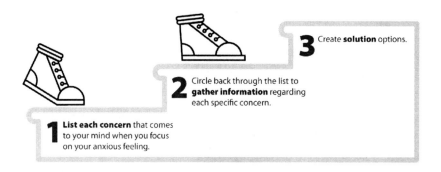

3 Create **solution** options.

2 Circle back through the list to **gather information** regarding each specific concern.

1 **List each concern** that comes to your mind when you focus on your anxious feeling.

Step 1 | List your concerns

Writing a list of your concerns launches a transition from frozen thinking to active problem-solving. Writing your worries onto paper lifts them out of the mental fog in the back of your mind to a place in front of you where you can see them clearly. Writing a list also organizes your thoughts. Now they become like children who are lined up in front of you to take turns instead of crowding around you in an agitated clump, all vying for your attention.

> Charlotte felt anxious as she thought about the weekend ahead. She and Cooper, her husband, would be visiting her brother Jeff. In the past, visits to Jeff had consistently led to marital clashes.
>
> Writing down the concerns that seemed to be creating her anxious feeling, Charlotte listed:

1. When I'm enjoying time with my brother, Cooper will begin to stew.
2. Cooper will think I love Jeff more than him.
3. Cooper will accuse me of not treating him as lovingly as I treat Jeff.
4. I'll get defensive because I do treat Cooper well.

Step 2 | Gather information

The best antidote to anxiety is information.

When anxiety creates viscerally unpleasant physical sensations, looking away from the situation that triggered these unpleasant feelings can feel tempting. Yet, paradoxically, focusing your gaze directly onto your anxiety-producing concerns about the situation is calming. Ask questions and gather information to understand the situation more fully. The following script is from almost verbatim notes of a therapy session with Cooper and Charlotte.

Dr. H:	Talk with each other about what has happened in the past when you have visited with Jeff and his family.
Cooper:	(pausing, and then turning to his wife, Charlotte) I'm picturing the way you treat Jeff. It's so loving. I feel jealous when you laugh with him. I notice that you ask what he'd like to eat for breakfast and then make it for him in such good humor. That's such a contrast with your attitude toward me in the mornings. I get what feels to me like either obligatory niceness or irritation.
Charlotte:	Hmm. You're probably right. I do feel accommodating toward Jeff and eager to help him.
Cooper:	We both really like Jeff. When we're visiting him, we both treat him lovingly. We often treat each other irritably, sending each other pointed barbs, at home as well as at Jeff's. However, I see it more at his house because I find the contrast so painful, especially when I start thinking that you love your brother more than you love me. Then I get mad and say something mean to you. Boom, we're arguing.
Charlotte:	I agree that we do act pissy toward each other, a lot. I don't know how to stop the merry-go-round to get off it. I see now that I often get critical of you—and all the more when we're at Jeff's. No wonder I've been anxious about the visit coming up.

I first learned the mantra *The best antidote to anxiety is information* many years ago from a treatment strategy called transactional analysis. As a means of relieving anxiety, this short mantra has proven to be of lasting value. The best antidote to anxiety *is* information.

Step 3 | Create solution options
Creation of a plan of action completes the three-step anxiety-reduction process. Even before the solution plan has been implemented, anxiety tends to lift.

Charlotte: I'm willing to decide to make a fresh start. How about you?

Cooper: Making a fresh start sounds like a good plan to me too.

Dr. H: Do you remember the exercise *Put Your Past in the Past* (Rx 3.9)?

Charlotte: (closing her eyes) I'm picturing all the stuff I'm mad at you about and bundling it up. I'm putting it in a big balloon that I'm blowing up bigger and bigger . . . Now it's exploding. I'm standing on the edge of the world, along a cliff, and I see everything that I was mad at exploding into dust. I wave the dust behind me . . . I feel calmer, and empty inside, a good kind of empty, more open, like I can breathe. Phew. I see you now in front of me. Instead of looking like a big ogre, now you're small, like a statue of the Virgin Mary. That's weird, but, oh well. I feel affectionate now when I look at you. I pick you up, the statue. It's weird, but I feel good now and want to hug you.

Cooper: Okay. A Virgin Mary statue is not quite how I think of myself, but I'm fine with it. The part of your visualization about you letting go of the balloon of all the anger you've been holding onto toward me gave me a calm, relieved feeling.

Dr. H: Great, Charlotte. Looks like you did it. Your past is now in the past. Cooper, your turn now to close your eyes.

Cooper: I see myself standing by a lake, looking out at the water and the trees. I feel really good. I don't seem to carry the past with me into the present. I just need to put myself in a calm place instead of letting myself get anxious and then angry . . . Can I open my eyes now?

Charlotte   (tenderly reaching out to touch Cooper's knee): I do love you. Jeff has so many medical problems and lives alone without a spouse, so when we visit I do want to give him lots of loving attention. I'm clear though that you are my husband, the one who is for me my number one.

Charlotte and Cooper illustrate the *Three Steps to Alleviate Anxiety*. Charlotte first clarified the concerns that had been generating her anxious feelings. Second, she implemented the mantra *The best antidote to anxiety is information*. Her anxiety diminished all the more when, third, she and Cooper co-created a plan of action which was to make a fresh start. Putting the past in the past helped to implement this plan.

In summary

Remember the Hand Map? The alternative to freezing, to immobilization in the face of a frightening situation, is to return to problem-solving via the three steps above. By the end of these three steps, your anxiety is likely to have vanished.

R̽ 4.2: VISUALIZE ANXIETY: *WHERE IS THE FEELING WITHIN YOUR BODY?*

Enhance the *Three Steps to Alleviate Anxiety* by using a visualization to locate the anxious feelings in your body.

> *Please refer to the Introduction for suggestions on how to do the visualization prescriptions. See also prescriptionswithoutpills.com for video examples and downloadable worksheets.*

Begin by finding a comfortable place to sit and closing your eyes. As I explained in the Introduction, closed eyes help you access subconscious concerns. Then answer the following series of questions:

- Where is the anxious feeling located in your body?
- Describe how the feeling looks and feels. The more details of size, shape, and anything else you notice, the better.
- What thoughts would make that anxious feeling in your body grow even larger? Write these thoughts down as your list of concerns.
- Circle back through your concerns list to gather information relevant to each concern.
- Create a plan of action.
- Check again on how the anxiety looks and feels in your body. The area where you felt it before will most likely feel quite different now.
- If anxiety remains or if additional anxious feelings or thoughts arise, repeat the above procedure.

The following case illustrates this procedure.

Joyce was a single woman in her early fifties whose mother had died the prior week. She was distraught about her mother's death. At the same time, she felt even more distraught by what had transpired in her family since her mother's passing.

Where is the anxious feeling located in your body?

Dr. H: Close your eyes. Notice in your body where you feel the anxiety.

Joyce: I feel it in my chest.

Describe how the feeling looks and feels. The more details of size, shape, and anything else you notice, the better.

Dr. H: Describe to me what you feel in your chest.

Joyce: It's like a hot place, like a ball of fire.

Dr. H: What color is the ball of fire? And how big?

Joyce: It's a hard, round, yellow ball of fire, about the size of an orange.

List the concerns that are generating anxiety.

Dr. H: What thoughts come to mind for you that might enlarge that orange-sized ball of fire in your body? I'll write them down as you list them.

Joyce: There's a batch of them, all rushing to my mind, all whirling around.

1. I'm worried that my sister and brother-in-law are stealing my inheritance.
2. I'm worried that they are emotionally, and maybe even physically, abusive to their son, my nephew.
3. I'm worried that my nephew has no one to talk with.
4. I'm worried that if my sister and brother-in-law steal my inheritance, I will have no recourse.
5. I can't afford a lot of legal fees.
6. I was supposed to inherit my mother's house, but my sister and brother-in-law seem to have gotten my mother to sign it over to them before she died.
7. I'm worried that all this worry will cause my health to deteriorate. I feel fragile.

Dr. H: Any more thoughts?

Joyce: Yes. I have no one to help me fight back. The situation is so unfair.

Dr. H:	Any more?
Joyce:	No, that feels like it.
Dr. H:	Now we have a list of the thoughts that make the anxiety worse. Let's add any thoughts that come to mind that seem to have a calming impact. They are the positive concerns.
Joyce:	I already feel some relief, just from making that list so my worries stop spinning around in my head. My chest feels like the ball of fire is cooling. I'd like to think if there's any other thoughts that feel calming . . .

8. I feel gratitude that I have a good job.

9. I feel gratitude too toward my mom. Even when she was so sick, her presence kept my sister and her husband from acting with overt evil like they are doing now.

Joyce wrote both the fearful and the soothing thoughts all on one list. Both positive factors and negative concerns can prove helpful in finding solutions to a dilemma.

Gather information about each concern and create solutions.

With her swirling thoughts listed, numbered, and even written down, Joyce now could proceed with the next two steps for anxiety reduction: gathering information and creating a plan of action.

Dr. H:	Let's circle back to see what information will help you figure out what to do about each of your concerns.
Joyce:	Okay. Can you read me the concerns?
Dr. H:	Yes, one at a time. About your sister and brother-in-law stealing your inheritance . . .
Joyce:	I could go to legal aid to see if they can tell me more about my legal options. Once I have more legal information about the inheritance process, I'll map a plan. I'll either rescue my share of the inheritance or give up on it, grieve, and move on.
Dr. H:	About helping your nephew . . .
Joyce:	I need to talk with him to find out what's been going on. I could arrange to hike with him in the mountains. He'll feel safer opening up to me if we're walking out in nature, far away from his house where his parents might hear what he says. After I know what his parents have been doing to him, I'll contact

child protective services to figure out what, if anything, I can do to help.

Dr. H: Your health concerns...

Joyce: I'll ask my doctor to check my blood pressure and cholesterol to be sure my health doesn't fail from the stress. I'm sure glad my health plan pays for preventive healthcare.

Dr. H: How are you feeling now?

Joyce: Way calmer. I still don't like the situation. I profoundly dislike my sister and brother-in-law for acting so selfishly. At the same time, they've shown these traits before, so it's not really new news. I feel a lot better with a plan for moving forward—sad but way less anxious. I accept that it is what it is. I'll try to get what I can from what was supposed to be my part of the inheritance, and I'll try to find resources to help my nephew. Then I'll focus on feeling gratitude for what I do have in my life and moving on.

Return to the somatic visualization to check progress.

Dr. H: Focus again on that ball of fire. How does it look now?

Joyce: The ball of fire is still there, but just the size of a pea, maybe even smaller. And instead of being bright orange, it's a pale yellow. It's like a yellow lentil, small and flat and pale-colored. Big difference. As to the inheritance, I keep hearing in my head the words to that old Everly Brothers song: "Got along without you before I met you, gonna get along without you now..." I'm sad to lose my mom. At the same time, I'll be okay.

Visualization of where an emotion is located in your body and how it looks begins to give you control over it. After completing then the *Three Steps to Alleviate Anxiety*, re-visualize where the emotion is in your body and what it feels like. The images validate your progress and also let you know if pieces of the problem still remain.

R$_X$ 4.3: REDUCE ANXIETY WITH *THAT WAS THEN, THIS IS NOW.*

If no specific concerns in a current situation appear sufficient to account for current anxious feelings, a distressing earlier experience may be causing your malaise.

Old anxious feelings that have not been fully digested can bubble up when a present situation has ingredients that feel similar to the past experience. To access and root out the problematic subconscious earlier life experience influencing your current edgy feeling, use *That Was Then, This Is Now*. This multi-purpose visualization, introduced for depression in Rx 2.5 and for anger in Rx 3.7, enables you to identify the culprit so that you can free your current reactions from the old template.

Please refer to the Introduction for suggestions on how to do the visualization prescriptions. See also prescriptionswithoutpills.com for video examples and downloadable worksheets.

Exercise: *That Was Then, This Is Now*

- **Close your eyes.**
- **Picture, as in the prior exercise,** where the feeling is located in your body and how it feels.
- **Allow an image to appear** on your visual screen of an earlier time when you experienced a similar feeling. How old were you then?
- **What is the same** then and now? Give details.
- **Identify what is different** now that can enable you to feel more safe and to handle the situation with an option available to a grown-up.
- **Older consoler**: Is there an older part of me that can console the younger distressed part of me? If so, let that voice console the younger me.
- **New solution plan:** Given these deeper understandings of myself, what might be more effective ways of handling the present situation?
- **Check again how the feeling looks** and feels in your body. If pieces remain, find solutions for these, perhaps with *Do or Become* (Rx 6.8).

Chris, a man in his mid-forties with a wife and three children, had been waking up most weekday mornings with stomachaches and overwhelming feelings of anxiety. His anxiety was so intense that sometimes he would vomit.

Chris sensed that his anxiety had something to do with the fact that his current job as a high school soccer coach in an elite high school was not a good fit for him, but he felt immobilized with regard to finding what to do next.

Dr. H:	Close your eyes. Take a deep, cleansing breath. Then focus on your body. Where do you feel the anxiety?
Chris:	It's a swirling sensation in here (moving his open hand over his stomach and lower abdomen). Like a windy storm covering all of that area.
Dr. H:	Allow an image to come up of another time earlier in your life when you may have had a similar feeling of a windy storm covering all of that area.
Chris:	I'm seeing images of when my mother and dad left me off at boarding school. I was about fourteen. I felt totally panicked. I was terribly afraid of whether I would be able to make friends and do the work. The school was in a different language from what we spoke at home. We spoke Spanish, and at the school, everyone spoke English. And I hated being away from my family, especially my sisters.
Dr. H:	What feels the same in this incident as something in your present life?
Chris:	I feel a similar feeling of fear and grief at work. I feel stuck in a place where I don't feel like I belong.
Dr. H:	What is different now from back then?
Chris:	(smiling) I'm a grown-up now. I can take care of myself—at least better than when I was fourteen. I'm married, so when I leave my wife in the morning, it's just for the workday, not for months at a time like then when I left my sisters and parents. I speak English fine now. And work is far less scary than boarding school was. I know that I'm good at what I do.

The visualization above reduced the potency and frequency of Chris's anxiety episodes. Yet Chris still sometimes woke up with stomachaches and during the day he continued to feel chronic rumbles of low-level anxiety. We therefore repeated the procedure to see if prior to the boarding school incident there had been an earlier root experience.

| Chris: | As I focus again on that anxious feeling in my stomach, I'm remembering now a moment I haven't thought about for years. I was seven years old. My parents had just left me off at a summer camp. I looked out the window in my bunkroom and saw my |

parents' car driving away, heading down the long driveway. I totally panicked. I ran barefoot out of the bunkhouse, chasing after my parents' car, waving and shouting to them. The car continued to drive away. My parents never noticed me. I felt terrified.

Dr. H: What's the same then and now?

Chris: When I go to work, I feel like I'm going to a place where I don't belong. I don't like my boss, and I didn't like the counselors at that summer camp. I wanted to be home with my family, like now I'd rather be home with my wife and kids.

Dr. H: And what's different?

Chris: I'm a grown-up now. I'm not helpless. As I think about it now, maybe I could look for a different job. I don't think I've realized how much I really, really dislike where I'm working now. I would much rather work in a place where I feel more at home.

By the end of this session, Chris felt "lighter."

Dr. H: Check in with your body. What are you feeling now in your stomach and lower abdomen?

Chris: That's amazing. There's no more swirling wind. It feels calm, like the feeling I get when the sun is shining on a summer day.

Chris woke up the morning after this session feeling essentially normal, with almost no anxiety. Within a few days, the anxiety and stomach pain faded further, closer to zero. Chris could enjoy his family in the mornings before work without nervous episodes. He no longer felt background anxiety at work during the day.

Within the next few months Chris found a new job. As athletic director in a Hispanic neighborhood recreation center where the staff and clients all treated him like family, he felt great. Mission accomplished!

R_X 4.4: CHOOSE FROM TWO CALMING OPTIONS FOR ANXIETY SURGES.

Do you from time to time find yourself experiencing a sudden surge of nervousness? If so, what are your immediate options for calming yourself? In this kind of circumstance, distraction can give your body time to metabolize the chemicals of anxiety. Paradoxically, the opposite strategy, focusing on your feelings with full mindfulness, offers an equally effective alternative.

Distraction

Distraction, introduced in Rx 3.5 as a self-soothing technique for calming anger, calms anxiety as well. Because your mind can think about only one thing at a time, focusing on something highly engaging but pleasant makes you unaware of anything else. During a distraction interlude, your body's chemistry will match your thoughts. Pleasant thoughts yield a pleasant emotional state irrespective of whether the prior feeling had been anger, anxiety, joy, or sadness.

For instance, if you feel anxious before a brief medical procedure such as having blood drawn, give yourself a mental challenge that will occupy your thoughts.

Maria hated getting blood drawn. Her strategy: she would focus on her fifteen grandchildren, giving herself the assignment of listing them in age order. Since the children were spread out over four families, lining them up by age posed a relatively challenging mental task. Well before she had reached the youngest child, the blood had been drawn.

Serial Sevens, a challenging mental task that psychologists use to test concentration ability, can similarly serve to distract your thoughts away from an anxiety source. Start at one hundred and keep subtracting seven from each total until you make it down to zero. Distraction by reading a magazine or checking your cell phone can accomplish a similar anxiety reduction.

Tanner, who often traveled for business, loved his twenty-sixth floor hotel room. It was spacious and sunny, looking out over a rooftop view of New York. At the same time, every long elevator ride triggered an anxiety rush.

Tanner decided to take out his cell phone and send text messages as he rode up or down. As long as he could distract himself this way, elevator anxiety no longer overwhelmed him.

Mindfulness

Mindfulness techniques derived from Buddhist teachings ease anxious and other negative feelings by focusing directly on the uncomfortable feeling. In a mindful state, there is no judging about what should or shouldn't be. There is only awareness and acceptance. Feelings flow—that is, they keep changing. Watching your anxiety rise and eventually fall occupies your mind until eventually you note that the uncomfortable feeling has passed on.

Where can you find further explanations and practice exercises for using mindfulness to cope with physical discomfort? I especially like the engaging and easy to read book by a former law professor who suddenly contracted an intermittently painful and often debilitating chronic illness. Buddhist mindfulness concepts and techniques helped her to "wake up" to ever-increasing awareness. "Waking up" in Buddhist terminology leads to finding inner peace. See *How to Wake Up* by Toni Bernhard.[51]

R_X 4.5: MINIMIZE PERFORMANCE ANXIETY.

Do you sometimes feel anxious in the face of performance situations such as test taking, public speaking, music or theatrical productions, and athletic competitions? Being evaluated or watched by an audience can feel dangerous, especially when you fear being judged, lacks confidence in your readiness to perform the task, or is shy about being in the spotlight.

What thoughts typically trigger performance anxiety?

Working for the past decade as a mental coach for professional tennis players I was surprised to see that even these athletes, ranked among the top in the world, sometimes found their level of play cramped by anxious feelings. Anxiety contracts muscles and constricts thinking, hindering highest level performance, so upgrading their anxiety-prevention strategies turned out to be vital.

The tennis court proved to be an excellent laboratory for exploring performance anxiety triggers. As my players and I debriefed after instances in which sudden nervousness had tightened them up on court, we gradually teased out a relatively small number of thoughts responsible for most of their anxiety reactions.

These anxiety triggers turned out to be variations on the same themes as the thoughts that provoke anxiety reactions in the clients in my clinical practice. Which of the following thoughts trigger anxiety for you?

❏ Fear of fear

Most athletes realize that anxiety can undermine their athletic skills. Consequently, when they feel anxiety rising, they become at risk for becoming anxious about feeling anxious.

To counter this risk, a standard sports psychology trick is to encourage athletes to label their pre-performance feelings as *excitement* instead of as anxiety. Many athletes report that this simple reframe enables them to convert their anxiety to a helpful source of extra energy.

> Ron, an eighteen-year-old tennis player, had professional tennis aspirations. For some time, he had been performing exceptionally well in practice sessions. In tournaments, however, anxiety sometimes surged up, seemingly out of nowhere. Ron's arm then stiffened. His feet moved heavily, slowing his movement; he felt awkward and robotic.
>
> Telling himself that he was excited helped Ron to experience the extra energy surge as energizing rather than as a detriment. Whereas defining his feeling as anxious had led to cautiousness, defining the same nervous feeling as excitement increased his aggressiveness in attacking the ball. Ron's confidence that he could win gradually rose, and with it, his ranking.

❏ "Will I or won't I . . .?"

"Will I or won't I . . .?" That question triggers uncertainty. "Will I or won't I win that match?" "Will I or won't I get that job?" "Will I or won't I get invited to the prom?" Uncertainty breeds anxiety.

While no one can tell the future, contingency planning can help. That is, create a backup plan, a Plan B. That way if Plan A does not pan out, the consequences look less worrisome.

For example, you might think to yourself, "If I don't win the match, I'll find a new coach to help me strengthen my serve." Or, "If I don't get this job, I think I'll refocus my job search onto . . ." Or maybe, "If I don't get invited to the prom, I think I'll call my cousin Sherwin and ask him to go to the prom with me."

Assume that Plan A will work. At the same time, knowing that you have given yourself a Plan B safety net can reduce unhelpful worrying.

❏ **The "bigs"**

The big point, the big game, the big tournament, my big chance—all these phrases trigger anxiety. So do the *have tos*: "I *have to* make this shot!"; "I *have to* get a high score on this exam!" Inflating the importance of an event increases performance anxiety, lowering your success odds as anxious tension rigidifies both your thinking and your muscles. Fluid, flexible thinking improves access to memory and increases creative thinking, the same as fluid, flexible muscles improve athletic, musical, and any performance.

> Ron learned to remind himself that games are not won by any particular big point, but rather by how he played throughout a match. A high tennis ranking similarly results from a pattern of wins, not from any one point, game, or tournament.

Similarly, careers are built on collecting many fine performances, rarely on any one particular one. Win or lose, there's almost always another performance opportunity in the future. Life flows.

❏ **"New" or "the first time"**

Words like *new* and *for the first time* can have similar anxiety-inducing impacts as big. Thoughts like, "This is the first time I've ever . . ." increase excitement because first times elevate emotional intensity. New is the final depression antidote in the *AGGRESS-N* formula. The excitement generated by newness may be why you probably enjoy travel, going to a new restaurant, meeting new friends, and wearing new clothes. At the same time, excessive excitement can easily slip into anxiety.

> Ron was wary of anything new. One day at a friend's house, his friend had no coffee. "Try this Postum instead," his friend suggested. "Postum is what they used to drink in World War II when coffee wasn't available."

Ron suddenly felt nervous. He was used to real coffee. Trying something new, coffee-like but not the real thing, scared him. So did playing a tournament in a new city or playing for the first time at a higher level of competition.

❏ Misplaced focus: What will they (the audience, other players, etc.) think about how I'm doing?

Peak performance requires entering a state of flow. Flow occurs when your attention, which you can think of as being like a beam of light, focuses steadily and entirely on the task you are doing, without interruption. Immerse yourself in the activity you are doing—in the content of your speech or the music you are performing—to enter that state of total concentration.

By contrast, watching yourself as you are performing undermines quality performance by giving you a dual role. Sex therapists have coined the term *spectating* for the self-defeating habit of performing and simultaneously being a spectator to your performance. Observing to yourself, like a sports commentator who judges what you are doing while you are doing it, requires mental hopping back and forth between the doing and the watching perspectives. Each hop interrupts your focused concentration on the task at hand.

If you do watch yourself as you perform, evaluating yourself positively as in "Great job!" can prove to be as pernicious as judging yourself negatively. Evaluating yourself in either way breaks the flow of being in the moment. Again, interruptions in your concentration can be costly. So can either excitement or concentration.

Ron would get excited after a great shot. He gradually learned that he could enjoy these successes, but only if he kept his enjoyment brief. Otherwise, in his delight he would begin to hit the ball wildly or go for shots that were low odds in order to repeat the fun of showing that he could do the impossible.

While spectating on yourself is problematic, guessing others' reactions to you can be even more undermining. When you speculate on what others think of you, do you become at risk for assuming they are viewing you critically? Many people do, needlessly raising anxious feelings.

When Ron, then in his teens, first started playing tennis tournaments, he was acutely aware of his dad's presence at the game. "I wonder what Dad thought of that serve?" he'd speculate. Or, "Oh, no. Dad's going to think I have no talent since I missed returning that easy serve."

Each guess about what his dad might be thinking worsened Ron's internal chatter and emotional surges. When intrusive thoughts about what others think interrupt mental focus during matches, they can undermine success in even the most skillful players.

Focusing on what others think is not your job. To minimize anxiety, stay fully immersed in what you yourself are doing, which is your job.

❏ The mistaken belief that anxiety is a red light

Do you react as if anxiety is a red light, telling you to stop? Anger is a red light, a stop sign that does tell you to pause immediately from what you were doing or saying.

Anxiety, by contrast, is a blinking yellow light. What do you do at a blinking yellow light? Proceed with caution. When you feel anxious, reassure yourself with the mantra, "I can feel anxious and still go ahead and do what I need to do."

Ron often felt nauseously anxious in the hour or so before his first match in tennis tournaments. To escape this extreme physical discomfort, Ron wanted to leave. He wanted to withdraw, claiming an injury, or simply run away.

Putting on earphones to distract his thoughts with music helped. In addition, to counter the impulse to run away, Ron repeated to himself the mantra, "I can feel anxious and still do what I need to do," refocusing then on his pre-game preparation routines.

Once the game had started, Ron learned to focus intensely on the ball when the ball was in play. Between points, he focused on strategy. With these techniques, within minutes after the start of the match his anxiety would vanish.

Forgetting to focus on the very next step

Sometimes, even if you believe that anxiety is just a blinking yellow light and even if you have reframed your nervous jitters as excitement, you may feel anxious as you get started. Fortunately, focusing on the very next step raises the odds that you will soon get into the flow and perform your best.

During pauses in the action, anxiety is especially likely to surge. Again, keep your focus on your very next step. Planning and visualizing what you will do next occupies your mind, crowding out anxiety remnants. At the same time, a focus on the very next step gives you an opportunity to review or revise strategy decisions, to correct for technical mistakes, and to engage in behavioral rehearsal, that is, in visualizing what you will do next and how.

> Ron learned to use his twenty-five allowable seconds between points in tournaments to plan his next point. He reminded himself of the strategy and tactics he and his coach had decided upon. He visualized to correct technical errors he may have made in the prior point, errors such as needing to bend his knees lower or move his feet more quickly. Before launching his serve, he envisioned the single-most critical aspect of his next action, for instance, his service toss.
>
> In these ways, instead of wasting precious moments on worrying he used all of his between-points time to optimize his performance.

❑ Jumping ahead and *what ifs*

"Oh, no, I'm going to lose!" That thought is a killer, and so is its opposite: "Wow! I'm going to win!" Guessing outcomes in either direction indicates that your thoughts have jumped ahead from a focus on the immediate present to the future. A focus on outcomes, on whether you will win or lose, invites losing. Like spectating, thoughts that jump ahead distract you from the task at hand, disrupting your concentration. They undo the state of being "in the zone."

Speculations about the future also inadvertently stimulate excited or nervous feelings: "I wonder if giving this speech will get me a promotion," or "My current illness could lead to something much worse."

> All week Ron had been playing his best tournament tennis ever. Now he was in the finals and approaching the last point of the match. Seeing that his opponent had hit a relatively easy serve, Ron's thoughts suddenly jumped ahead. An image of how happy his girlfriend would be rose in his mind's eye.

In that brief microsecond, his eyes lost their focus on the ball. He hit the ball off-center, sent it out of bounds, and lost the point.

Ron's mind then jumped ahead again, this time with a *what if*: "What If I miss the next two points?" With the image of losing the next two points now in his mind, he did. He lost the match and, with it, the tournament championship.

In contrast with those who jump ahead to guess outcomes in a performance or game situation, psychologically skillful performers stay in the moment. As the famed baseball star Yogi Berra once said, "The game's not over till it's over." Or as the country-western singer Kenny Rogers crooned, "There'll be time enough for counting when the dealin's done."

If you have inadvertently jumped ahead to guess an outcome, calmly take your mind by the hand and bring your thoughts back to the immediate present.

In a subsequent major tournament, Ron again played well. This time he again reached the finals, finding himself once more at what could be the winning point. Ron steadied himself: "Stay focused on now. Keep your eyes on the ball."

Ron consciously relaxed the muscle in his serving arm. He visualized the spot where he was aiming his serve. He visualized how high he wanted his serving ball toss to go. He launched his service swing, and he aced in a winner.

R$_X$ 4.6: HALT AGITATION OVER DECISIONS.

Do your attempts to make decisions ever get mired in mental wheel spinning? If your thinking stalls, spinning like wheels in a snowy rut, or if your thoughts agitate back and forth like windshield wipers, your thinking will create anxiety instead of solutions.

Agitation can cause tension whether a decision is within your own thoughts or involves two or more people. In both cases, agitation blocks progress toward finding a solution. Constructive thinking, by contrast, gives you a feeling of forward movement.

What accounts for stalls and agitation in decision-making? Often it's a surprisingly powerful three-letter word. See if you can spot the problematic word in the following self-talk.

"I'd like to go to the mountains this weekend. But there's no way I can do that with my house needing to get cleaned up . . . Maybe I can clean it up after work on Monday. But I know I'll be too tired to tackle it then . . . But it looks like such beautiful weather, and it's been so long since I've gone hiking."

What word made this inner dialogue so frustrating? If you guessed that the culprit was *but*, you guessed right. Each time the thoughts in this inner dialogue began to move forward with the addition of new data, *but* shifted the thoughts back to the starting line. How did *but* accomplish that unfortunate feat? *But* deletes whatever came before.

But deletes whatever came before

Rx 6.2, which explains how *Word Patrol* can help you stay in a mode of collaborative dialogue, will clarify more about the unfortunate impacts that the potent little word *but* can have on relationships. For now, however, notice what happens if you shift from *but* to *and*, or better yet to *and at the same time*.

"I'd like to go to the mountains this weekend . . . *And at the same time*, there's no way I can do that with my apartment needing to get cleaned . . . Maybe I can clean it up after work on Monday . . . Yes, *and at the same time*, I know I'll be too tired to tackle it then . . . *And* it does look like this weekend's weather will be beautiful, perfect for hiking. I know! I'll skip cleaning the apartment this weekend. I can live with some mess for a week. Then next weekend I'll do an extra-thorough cleaning. Maybe I'll ask a friend to come over to help. We could clean my house together and then switch to cleaning his place, *and* maybe drink a beer *and* put on music."

The impacts of *but* versus *and* or *and at the same time*

Within your thoughts, *but* creates tension. With *and* you are adding data, that is, you are doing addition. Each time you respond to a prior idea with *and* or *and at the same time*, you are augmenting the information in your database. When you link ideas with *and*, each additional piece of information propels your thinking forward, expanding your data base and inching your thoughts ever closer toward a creative solution.

In discussions between people, the little linking words *but* versus *and* also matter.

And or *and at the same time* sustain positive feelings. *But* versus *and* determine whether you will emerge from a problem-solving discussion feeling anxious or feeling relieved, satisfied, and happy.

R̴ₓ 4.7: END WORRYING BY SEEKING INFORMATION.

This prescription re-focuses you on the mantra, *The best antidote to anxiety is information.* Information about what?

Anxiety usually arises in response to a sense that something dangerous lurks ahead on your path to the future. The threatening potential calamity may harm your physical health, your financial health, your job, your emotional health, a personal relationship, or any aspect of your life.

Anger tends to be about something that has already happened, something in the past. Anxious thoughts by contrast hover over the future, on a development that you are concerned will or will not happen, and if so with what consequences. Worrying is the repetition of anxious thoughts about the future.

Worrying often centers on relationships. People need people. While some folks are loners, most turn to family, friends, and community to enhance their well-being with affection, enjoyment, and support in difficult times. Even most animals tend to form herds, flocks, packs, prides, or gaggles. Relationship threats therefore are especially prone to trigger worrying.

Perceived threats in relationships typically revolve around two deep and quite universal concerns:

- Whether the bond that holds your relationship together will stay securely attached
- Whether you will be safe from injurious comments or actions

While many situations can evoke these concerns, three mental habits are especially likely to perpetuate relationship anxieties.

- Guessing others' thoughts
- Anticipating and then believing worst-case scenarios
- Avoiding explicit discussion of potential problems

Fortunately, all of these common anxiety-exacerbating technical errors can be remedied, primarily by reminding yourself of the mantra *The best antidote to anxiety is information.*

Guessing others' thoughts and feelings

Most worries in relationships are based on guessing what people of importance to you think, e.g., "He doesn't really love me!" or "She's going to leave me!" Guesses occur when you extrapolate meanings from small clues. For instance, if your friend seemed grumpy when he left after dinner at your house, you will worry about the friendship if you interpret his grumpiness as disgruntlement with something that you have done. Maybe he was really worrying about having to get up early the next morning. Maybe he had a headache. Maybe he had received a troubling text message. Guessing converts clues to needless worries.

Often, guesses are projections onto your partner of what you yourself would have thought or felt in that situation. "He's mad at me because I . . ." or "I know that he thinks I . . ." See Rx. 2.8, 3.3, and 3.10 for explanations in earlier prescriptions of the phenomenon of projection.

Instead of guessing, ask. *The best antidote for anxiety is information.* Fortunately, reality is generally more benign than the worst-case scenarios that anxiety-prone people create.

Eve guessed that her husband Gary cared more about his ex-wife than he did about her. Why else would he be so financially generous with an ex-wife?

Believing her interpretation, Eve felt anxious and then angry. She then withdrew emotionally from Gary, not wanting to make the situation even worse by berating him for treating her as a second-class citizen.

Confused by Eve's distancing, Gary felt rejected. He coped by stretching out his business trips to avoid the pain of experiencing his wife as cold and unloving. When he traveled, he could enjoy himself, burying his anxieties in long workdays and TV watching in his hotel room at night. Eve, however, interpreted Gary's increasingly lengthy business trips as further signs that her husband did not love her.

By contrast with guessing, assuming, and interpreting others' thoughts, asking gathers reliable data. Even bad news is better than no news because information enables you to build realistic action plans. *Information is the best antidote to anxiety.*

> Eve continued to worry about whether her husband really loved her. "Time for asking," she decided. "I'll just ask Gary outright."
>
> "Gary," Eve asked, "how do you feel toward me?"
>
> "Scared. I love you so much. But do you love me? I'm always afraid I'm letting you down, especially when you get quiet. I worry, too, that you may be angry at me. My parents, and my first wife also, were pretty much always mad at me. I do get terrified that you are mad at me too, just nicer about it."
>
> "Hmm. That surprises me. And how do you feel toward your former wife?" Eve continued. "When I hear you sounding so kind when you're on the phone with her making arrangements for the kids, and especially when you give her extra money, I feel less-than in your eyes."
>
> Gary answered, "You and she are day and night. I love you. I'm terrified of my ex. She rants and raves, just like my father used to. It's now five years after our divorce, and I'm still afraid to stand up to her when we have to discuss anything. I turn back into the ten-year-old kid who was afraid of his dad. As to why I gave her a too-generous divorce settlement. I still pay her off so she won't get mad at me. It's pathetic."

Asking yielded reassuring information. With the answers Gary gave her, Eve's worries evaporated.

> "Gary, I love you too. Who would have thought!"

Anticipating and then believing worst case scenarios

Worrying involves a mental habit envisioning bad outcomes when you look ahead, and then spinning your wheels as you ruminate about these negative scenarios.

The recipe for worry is simple, though not one that I would prescribe for you unless you like feeling anxious. Keep your focus ahead on future events rather than staying primarily present-focused. Anticipate worst case scenarios. Assume that your dark crystal ball gives you truth. As you see painful illnesses, financial disasters, relationship endings, and worse in your future, keep repeating the thoughts to insure a steady stream of anxious feelings.

By contrast, a long-popular 1960's song sung by Doris Day began, "Que sera, sera; Whatever will be, will be." My mother-in-law, Dorothy, a woman of wisdom, used to love that song. The song offers a reminder for you if you want to enjoy your present life. Beware, the song suggests, of letting the present slip by while you preoccupy yourself with guessing what might, or might not, happen in the future.

Planning ahead for known future challenges of course makes sense. Work hard in school. Get a solid education to give yourself a platform for earning a good living. Choose carefully whom to marry. Learn the skills for collaborative interacting to increase the likelihood that both your marriage and your work-life will bring you blessings. Save for your retirement.

In sum, put a stop to excessively focusing on what might happen in the future. Make a decision instead just to stack the odds in your favor. Plan for known challenges. Take the thumb route of problem-solving to Find Solutions in response to current difficulties. And then take a grand leap of faith onto truly believing that the future ahead for you will work itself out for the best. *Whatever will be, will be.*

Avoiding discussion of the problem

Avoidance may feel like it's going to be less frightening than dealing directly with concerns that scare you. Unfortunately, avoidance, a form of becoming immobilized and Freezing, perpetuates anxiety.

My client Eve refers to this reaction as turtling, an apt metaphor for how she "stuffs" her emotions and the concerns that raise them, hiding them under her thick and strong shell.

Eve had made a brief attempt to tell Gary her feelings of being less-than in his eyes. Unfortunately, by raising the issue in a way that sounded accusatory, she invited a defensive retort. After that initial abortive attempt, Eve had avoided further discussion lest it lead to a fight.

In spite of her success in asking Gary how he felt about his ex-wife, Eve still remained concerned that he ignored her in the evenings. Why was he so absorbed every night in watching televised sports?

Eve finally decided to ask Gary if he would discuss his TV watching. He readily agreed. They talked quietly. Gary had had no idea that his sports viewing left his wife feeling abandoned. Ever since his teenage years Gary had turned on the TV at night and mostly stayed glued to it until bedtime.

In response to his new perspective, Gary volunteered to remove the TV to a back room in the house. He might still occasionally choose to watch a major sporting event. Overall though, he would be far less likely to be tempted every night to slip back into his chronic TV habit.

Eve gained a surprising new understanding of herself from discussing her TV concern with Gary. She realized that because she had felt abandoned when her husband watched nightly TV sports, she had pushed him away. It felt safer to push Gary away than to feel pushed away herself, so she had been offering Gary less and less warmth, appreciation, or sexual connecting. She had been serving him distance and irritability instead of affection.

Now in the evenings Gary and Eve talk together about their day, play Scrabble, put on music, and often read side-by-side on the couch as they had when they were first married. Both of them are delighted.

Thinking back on the widening canyon that had distanced her from Gary, Eve recalled the words of a neighbor. "Worry is the interest you pay on something you haven't yet purchased."

You now have two mantras to use as antidotes to anxiety.

Eve recalled then the anxiety mantra *Information is the best antidote to anxiety*. "That mantra really works!" Eve concluded.

The same mantra can work for you, especially in combination with the anti-anxiety mantra *Whatever will be, will be*. Are you ready to take this leap, leaving your worries behind? _____

What might hold you back? _____

What can you do to let go of worrying nonetheless? _____

R$_X$ 4.8: THINK OF PANIC ATTACKS AS *FIND THE BUTTERFLY* PUZZLES.

Panic attacks are bursts of high-intensity anxiety that arise suddenly, often with no apparent cause. Fear usually has a visible trigger, maybe indications that a spouse could be having an affair, a work task that looks too difficult, the appearance of a potential attacker on a dark street. With panic attacks, by contrast, the anxiety seems to erupt like a random geyser.

For some people, a sudden surge of anxious feelings induces a secondary wave of fear. This fear is about the panic itself. Does this panic feeling mean I'm going crazy? Does my fast-beating heart mean that something dreadful is about to happen?

Women most often interpret the sudden wave of fear as a first sign of going crazy. Men tend to fear that the out-of-the-blue anxiety eruption with its surging heart rate and sudden breathlessness are first signs of an imminent heart attack. Fortunately, a panic attack is generally far more benign than either of these mistaken guesses.

During a panic attack, you can use the techniques from Rx 4.4, distraction and/or mindfulness, to wait out the rise and then gradual reduction in anxious feelings. Either during that time or after the attack has subsided however, think about butterflies. Generally the butterflies technique still works to help you understand the attack days or even weeks after the panic has passed.

Think about butterflies

Butterfly thoughts is my term for the fleeting thought-fragments that trigger panic attacks. Imagine the flight path of a butterfly. Butterflies zig and zag, darting so quickly into and away from your vision that their flight path is difficult to track.

Just before a panic attack, an idea or image has briefly darted in and then immediately out of your mental vision. Before you could catch and bring the thought to conscious awareness, Zap! Adrenalin has flooded your body, creating a live wire of potent anxiety. Meanwhile, having triggered a nauseatingly fearful feeling, lightness in your head, a pounding heart, and shallow breathing, the butterfly thought has quickly flitted afar and disappeared.

No problem. Here's the game plan.

First, reduce the immediate feelings of panic. Sitting quietly, close your eyes and focus on relaxing the tension in your arm, leg, and facial muscles. Breathe several slow, deep breaths as you visualize yourself in a calming environment like a beach or a flowery meadow. Or distract yourself by doing something that absorbs your attention. Sing a song, hum a tune, or think about a recent enjoyable activity.

As the panic feelings abate, close your eyes so that you can reconnect with the idea or image that the butterfly had darted in to share with you. Allow yourself to become aware of the last image or thought that had darted through your mind in the moment before the anxiety had welled up. If you are relaxed, the message will gradually resurface to your consciousness.

Having found your butterfly thought, use it to clarify the panic attack mystery. Notice in the four case examples below how *Find the Butterfly* works.

Ryan, an entrepreneur in his forties, had been sitting with a friend in a restaurant waiting for lunch when he suddenly felt flooded by a wave of intense feelings of panic. He had experienced panic attacks before so he knew to relax in order to recapture his butterfly thought. Darting through his mind just prior to the surge had been the words, "What if I've taken too much risk this time?"

Ryan's newest venture, a high-end restaurant, had all the right ingredients: a central location, a great chef, upbeat decor, and the latest in culinary trends. At the same time, the loan he'd taken out for the business was huge, the interest rate high, and the rent on his space was more than he'd hoped to pay.

Ryan's friend, as they chatted, had mentioned a gloomy newspaper report on businesses that were folding in their neighborhood. That's when the butterfly fluttered in.

***

Jeffrey, a young fellow in his twenties, had been sitting in a friend's living room when a panicked feeling came out of nowhere. Tracking down the last thought he'd had before feeling flooded with anxiety, Jeffrey recalled a visual observation. A bright red spot on an abstract painting on the wall had caught his eye.

Jeffrey at first felt confused. Why a red spot? He then remembered that the red color was the same as the intense red of the high-heeled shoes his mother had worn the prior evening when they were sitting in her living room.

Jeffrey often found his mother provocative. That evening at one point he felt totally enraged. He had felt a powerful urge to haul off verbally, to tell his mom he never wanted to see her again, and even to punch her mouth to make her stop talking.

The red on the painting that was the color of his mother's shoes had reminded Jeffrey also of his anger and of how fearful he had felt of losing his self-control.

***

Jane's last thought before her panic attack had been, "I'm going to the Safeway." The Safeway is a grocery store. What could be so frightening about going into the grocery store?

As she focused on the word Safeway, Jane's butterfly thought suddenly came clear. Several years prior, Jane had thought that by turning down a job offer with a fun, new startup company and instead taking a relatively boring job at a long-established company she had been taking "the safe way." In the past year, however, the startup had grown steadily while the profits at her older and more traditional company had dwindled. Her employer now was considering closing the company's doors. Jane's choice of jobs had not put her onto a safe pathway after all.

***

Michele, a recently engaged woman in her mid-twenties, also had a panic attack in a grocery store. As Michele entered the store, a brief thought wafted by. "That's the aisle I need to walk down."

Michele's fear? Her butterfly thought had metaphorically expressed her anxieties about "walking down the aisle," that is, about her forthcoming marriage. Had she chosen someone who would be right for her? What if the marriage proved to be as painful a mistake as her parents' marriage had been for them?

Ryan, Jeffrey, Jane, and Michele all succeeded in identifying the butterfly thoughts that induced their panic attacks. In each case, once they understood what about the thought had triggered their adrenaline surge, they felt relieved. The butterfly thought had helped them to clarify a genuine, albeit worrisome, life dilemma.

With the source of their anxiety now clear, thinking about what to do about the real problem could begin. Thank you to butterflies!

R$_X$ 4.9: ALLEVIATE CHRONIC STRESS VIA THREE STRATEGIES.

Stress is the generic term for your body's response to a situation that needs your attention and action. As earlier chapters have mentioned, when your body has a stress reaction, your amygdala rings a "Do something!" alarm. Like the American Revolution's Paul Revere, the silversmith who "rang the alarm in every Middlesex village and farm," your amygdala mobilizes your body for an immediate response. Cortisol and adrenaline raise your heart rate, quicken your pulse, speed up your breathing to infuse extra oxygen into your body, and prepare your muscles for action.

A life without sufficient challenges would become boring. When your body responds to a stress trigger by ringing the amygdala alarm, cortisol, the stress chemical produced in your adrenal glands, can be good for you. Episodic stress keeps you in shape, much like exercise keeps your body well-tuned and puzzles keep your mind sharp.

Excessive stress, however, can overload your response system. Troubles emerge if the following occur:

- Your amygdala frequent rings false alarms when no real danger is present.
- The danger was overrated, so your reaction is inappropriately intense.
- Your stress response keeps flooding you like a gas pedal stuck to the floor.
- You function in stress mode over too long a time period.
- You do not alternate periods of stress with pauses for relaxation.

Too much stress plus insufficient relaxation periods to let the cortisol subside can cause your cortisol to build up excessively. Continual alarms of "This is an emergency!" train your adrenal glands to believe they have to manufacture cortisol incessantly. Your adrenals may then become exhausted.

Adrenal fatigue results in insufficient cortisol in your body, which in turn creates a further set of problems. If you suspect that your adrenals have been working overtime and may be exhausted, be sure to get them checked by your doctor. Chronic stress invites a broad range of other medical difficulties as well.

With regard to its mental health impacts, chronic stress creates emotional brittleness, energy depletion, quickness to anger, and on-going feelings of tension and anxiety. These excessive emotions can harm your relationships, cause sleep problems, make you prone to depression, and reduce your overall sense of well-being.

If you feel excessively pressured or anxious, what can you do to calm your system? You might start with one or more of the following three stress-reduction strategies:

- Address unnecessarily anxiety-arousing beliefs.
- Change the circumstances that have been causing anxiety and stress.
- Utilize *AGGRESS-N* plus the *Three M's* of *Meditation, Music,* and *Mother Nature.*

Address mistaken beliefs that keep you anxiety prone

Overly frequent and intense emotional responses can be based on what cognitive therapists refer to as mistaken beliefs. When beliefs and expectations do not line up with reality, stress and anxiety emerge at each disjunction.

Quentin was enjoying dinner with his family when he said to his young son Bobby, "Pass the salt, please." Bobby, in typical kid fashion, was absorbed in playing with his food. He didn't realize that someone just asked him to do something.

"I told you, pass the salt!" Quentin repeated, this time with irritation. Bobby continued to play with his food, still too lost in fantasy to hear his dad's request.

Quentin then blasted out in a full fury, "I am sick of you ignoring what I say! Pass the salt now!"

Where does anxiety come into this picture? Not receiving instant attention from his children tapped Quentin's fear that his children did not respect him. Once that fear had been triggered, Quentin would flip almost instantaneously from anxiety into aggressive responses. As the Hand Map in Rx 1.1 conveys, once people respond to a difficulty by heading down one of the four finger routes, they may easily shift from one to another of these counterproductive pathways, e.g., from anxiety to anger.

Quentin habitually overreacted to Bobby's normal-child behaviors, in large part because of mistaken beliefs about parenting. Quentin believed he was entitled to "respect." Respect, to him, meant that his child should snap to attention every time he spoke. That mistaken belief kept him on chronic alert for signs that his son did not respect his authority.

Looking back at its source, Quentin quickly understood where he had learned this unrealistic belief about father-son relationships. Quentin's own dad had been a military officer. He had parented with a similar mistaken belief that military notions of hierarchy were appropriate for parenting children.

Cognitive Behavioral Therapy (CBT) identifies mistaken stress-inducing beliefs such as these. In addition, CBT pays attention to common stress-inducing mistaken thoughts like the six below.

If some of these beliefs are causing you to feel needlessly anxious, awareness offers a first step toward change. With awareness, you then can choose to replace the mistaken beliefs with more helpful understandings. Which of these anxiety-inducing beliefs may be stressing you?

❑ **Perfectionism, such as believing "I have to be perfect" or "My children have to be perfect"**
People, and especially children, are never perfect.

> Quentin believed that children should behave perfectly, which to him meant following orders without question. Each time his son Bobby acted instead like a normal child, Quentin would feel a surge of anxiety. Bobby was not acting perfectly, which meant that Quentin was not being a perfect parent.

Replacement beliefs for "I have to be perfect" might be "All people make mistakes" or the mantra *Mistakes are for learning*. Also, *That Was Then, This Is Now* can explore the source of this belief. That understanding can take away the belief's potency.

❑ **Believing "I'm not lovable"**
When parents speak to their children in irritated voices or criticize their children too often, they inadvertently convey to their children that they are not lovable. Mean, teasing, or bullying peers at school can do the same.

> Growing up with incessant criticism from his father, Quentin had interpreted his dad's frequent annoyance at him as meaning that he was unlovable.
>
> A more sanguine belief would be "I am lovable." To change deep-rooted beliefs like this, specialized therapy techniques can help. My colleague Dale

Petterson and I use a technique created by Bradley Nelson called Emotion Code. At the same time, *That Was Then, This Is Now* is likely to work well also.

❑ Awfulizing

"Bobby's ignoring me is awful!"

Awful situations evoke strong anxiety. Replace *awful* with more neutral, observational words. Bobby's behavior was the normal response of an imaginative child who enjoys engaging his active mind in fantasy-story creating.

❑ Personalizing, or believing "It's all about me"

Personalizing, explained in earlier prescriptions (Rx 3.1, 3.3 and 3.9), rests on the often-mistaken idea that others' behaviors signify how they feel toward you when in reality their behavior is motivated by other factors. Taking others' words, feelings, or actions personally evokes anxiety because you, if you are like most of us, want to feel liked. Belonging feels safe. Feeling rejected or criticized evokes anxiety because losing the connection with attachment figures, other family members, or friends creates feelings of vulnerability.

"If he loved me, he would have passed the salt right away."

Quentin's anxiety calmed as he began to understand that Bobby's non-responsiveness to his request stemmed from Bobby's absorption in his own thoughts, not from negative feelings toward his father.

For young children, a belief that "I am the center of all that happens" is developmentally normal. For adults, however, all-about-me thinking and the taking-things-personally mindset that it breeds invite needless anxiety and stress.

Instead of personalizing, cultivate a habit of curiosity about others' perspectives. Ask questions to others about what they think and feel.

❑ Overgeneralizing from a specific behavior to a broad conclusion about character

Overly broad conclusions long-jump minor fears into major anxieties.

Quentin observed, "Bobby isn't passing the salt." Leaping to the overgeneralization "I have a disrespectful son" made Bobby's momentary action feel to Quentin like an alarming danger.

Instead of making this cognitive error, tether your focus to the specific behaviors.

❏ Musterbation

Albert Ellis, one of the originators of CBT, noted the negative potency of words like *must*, *should*, and *have to*. A fan of provocative phrasings, Ellis coined the term *musterbation* to convey how these words augment stress.

"I *must* get Bobby to listen to me!"

"Bobby *should* pay attention and respond right away when I ask him to do things."

Yes, it would be nice if Bobby heard the request and immediately passed the salt. At the same time, *must* and *should* cause needless emotional inflammation. Better to use calmer words like *would like to* and *could*.

"I *would like to* get Bobby to listen to me."

"It *would* be nice if Bobby could respond right away when I ask him to do things."

"Lucia [Quentin's wife], *could* you pass me the salt, please? Bobby seems to be in outer space, or maybe that's inner space. Do you think that when he grows up he'll write fantasy books?"

For Quentin, eliminating mistaken beliefs enabled him to let passing the salt shaker become just about passing the salt shaker.

As Quentin replaced his anxiety about Bobby disrespecting him with appreciation that Bobby was a boy with a creative imagination, he began to devise playful games to catch Bobby's attention. Before issuing requests, he would call out in a funny raspy voice, "Bobby, paging Bobby. Earth to Bobby.

You there, Bobby?" Bobby loved it. The games became rituals Quentin could use again and again in situations that he used to react to with stress.

What situations and thoughts produce stress for you?

Make changes in your circumstances

If you have been living for quite a while with an ongoing stressful circumstance, anxiety can begin to feel like your normal emotional state. In that case, you may be surprised to discover the extent to which a decision to make changes in your circumstances can change how you feel.

> Henry felt chronically stressed. While he liked his work as an interstate truck driver, to meet the timetables demanded by his employer Henry had to defy state and national safety regulations on the number of hours he drove per day. Worries about being caught when he was driving beyond his legal limit and about having an accident from falling asleep at the wheel kept him constantly on guard.
>
> When Henry returned to therapy after a pause of several months, I saw immediately that something had changed. Henry looked relaxed and happy. He greeted me with a broad grin. What had happened?
>
> Henry's employer had been paying top truck-driving wages. At the same time, the stress eventually made the money feel secondary. Henry quit. He took a job shortly after with another trucking company, one that expected its drivers to follow the rules.
>
> Henry's health, marriage, and personal well-being all quickly improved. With his shorter driving hours and consequent more relaxed state when he was home, everyone in his family fought less and laughed more.

Work challenges and family relationships tend to be the most common sources of excessive stress, particularly if you need to deal frequently with an emotionally unhealthy and often angry other. The stress in the following case came primarily from an adult's relationship with his difficult father. Adult women suffer similar challenges when they have a difficult parent.[52]

Jules had grown up as an only child. As an adult, responsibility for aiding his aging and long-divorced parents fell totally on his shoulders.

With his father, who fortunately lived out of state, Jules felt highly anxious before and distressed after even the shortest of phone conversations. His father specialized in appearing to be affable while sliding snide, deprecating remarks about Jules into every conversation.

One day Jules realized, "I do not need to continually expose myself to this source of stress. Sure, I'd like to rise above letting my father upset me. I've been trying that unsuccessfully all my life. I'll talk from time to time with Dad's brother to be sure that Dad has a roof over his head, clothing, food, and access to medical care. Beyond that, I want no further contact. Phew. What a relief!"

Utilize *AGGRESS-N* plus the *Three M's: Meditation, Music,* and *Mother Nature*

In the chapter on depression, the acronym *AGGRESS-N* prescribed eight factors that can place you into an emotionally healthy zone. These same factors work with similar effectiveness if your starting point is anxiety.

For instance, exercise, the E in the *AGGRESS-N* formula, stimulates the flow of GABA and other calming body chemicals. Studies have found that exercising with yoga in particular increases the body chemicals that reduce anxiety. In one study, yoga exercise was compared with walking. While both yoga and walking did increase GABA, yoga stimulated higher increases.[53]

Three additional factors, the *Three M's* of *Meditation, Music,* and *Mother Nature,* can add further calming relief for anxiety and stress. Interestingly, M sounds are associated in many languages with the word for mother. *Mama, mom, ma, eema, mamam, mere, madre,* and many more similar m-based words tend to be among the first words that infants learn, perhaps because a mother is the primary source of calming for babies and young children. Yoga sessions generally begin and end with chanting of the sound "Om," a sound that vibrates at the frequency of 432 Hz, a calming vibrational frequency found throughout nature. Similarly, to express contentment you may emit a version of "ummm" or "hmmm." So next time you feel stressed, consider using the Three M's.

Meditation reduces stress via sitting still. Humans are paradoxical beings. Opposites *distraction* and *mindfulness* both can ease anxiety. Similarly, both *movement,* via exercise of almost any sort, and *stillness* can create calming body reactions. Exercise optimizes your body's functioning. Research also has confirmed that meditation causes anxiety to flow away, leaving a state of calm well-being.[54]

Music sets moods. Depending on your preferences, you can choose to set an energizing or a calming tempo.[55]

Mother Nature offers surprisingly potent stress relievers as well. Sitting or walking in a natural environment among trees, flowers, grass, and sunshine has a calming impact.[56] Seashores, mountains, forests, and plains all can ease and uplift you. Green plants in your home and office[57] and a window that looks out on trees or grass[58] can grant you similar physical as well as emotional benefits. It makes sense that people send flowers to friends and family who need to spend time in a hospital. Flowers speed healing.[59]

If you live in an urban environment, take advantage of your city or town's parks and gardens. Stanford University tested thirty-eight San Francisco city dwellers, comparing the impacts on stress if they took one ninety-minute walk in a lushly green, natural environment each week to the impacts of a similar walk on a three-lane busy city street. Walking in the natural environment more effectively lowered negative ruminations. It lowered activity in the right prefrontal lobe, the side associated with depression. The natural green environment also decreased the frequency of mental health problems.[60] The bottom line: instead of taking pills, head for the hills—or fields, lakes, or seacoast.

In contrast with the positive impacts of *Meditation, Music,* and *Mother Nature,* computer screen time has anti-health impacts.[61] So do air pollution, traffic noise, congestion from many people living close together, and other features of city living. According to a recent Scientific American article, urbanites suffer more anxiety and depression than their country-living counterparts.[62]

In addition to the eight *AGGRESS-N* factors and the *Three M's,* any activities you enjoy are likely also to be stress-busters. Coffee breaks? Tea-time or a cold beer on a hot day with friends? Prayer? Riding a motorcycle? Walking a dog? Singing? Hugging children? Holding newborns as a volunteer in a hospital maternity ward?

Identify and make a priority of whatever activities are relaxing for you. List three here for starters: _____, _____, and _____.

R𝗑 4.10: REMOVE INTENSE ANXIETY AND ELIMINATE PTSD WITH EFT.

Post-Traumatic Stress Disorder, or PTSD, is a psychological reaction that occurs after an extremely stressful, painful or frightening event. Physical violence, natural disasters such as tornados, military combat, and other dangerous and frightening events can trigger it. So can verbal, physical, and sexual abuse, especially of children.

If you are in state of extreme panic or intense anxiety, or if you have been experiencing post-event symptoms such as flashbacks, nightmares, emotional brittleness and quickness to anger, there is good news. A treatment called Emotional Freedom Technique (EFT) is highly effective for relieving both strong anxiety reactions as they are happening and their aftermath of PTSD.

EFT, also known as acupoint tapping because it involves tapping on acupuncture points, is remarkably quick to do. It generally takes less than half an hour. It brings total and long-lasting relief. It requires no recall or re-living of painful past memories. And there seem to be no negative side-effects.

EFT mainly involves tapping with fingertips on specific acupuncture points on your fingers, the side of your hand, your face, upper chest and under your arm. At specific times you say aloud a sentence that expresses self-acceptance such as, "Even though I feel extremely anxious, I totally and profoundly accept myself."

Adding a sequence of eye movements, humming, and counting aloud further integrate the changes on both sides of your brain. These benign actions together facilitate profound reductions in intensely anxious emotions and their aftermath.

First created by psychologist Roger Callahan who named the technique Thought Field Therapy (TFT), the tapping treatment was later simplified and renamed EFT by Gary Craig. Most therapists who do tapping now use Craig's simplified procedures.

Because EFT has been around for several decades, the technique has been studied by many researchers who have validated its effectiveness with evidence-based testing procedures. Psychologist David Feinstein has written a particularly comprehensive review of this research. His article, which was published in a respected psychological journal, is accessible on the Internet by searching the author's name. Feinstein concludes that acupoint tapping procedures do rapidly remove PTSD symptoms and do yield lasting, not just temporary, relief.

Most interestingly, in studies comparing EFT with other PTSD treatment methods, tapping appears to be both the fastest treatment method and the most effective. Only the eye movement desensitization technique called EMDR (Eye Movement Desensitization and Reprocessing) shows similar effectiveness. EFT treatment however is a shorter procedure. [63]

To use EFT, one option is to do the tapping on your own. Learning how is surprisingly feasible. The Internet has many free instructional videos, including those on prescriptionswithoutpills.com. Gary Craig's free website offers especially clear instruction for self-administration.

A second option would be to find a local therapist who has been trained in the procedure. Many psychotherapists now utilize EFT techniques. An Internet search should identify EFT therapists in your geographic area. As you search, you may notice that a second psychotherapy technique, emotion-focused therapy, goes by the same EFT initials. For that reason you might do best by searching *EFT Tapping*.

In the following case, I invited my colleague Dale Petterson to do an EFT treatment with a client of mine who was too agitated and frantic to benefit from standard talk therapy. Reducing the intensity of his anxiety was essential before he would be able to begin to face the problem that had triggered his panic, gather further information, and eventually consider solution possibilities.

For the past several months, Perry had been telling his wife lies about their financial situation. When his wife discovered the reality of their debts, she told him that she was leaving their marriage. Perry was in a state of panic.

Perry had lied to his wife because what they owed was so much more than they would possibly be able to pay. He had feared that if he told her the reality, his wife would decide to divorce him. Now, days after a distressing discussion in which he did confess the realities of their financial situation to his wife and his wife had demanded that they divorce, Perry still felt too anxious to think coherently or even go to work.

EFT tapping reduced Perry's anxiety levels within less than ten minutes from an initial level of 10 on a scale from 0 to 10 to a level 4. Perry felt significantly relieved with this reduction. Further tapping for several more minutes continued to lower his anxiety.

By the end of the session, Perry felt calm enough that he felt he would be able to return to work. In a subsequent session with me, Perry reported that he had continued to feel relatively calm the rest of the week since the initial EFT treatment. From this emotionally manageable state, he now could utilize the techniques I describe earlier in this chapter, listing the thoughts and concerns associated with his anxiety and then circling back to figure out how to address them.

Looking back

This chapter began with a basic formula for reducing anxiety by listing concerns, seeking out additional information, and finding solutions to the problem that had triggered the anxious feelings. Prescriptions for anxiety prevention came next. The chapter concluded with treatment methods for eliminating panic attacks and post-traumatic stress. May calm now prevail.

Chapter 5

Addictions

When your travels down the road of life hit a bump, the fourth alternative to effective problem-solving is the escape route. The Fold, Fight, and Freeze Pathways to depression, anger, and anxiety all lead to unpleasant feelings, so the Flee Route can seem more appealing. However, like Alice's long fall down a rabbit hole into Wonderland, addictive escapes can lead you into further difficulties.

In addition to offering an enticing escape route from troubling situations, addictions beckon by tempting you with the promise of positive feelings, a high.

My fellow psychologytoday.com bloggers and I chuckle together about how easily we can become addicted to checking our numbers. How many readers have clicked on our most recently posted article? How do today's clicks compare with last week's? And how many likes?

Numbers that keep edging upward feel exciting. Yet excessive number-checking wastes time that could be better spent enjoying friends and family, reading, exercising, or even writing a next blogpost.

This chapter uses the term *addictions* in two ways: to refer to addictive habits and also to refer to full-fledged clinical addictions.

Addictive habits develop when a pleasurable or escape activity has become a compulsion, a habit that you keep doing even though it has become more self-destructive than life-enhancing. Addictive habits can range from mild to severely detrimental. Excessive eating can cause you to add a few less-attractive pounds. In the extreme, overeating to obesity creates a host of social and medical problems. Compulsive lying similarly can mildly impair or totally destroy your happiness and relationships. The prescriptions in this chapter mainly address mild to moderately self-harming habits.

A full clinical addiction brings physical suffering when the addictive substance or activity is not available. Cravings, physical withdrawal, and brain changes can make ending a serious addiction close to impossible for any except the most strong-willed to accomplish without support from an addictions program, professional counseling, and sometimes also medical and medication support. Do get help if you need it.

R_X 5.1: RECOGNIZE YOUR SELF-INJURIOUS HABITS.

Habits make your world go round. Habits of making your bed as you get up each morning, putting dirty clothes into a laundry basket instead of on the floor, and cleaning up the kitchen after meals serve you well. Personal hygiene habits like tooth-brushing and showers keep you safe to sit next to. Good nutritional and exercise habits keep your body humming optimally. Manners like saying thank you and chewing with your mouth closed make you look classy. How aware are you, though, of the habits in your life that are hurting instead of helping you?

In what way are all self-injurious habits chemical addictions?

All addictions involve a chemical component. The chemical may be exogenous, that is, a chemical from outside your body like alcohol, caffeine, sugar, or cocaine that you ingest. Alternatively, addictive chemicals that feel good and therefore demand "Give me more!" may be produced within your body.

Your body naturally produces "happy chemicals," a term that writer Loretta Breuning aptly coined for the pleasure-enhancing neurochemicals such as oxytocin, serotonin, dopamine, and endorphins. In her book *Meet Your Happy Chemicals*, Breuning explains that the chemical of bonding, oxytocin, flows when you feel close or affectionate toward someone. Winning and feeling more successful or ranked higher than others trigger a serotonin surge. Going on the

Self-Injurious Habits
Download this worksheet at *prescriptionswithoutpills.com.*

Do you have self-injurious habits that feel too enticing for you to resist in spite of their downsides? On the following activities checklist, note which may be controlling you:

I ENJOY	DOING TOO MUCH?	ADDICTION STAGE: I, II, III
Drinking alcoholic beverages	❏	
Using marijuana	❏	
Watching sports or other television programs	❏	
Working long hours, well beyond a standard workday	❏	
Shopping to feel good	❏	
Frequent checking of email, social media, and texting	❏	
Frequent number-checking, e.g., sales numbers, "likes," etc.	❏	
Playing computer or other electronic games	❏	
Sexual or emotional connecting with an inappropriate partner	❏	
Pornography viewing or other illicit sexual activity	❏	
Gambling, including obsessive stock market involvement	❏	
Thinking that you have illnesses (hypochondria)	❏	
Obsessive thinking, ruminating on negative thoughts	❏	
Under-eating, overeating, or binge-purge eating cycles	❏	
Bingeing on sugary foods or chocolate	❏	
Smoking cigarettes or cigars	❏	
Drinking excessive coffee, caffeinated sodas or energy drinks	❏	
Stalking	❏	
Excessively craving fame, status, popularity	❏	
Compulsively seeking risk and thrills	❏	
Acting sadistically	❏	
Committing crime or violence	❏	
Sniffing solvents	❏	
Overachieving	❏	
Over-exercising or weight-lifting	❏	
Collecting (coins, cars, etc.)	❏	
Cleaning compulsively	❏	
Another habit	❏	

prowl to pounce on prey or accomplish a goal stimulates dopamine. Endorphins surge with intense physical exercise. [64]

Take, for instance, checking email or a Facebook page. When a message on either evokes a gratifying "Wow!" response, your body responds with a spurt of pleasure neurochemicals. Similarly, you feel delight from seeing a higher golf or bowling score than you've earned in the past. Watching rising stats of your favorite sports star or team, or increases in the value of your stocks on the stock exchange, probably can give you a similar happy chemical surge. Ever-higher numbers of any type, along with winning at just about anything, stimulates release of neurotransmitters that give you a momentary natural high.

Happy chemicals train you to return for more, and more, and more, even after the action has become potentially self-harming. Beware of allowing good feelings to smother the little voices of caution within you. Otherwise, you may be at risk for continuing the costly habit, an addiction created from internal chemicals.

The shift from enjoyment to addiction may be subtle. To evaluate the pleasurable activities that bring forth your happy chemicals, consider the following questions:

In what ways does the activity bring net harm to your life?

_____

If you were to decide to end the habit, to what extent might the pull to resume it overwhelm the part of you that wants to quit?

_____

Do you now need more of the habit to get the same enjoyment you used to get with less?

_____

Does the habit cause you to invest less energy in work, friends, family and other realms that used to be meaningful to you?

_____

R$_x$ 5.2: IDENTIFY FOUR STAGES IN THE JOURNEY FROM HABITS TO ADDICTIONS.

In his classic book *The Addictive Personality*, family therapist and addictions specialist Craig Nakken clarifies three stages in the development of a drug or other major addictive disorder. Each stage is like a stop along a railroad line. The sooner you get off the train, the less likely you will end up stuck at the final station. [65]

Stage I: Internal changes

The journey begins with an experience of a high. This first intensely pleasurable moment could be produced by a big gambling win, buying something new, an illicit flirtation, intoxication from a drink or a pill, the thrill of control from not eating that can herald the beginning of anorexia, or any action that evokes a spurt of intensely positive feelings. Desire to repeat this high starts you down the tracks toward full addiction.

Stage II: Lifestyle changes

Addictive behaviors then continue, potentially increasing in frequency. So does preoccupation with when and how to accomplish the next high. As bonding to the addictive habit increases, attachment to normal relationships and activities decreases. Relationship and work troubles brew. If family or friends become aware of the addiction, they want it ended.

Stage III: Life breakdown

The addiction now is in total control. Self-defeating behaviors have become so pervasive that they scare even the addicted person. By this stage, intervention by others can make a huge difference. When addiction becomes this deeply entrenched, even a highly motivated addict is likely to have trouble ending the habit without outside help.

R_x 5.3: CLARIFY THE SOURCES OF YOUR ADDICTIVE HABITS.

Pleasure tells your brain to get more of what brought you that good feeling. Unfortunately, alas, any initially enjoyable activity can gradually take control of you. Tasting one spoonful of ice cream may tempt you to take another, and then another, in spite of your determination to stick to your weight-loss plan. What causes that strong pull to repeat doing something that felt good in spite of its longer-term detrimental impacts?

Fascinating brain studies now are producing clues about what goes on in your head to lock you into bad habits that may ultimately hurt you. Conventional psychological theories, reported toward the end of this prescription, also suggest helpful hypotheses.

Brain asymmetry

Addiction researchers from Duke University's Neurogenetics Study report surprising findings. In a recent, ground-breaking article they explain that tendencies to addictive habits increase when participants have asymmetrical amounts of energy activation in two specific parts of their brain.[66]

The ventral striatum, located deep inside your brain, is associated with reward-seeking behavior. The amygdala, the threat-assessment brain part discussed in several earlier prescriptions, is a second brain part involved in addictive potential. The Duke researchers used non-invasive MRI imaging to measure brain activation in these two areas.

If the levels of activation were at similar levels in both of these brain parts, either both high or both low, then susceptibility to addiction was relatively low. Impulses to gravitate toward enjoyment of pleasures and sensors that detect potential danger kept each other in check.

By contrast, for individuals in the study with one brain area that was highly energized when the other was underactive, addiction risk was high independent of which was the greater and which the lesser. That is, asymmetrical activity in these two brain organs (one high and one low) predicted problem drinking irrespective of which was the higher or the lower. In fact, an asymmetrical pattern predicted problem drinking not only at the time of the scan but again three months later, suggesting that addictive potential may be a fairly stable phenomenon.

Why does asymmetry in energy activation in these two brain organs predict increased addictive risk? Two different addictive patterns emerge. If your ventral striatum has a higher level of energy activation than your amygdala, you may tend to be impulsive, giving little thought to the long-term harm that may come from addictive actions. You become at risk enhancing good feelings with little worry about tomorrow. In contrast, if your amygdala has a high level of emotional reactivity, you are likely to experience frequent and intense negative emotions like anxiety, sadness, or anger. In this case, you could become at risk for succumbing to an addiction in order to obtain relief from too much distress.

As the Duke scientists explain, one addictive pattern is "associated with positive emotion enhancement . . . and another associated with negative emotion relief." Impulsive people who loved the feeling of a good drink perhaps underestimate the dangers of drinking too much, hence the dangers posed by a low-activation amygdala. Individuals who feel overwhelmed by emotional pain drink to seek emotional relief. Pleasure motivation plays little role in their decision-making.

Ahmad Hariri, the neuroscience psychologist who headed up this study, hopes that these findings will help therapists to tailor their treatments to their clients' specific type of addiction risk. People who drink because they impulsively do what looks gratifying without concern for negative consequences might benefit most from a therapy approach designed to help them gain control over their problem behaviors. For them, for instance, keeping alcohol out of their house might be essential. People with higher amygdala activation may benefit most from support with the stress factors in their lives to reduce their addictive impulses. For them, the prescriptions in this book for remedying depression, anger, and anxiety, and also the chapter ahead for sustaining well-being, could prove especially helpful.

Eye color

Could the color of your eyes possibly have anything to do with your susceptibility to addictions? University of Vermont researchers Arvis Saloveri and Dawei Li say yes to that question. From their database of over ten thousand individuals, people with blue eyes had the strongest tendencies to become addicted to alcohol.[67]

Why should people with blue eyes have any higher risk of alcohol addiction than people with brown eyes? The blue color itself is unlikely to be the culprit. A more likely explanation is that genetics plays a strong role in the tendency for alcohol to become addictive. Blue eyes correlate with other genetic factors that play a role in causing some people to have difficulty keeping their drinking within safe boundaries.

The bottom line: if you have blue eyes, take additional cautions to minimize your exposure to alcohol. If you do drink, set a firm limit to the number of drinks per sitting. If you drink with some frequency, limit the times and places where alcohol is available to you. If your drinking involves episodic binges, think through how best to protect yourself. Most importantly, if family members are telling you that your drinking concerns them, avoid the impulse to denial. Listen to what they are saying and take constructive action.

Other addiction risk sources

The National Institute on Alcohol Abuse and Alcoholism reports that while genes may account in part for who develops a drug or alcohol addiction, environmental factors such as cultural values, parental modeling, attitudes toward drugs, and availability of the addictive substance also play major roles.

What factors may be feeding your impulses to indulge excessively in your problematic habits?

_____

Beware especially if enjoyment in your relationships, work, and leisure activities begins to feel less compelling than the temporary high of the addictive habit. For instance, are you a sportsaholic who can't leave the TV screen to read to your children at bedtime? _____ A workaholic who works to the exclusion of love and leisure?_____ Addicted to Facebook or email? _____

Your risk for an addictive bond with a drug or activity will increase if your real-life relationships feel too thin. At the same time, the causation can be circular. That is, the more you invest your energies in an addictive habit, the more you will withdraw your energies and affections from life's ordinary pleasures like family, friends, and work. If these pleasures feel increasingly distant and of lesser importance, pay attention.

Cerise started looking frequently at Facebook. After dinner, and sometimes during the workday as well, she went upstairs to her desk to check her computer. She posted often. She loved the high when others clicked "like" in response to her writing or photos.

Eventually Facebook became more gratifying during daytime hours than her business. In the evenings Cerise interacted with Facebook instead of with her son or husband. Her teenage son began having problems at school and became surly at home. Her husband, who often brought work home on his computer, seemed not to notice how many hours Cerise spent on her computer until at some point he began to recognize how little connection he had with his wife.

Gradually Cerise stopped trying to keep her struggling business going. Facebook was more pleasant. Her husband began complaining about her Facebook compulsion and even mentioned divorce though he did reinvigorate his relationship with their son. The marriage bond became increasingly fragile.

Conventional psychological views of the sources of addictions

Conventional psychological wisdom hypothesizes that people prone to full-fledged addictions have had insufficient childhood experiences of being nurtured and soothed. Though no one explanation accounts for all serious addiction, I have seen many cases where this attachment-deficiencies hypothesis does apply.

> Leo's parents ignored and sometimes also verbally abused him. As he grew into adulthood and married, Leo's marriage relationship devolved into being similarly disconnected or hurtful. Bonding with a drug felt more gratifying—until the addictive substance took over his life.

A recent international discussion on LinkedIn about the sources of full-fledged addiction (as opposed to simpler addictive habits) offered a variety of helpful additional perspectives. Thank you to Ron Brown, Perry Kendrick, J. Craig, Joe Gitau, Ryan Cummings, Bema Yeboah, and others from the United States, the United Kingdom, and Africa for contributing your thoughts to this discussion.

> Addiction arises when the drug of choice hijacks the reward circuits of the limbic system, with the result that the addict comes to believe that the drug of choice is the most important thing in life, and using it becomes the addict's purpose in life.
>
> * * *
>
> Any over-indulgence in anything, sex included, alters the brain to crave and need that same feeling all the time to feel level or good or to just get through the day.
>
> * * *
>
> Addicts believe themselves to be "victims." They feel helpless and subsequently (often) turn to "self-medicating" as a means to numb or avoid their sources of pain . . . Eventually, the drugs become the new source of more pain, but then,

they come to love the high from whatever means they use. We are pleasure-seeking creatures.

* * *

Some people want to lose touch with reality. What is real may be painful or angering to an addict, so they attempt to avoid those feelings by doing drugs. They may have memories that they want to forget too.

* * *

I encountered two curious cases of early childhood traumatic experiences and deprivation, which I believe inform on this question . . . The first was of a sixteen-year-old boy who already, the previous four years, had been abusing cannabis. He and a sister were abandoned by their mother, a single parent, at four years of age, and she has never been seen again . . . To this day, he continues to abuse cannabis, and my hunch is that he is still self-medicating against the abandonment and lack of attachment.

* * *

There are a host of reasons why one can become addicted. Traumatic, early-life experiences can lead to people turning to drugs or alcohol to block out the pain of their trauma. I have experience of working with homeless people who become dependent on drugs or alcohol as it enables them to forget their current situation.

* * *

While life events may trigger an addictive response, it would appear that this is more likely to occur when people are in a state of psychological uncertainty. Developing a deep sense of purpose, competence, confidence, interpersonal trust, and so on leads to robustness and resilience.

* * *

I believe that addiction boils down to individual differences. Escape from trauma, just plain landing in bad company, a chance encounter with drugs—the reasons vary.

R$_X$ 5.4: ASK THE *SIX QUESTIONS TO END BAD HABITS*.

What excessive habits would you like to reconsider?

Use the following six questions to clarify factors that trigger or sustain each specific habit that you want to change.

Six Questions to End Bad Habits

Precursors	**Cues**	**Goals**
Two backwards-looking questions	*The moment-before questions*	*The forward-looking questions*
■ When I first started this habit, what did I like about it?	■ What cues and thoughts come up in the moment before my addictive action?	■ If I look at my habit now in the best possible light, what is it meant to accomplish?
■ From what unpleasant situation or feeling may I have been trying to flee?	■ How might I eliminate these cues or counter the thoughts?	■ What might be a better way to accomplish that goal?

Precursors: Two backwards-looking questions

1. When I first started this habit, what did I like about it?
2. From what unpleasant situation or feeling may I have been trying to flee?

Identify the feel-good aspect of the habit and also what you may have wanted to escape from to clarify how your addictive habit began.

Both questions yield helpful information. For instance, cocaine is a highly pleasurable and rapidly addictive substance. Most people who use cocaine a first time enjoy it. At the same time, most realize that repeating the fun high is not worth the potential loss via addiction of all that is good in their life. If you had been feeling beset by a troubling home, work, or financial situation, though, you were at higher risk from the outset for continuing the habit until it became addictive, controlling you.

Cues: Two moment-before questions

1. What cues and thoughts come up in the moment before your addictive action?
2. How might you eliminate these cues or respond to the thought?

Most people operate most of the time on automatic pilot. Habitual actions, good and bad, generally occur in response to a cue. When someone gives something to you, for instance, accepting it cues your habit of saying thank you. When the clock reads five thirty, it may cue your habit of leaving work. Sitting in the driver's seat in your car cues putting the key in the ignition.

When you see cookies on your countertop, the cookies are far more likely to cue eating than if they are behind a cabinet door where they are not visible to you. If the cookies are no longer even in your house, the likelihood that they will trigger overindulging goes down almost to zero.

After you have spotted a cue, you may then have a green light thought that allows you to move forward or a red light that tells you to halt. "Well, just this time . . ." gives you permission to move forward with the action. Saying to yourself, "I don't do that anymore. It's totally out of bounds for me. I'm going in the other room," might block you from moving forward and doing the action.

Goals: Two forward-looking questions

1. If I look at my habit now in the best possible light, what is it intended to accomplish?
2. What might be a better way to accomplish that goal?

Do you ever scold yourself for having indulged yet again in a problematic habit? The *Best Possible Light* question, introduced in Rx's 2.9, 3.4, 3.5, and 3.9, can feel magical because instead of focusing on what you are doing wrong, it adds to your self-acceptance and self-appreciation. As it does with grieving, depression, anger, or anxiety, this question guides identification of the well-intended subconscious goal of your problematic habit. With this goal clarified, you no longer need to rely on your additive behavior as a solution. You can devise an alternative action plan that satisfies the concern with fewer side costs.

Here are several examples of using the *Best Possible Light* question to identify your concerns. Then you can create an alternative strategy for achieving the goal with fewer costs.

For evening nibbling, which puts on weight:
- *Best Possible Light:* You graze to feel good when you feel at loose ends or bored.
- **Alternative solution options:** Identify a positive project and absorb yourself in it. Put on music. Turn on the TV or a computer. Read a

book. Talk with family members or friends. Plan evening activities ahead of time so you are too busy in the evenings to feel unfocused or bored.

For drinking too much at parties and then getting belligerent:

- *Best Possible Light:* To feel like you fit in by doing what everyone else is doing.
- **Alternative solution options:** Dilute the alcoholic drink. Put the alcoholic drink in a smaller glass. Drink three glasses of ginger ale between alcoholic drinks. Make a Shirley Temple, a drink that looks like liquor but is alcohol free. Stop going to parties; instead do one-on-one activities with friends.

Ready now to implement this prescription?

Return to your checklist of self-injurious habits. Ask yourself the six questions for each that you noted. Writing down your answers will help to consolidate your learning.

Excessive Habit 1:

- What's pleasurable about it?

———————————————————————————

- From what problem am I escaping?

———————————————————————————

- What cues have been triggers?

———————————————————————————

- How can I remove them?

———————————————————————————

- Looking at the habit in the best possible light, what does it aim to accomplish?

———————————————————————————

- What alternative would accomplish that goal without the costs?

———————————————————————————

Excessive Habit 2:

- What's pleasurable about it?

———————————————————————————

- From what problem am I escaping?

———————————————————————————

- What cues have been triggers?

_____

- How can I remove them?

_____

- Looking at the habit in the best possible light, what does it aim to accomplish?

_____

- What alternative would accomplish that goal without the costs?

_____

℞ 5.5: LEARN FROM THUMB-SUCKING, THE EARLIEST ADDICTION.

When the last of my four children was still sucking his thumb in his preschool years, I asked our family dentist what to do. He advised me, "Trying to end thumb-sucking will do more harm than good." Our dentist had seen parents who fought with their child over the habit or who undermined the child's self-image by calling excessive attention to the sucking habit.

In response to similar advice, I had allowed my other children's thumb-sucking to continue for too many years, watching with chagrin as their mouths became molded around the shape of their thumb. This time I realized that my dentist's advice was mistaken. In response, I wrote _David Decides about Thumb-Sucking_, a story for children with an information section for parents.

From researching thumb-sucking habits for _David Decides_, I learned much about addictive habits that applies to adult addictions as well.

Addictions often start out as positive activities

Thumb-sucking enables a fetus, infant, or young child to self-soothe. Sucking eases a baby to sleep and calms a baby when it feels upset. As a result, newborns who suck on a thumb or pacifier spend less time crying. When they do cry, rhythmic sucking calms them, reregulating their breathing, heartbeat, and digestion, much like meditation does for adults. In a study of premature newborns' health, preemies who sucked a thumb, fingers, or a pacifier gained the initial weight that underweight infants need for survival more quickly than those who did not suck on something.[68]

Thumb-sucking toddlers benefit from the habit as well. If they feel stressed, they can self-soothe with a thumb instead of needing to find a parent for consolation. Compared with non-sucking peers, thumb-suckers can play longer on their own before returning to their caretaker to refresh the attachment connection.[69]

By the time children have reached age three or older however, the benefits of sucking habits no longer outweigh the detrimental impacts. Sucking habits can mold the shape of the roof of the mouth around a vigorously and frequently sucked thumb or finger. They can narrow the roof of the mouth, make front teeth protrude, and cause a gap between the front teeth. All of these impacts create facial features that look less attractive. Yet a child's appearance matters. Cute children attract more affection and positive attention from other children and from grown-ups as well. In fact, facial attractiveness fosters success throughout the lifespan.

Ending a habit starts with a decision

Desire to end an addiction usually begins with receiving new information about the habit's downsides. Initially, structure this conversation, which alcoholism counselors would call an intervention, around open-ended *How, What,* and *When* questions. Then add information about the habit's downsides.

- *What* are your thoughts about sucking your thumb?
- *When* do you put your thumb in your mouth?
- *What* does it do that you like?
- *What* do you dislike about it?
- *How* would you feel about ending the habit?
- *What* is your decision about whether or not to keep doing it?
- *What* would you need to do to end the habit?

Ending thumb-sucking habits often proves challenging. Because thumbs travel a well-worn path to the mouth on automatic pilot, ardent thumb-suckers typically have no conscious awareness of when or if their thumb is in their mouth. Sound like you when you put habitual sweets or drinks into your mouth?

Mobilize both fear and desire

While decisions to end addictive and other problematic habits generally include both fear-based elements and hopes of positive gains, the fears have the most influence.

> In the *David Decides* story, David looks in the mirror and has a heart-to-heart talk with himself. "My thumb in my mouth feels good, but I look silly. My thumb in my mouth makes me look like a baby. I want my teeth to stay just the way they are right now."

Expect habit change to take time

Ceasing entrenched habits is hard. We are all gradual learners. Conventional wisdom in behavior theory suggests that changing a habit takes at least three weeks. Addictive behaviors generally take at least that long to shed. For months and even years after, the behavior may keep trying to poke its nose back into your tent.

Track progress

A visual chart for tracking progress during this reprogramming period helps to keep motivation up long enough to make it all the way to the finish line.

> Michael, David's kindly older brother, explains to David, "Mom and I made a chart to keep count of the nights. On the chart we wrote how many nights I had to sleep without my thumb to earn my prize. Each night that I made it No Thumbs, we put a star on the chart."

Remove habit cues

Security blankets and stuffed animals that children hold when they are sucking in bed at night will trigger thumb-sucking impulses if the children carry them during the day. Limit the blanket or stuffie's travels to the bedroom if nighttime sucking will still be allowed.

For thumb-sucking to go away altogether, the blanket may need to disappear totally as well. It's a cue for sucking. Encourage your child to help you to design a goodbye ceremony. That way your child is less likely to feel that the blanket has been taken away from him or her.

My Thumb-Free Nights
Download this worksheet at *prescriptionswithoutpills.com*.
Add a star ☆ to the chart after each succesful night.

WEEK	SUN	MON	TUE	WED	THU	FRI	SAT
1st							
2nd							
3rd							
4th							
5th							

☆ The stars mean I am learning
WHAT A DEAL I HAVE MADE!
If I can sleep _____ nights within the next _____ months
without sucking my thumb, I will earn _____!

Removing cues against the child's will can trigger depression, which would make ending the sucking habit more difficult.

Where possible, block the habit

Block options that enable the habit to occur. Cutting off the thumb is clearly a non-starter strategy, but in the *David Decides* story, David's older brother Michael suggests a remedy for bedtime sucking that worked for him.

"I kept lying there without going to sleep. I felt like something was missing. I really wanted to let my thumb back in my mouth. I locked my hands between my knees. Some nights I had them under my pillow. Finally sleep would come. But during the night when I was sleeping, my thumb kept going into my mouth again."

Michael continued, "One night at bedtime I cried. I told Dad that stopping sucking was just too hard. I wanted to give up. That's when we came up with our best idea. We put socks on my hands. We taped the socks around my wrists so I wouldn't pull them off while I was sleeping. The socks made my hands sweaty, but they did keep my thumbs out of my mouth. And in the morning if I still had the socks on my hands, I knew I had made it the whole night No Thumbs."

Remember that addictions are contagious

Minimize exposure to others who still indulge in the habit to whatever extent is possible.

> After our first child turned out to be a confirmed thumb-sucker, my husband and I resolved with the second to use a pacifier, even though that meant many nights of wakeup calls to find the pacifier when it had fallen out. A pacifier, we assumed, was under parental control. When we felt that the time had come to end the habit, we could remove it.
>
> Which we did. Except that by then, our pacifier-sucking four-year-old had two younger siblings, both confirmed thumb-suckers. She took a look at them, tested the taste of her own thumb, and with consummate ease, proceeded to fill the space left empty by the no-longer-available pacifier with her newly discovered thumb.

Expect to need patience, persistence, and repeated problem-solving

To end even an addiction as simple as thumb-sucking, expect to encounter many slip-ups before the habit ceases. Without that expectation, each setback can feel hopeless. With the expectation that setbacks will recur, setbacks may still feel demoralizing. Hopefully, though, they will be less likely to tempt you to give up altogether on accomplishing your goal.

Turn to supportive allies for addiction-ending ideas

When success seems to be slipping away in *David Decides*, David talks with his big sister, his older brother, and later, with his parents. David's support team helps him figure out creative ways to overcome each barrier to success.

The same goes for adults attempting to end gambling, compulsive affairs, alcohol, or any addiction. Yet, as AA and Al-Anon often point out, supportive others need to walk a fine line. The person with the addictive habit must want to make the changes for him- or herself. If loved ones want the changes more than the person with the problem does, they risk over-involvement. Loved ones belong on the sidelines, where they can cheer for progress and coach by offering occasional suggestions. They do not belong on the playing field.

Ultimately, like David, only you can conquer your detrimental habits.

R̽ 5.6: BUILD NEW HABITS INSTEAD OF RELYING ON WILLPOWER TO RESIST THE OLD.

Habits that are good for you keep you on positive pathways with no willpower needed. The following reminders can help you to focus on building good habits instead of having to rely on willpower to refrain from bad ones. Which feel like they might work for you?

❏ Remove yourself from a situation you can't handle

A basic rule for keeping children well behaved is to *remove them from a situation they can't handle*. Even better, teach children to remove themselves from a situation they can't handle.

> Izzy used to have a problem with punching playmates who did not do what he wanted. He was increasingly frustrated with the friend his mother had invited to play with him for the afternoon.
>
> Twice, Izzy had given the boy blocks to play with. Twice, his friend came over and broke up the tower he had been building. The third time that the friend started breaking up his track, Izzy stood up in a fury and stepped toward the boy to punch him.
>
> Suddenly Izzy changed direction. He walked to the kitchen to find his mother. Izzy was four years old.

Exits protect adults similarly from having to use willpower to behave the way they would like. To end addictive habits, remove yourself from situations you can't handle. Remove yourself from the kitchen, for instance, when you have an impulse to reach out and grab cookies. When you feel anger welling up, walk to the sink to drink a glass of water or walk into the living room to turn on the television.

❏ Focus on *do's*, not *don'ts*, to build alternative habits

Your mind is designed to pay only minimal attention to the word *not*. It listens instead for images. Telling yourself, "Eating a cookie is *not* good for me, so I am *not* going to do it," programs your mind with images of eating a cookie. Each subsequent "Do not eat cookies" reinforces the cookie-eating image.

A better way to program yourself for ending an old habit and building a new one is to think positively. Think about what you *do* want to do. To build new eating habits, for instance, focus on what you *will* eat: fruit, vegetables, fish, chicken, cheese, and nuts.

> Beverly for many years had indulged in eating carbohydrates and sweets. She paid a high price in a plump body that had become too heavy for her to be able to enjoy the sports activities that she used to love.
>
> To lose weight, Beverly listed the foods she could eat. Instead of listing the pasta, pastries, and ice cream that she no longer would be able to enjoy, she wrote down a list of can-eats. She then cleared her house of foods not on her list and stocked her refrigerator with those that were. Within several months, twenty pounds had disappeared.

For every addictive habit, think about a counter-habit. Clarify what you *can* do. Instead of watching yet another sports event on TV, take the dog for a walk. Instead of sipping an alcoholic drink at night, drink juice or brush your teeth.

❏ In tempting situations, use the mantra *I think I'll wait this one out*

I think I'll wait this one out offers a one-size-fits-all mantra you can say to yourself whenever you have an urge to indulge in a habit you are trying to end. Skip the willpower. Instead, pause, take a breath, and say to yourself *I think I'll wait this one out*.

This technique uses constructive procrastination: "Maybe I'll do it later." Procrastination often feels easier than telling yourself, "Never again."

When the mantra *I think I'll wait this one out* becomes automatic, it offers surprisingly reliable protection through the several weeks necessary to extinguish old habits. Similar to mindfulness, this sentence works because of the wave nature of most impulses. Impulses rise and then fall. Got an itch? If you "wait this one out," you'll see that in a surprisingly short time the impulse to scratch the itch will have disappeared.

Have an urge to smoke a cigarette? *I think I'll wait this one out.* Want a shot of whiskey? *I think I'll wait this one out.*

❏ Draw bright lines

Paradoxically, the opposite technique also works. Instead of easing away from a problematic habit little by little with constructive procrastination, make a clear *never again* decision. "I don't eat cookies" draws a clear bright line. Do's and don'ts become clearly separated on either side of the line.

"I don't eat worms" is easy for most people. Putting cookies into a similarly clear-cut "I just don't do it" category can ease the need for willpower. Bright-line rules about what you do and what you don't do switch your decision-making to automatic pilot, bypassing the need for willpower. "I just don't eat worms." Or, as a Pakistani friend once said to me in his crisp British accent, "It's just not done."

R_X 5.7: BECOME SAVVY ABOUT THE ADDICTIVE NATURE OF ELECTRONIC DEVICES.

As a family therapist, I see much fighting between parents and children about frequency of use of electronic games, iPads, and the like. Alas, electronic equipment causes problems in adults' relationships as well. Mobile phones may be the most treacherous. They are conveniently small so that you can take them with you wherever you go, which is the good news and the bad. If you take your phone or other small electronic device into a bedroom you share with a loved one, your intimate relationship is likely to suffer from continual interruptions. Each time you switch from talking with your partner to glancing at your device, you will temporarily sever the emotional connection between you. Instead of building up feelings of intimate connection, you will keep going back to the starting line.

Phone calls, text messages, mobile device apps, and email deliver the time you would otherwise be devoting to a person in the room with you instead to someone or something in cyberspace. In this regard, electronic connections become like affairs. They sap attention from your loved ones at home, investing it instead afar.

Do you want to allow your devices to interrupt your home relationships now that you understand how detrimental they are?____If so, your resistance to change could signal that electronic connecting has become an addictive habit.

> Colin, a high school freshman, used to enjoy dinners and evenings with his family. His parents and siblings used to sit together around the kitchen table, lingering over dinner. After cleaning the kitchen, they would transition into their cozy living room, laughing and sharing stories of their day before heading to their rooms to do homework.
>
> Recently, however, Colin had begun texting to his friends, turning away from the family to connect via text with his girlfriend, his out-of-town athlete friends, or his best buddy at school. He was with his family in body, but no longer connecting with them in spirit.
>
> Colin's siblings and parents each in their own way felt saddened by Colin's being there yet not there. They asked Colin to leave his phone in his pocket during family times. Colin agreed but seemed unable to resist the temptation to respond to incoming messages. He had become addicted to his electronic connections.

Habit-forming electronic products, alas, can be good for business. The more addicted that users become to a website, phone app, or fun computer game, the more they will want to use it, tell their friends about it, and buy more of it. The book *Hooked* by Nir Eyal explains to business owners and executives how to build habit-forming factors into their products. Once a business has convinced you to buy or try its product, business will grow to the extent that you become a repeat user. [70]

What's good for business, however, may be bad for you, diminishing your well-being and eroding your close relationships. Rather than addicting yourself to excessive use of electronic devices, consider expanding your family interactions, your friendship circle, your participation in athletics and in creative activities like art and music. What for you would be the ingredients of a full and meaningful life? _____

Rx 5.8: PAY ATTENTION TO MARIJUANA USE.

I live in Colorado, one of the first two states to legalize marijuana, first for medicinal use and now also recreationally. My conclusion is that our society in general and teenagers in particular who are using this drug need to pay far more attention to when, how, and how much marijuana they want in their lives. While marijuana may not be physiologically addictive like cocaine and crack, marijuana habits can turn out to be a seriously consequential mistake.

Recreational marijuana first became available to middle class Americans, starting with college students, in the late 1960s. Many college students at that time experimented with the odd and often-gratifying mental states marijuana and other drugs induced. Compared with the hallucinogenic drugs like LSD that were emerging on the college scene at that time, smoking marijuana seemed safe.

No research existed then on the long-term impacts of marijuana use, so smoking it looked like a relatively risk-free experiment. Most students and young adults treated marijuana smoking "trips" like travel: "Interesting place to visit but I wouldn't want to live there." A small proportion, however, continued to smoke after their first exploratory attempts.

Two cases of excessive marijuana use in my clinical practice have sharpened my awareness of the risks from excessive marijuana use. In both of these cases, the addicted man had begun using marijuana in high school. This pattern accords with research suggesting that the younger the age of first marijuana use, the more likely that a user will end up using it addictively.[71] In addition, the younger the age of users, the more harm marijuana does to cognitive functioning.[72] Marijuana use by pre-adolescents and teenagers can cause serious and lifelong cognitive deficits.

> Joe was well educated, having completed college at a well-reputed university. He obtained a good job after college and at first worked successfully at the company. Then over subsequent years his work competence became increasingly questionable. When he needed to launch a project, and even worse when he needed to find new employment, he couldn't get himself going. Joe's daily marijuana use had burned out his starter engine.

Joe's inability to start larger projects like seeking employment and even small projects like initiating a conversation or loading the dishwasher stemmed from decreases in his ability to initiate action. This brain deficit, which also occurs with the dementia that sometimes emerges with aging, was one of the first cognitive deficits caused by long-term marijuana use to be identified by researchers.

A similar pattern of gradual degeneration of a cognitive ability proved to be at the core of the marriage difficulties of a couple with whom I worked some years later.

Corky and William looked like a perfect couple. Corky's stunningly attractive appearance and air of competence matched well with William's appealing smile and verbal cleverness.

William had succeeded as CEO of a startup, setting up the family to be financially comfortable for life. Yet at home, William's wife Corky complained that she seldom felt connected with her husband. He didn't share information with her about his work world. He didn't initiate conversations. The relatively rare times when William did engage in talking with her, Corky had a feeling that no one was home in the body across from her. "Our gears don't seem to mesh," she said to herself.

Eventually the truth came out. For the past several years William had returned to his high school years' marijuana-smoking habits. He had been smoking or ingesting marijuana as soon as he returned home from work. Corky returned from her job later, and she went to bed earlier in the evenings, so William fairly easily kept his habit hidden.

Recently a vicious cycle had intensified William's smoking. His wife, feeling chronically dissatisfied without understanding why, increasingly expressed her irritation at his remoteness. William then felt all the more reluctant to interact with her without first getting stoned.

The more William's mental state was skewed by marijuana, the more his wife felt frustrated and disconnected from him, further spinning the circle of mutual marriage distress. By the time that Corky discovered William's marijuana usage, she already had been questioning whether to stay in the marriage. When the extent of his habit became clear, she immediately filed for divorce.

With the help of an addictions therapist William totally stopped all of his marijuana use, but for his marriage the change came too late.

What can we do?

For starters, our society needs significantly more research and also public education about the dangers of marijuana. The detrimental consequences of frequent marijuana use, for younger people and for adults as well, can be irreversible.

In the meantime, if you suspect that a loved one is using marijuana, or if you have been using it habitually, open discussion about repercussions of the habit could be vital.

R$_X$ 5.9: PROTECT YOUR MARRIAGE BY REGARDING AFFAIRS AS ADDICTIONS.

Why are affairs being addressed in a chapter on addictions? Affairs are an addictive phenomenon. Appreciation of this addictive potential is an essential first step in affair prevention, just as awareness of the potency of cocaine's addictive potential helps most people to use good judgment in keeping their distance from the drug.

Along with Anger and Addictions, Affairs are one of what I refer to as the Three A's, the trio of actions that most frequently cause divorce. A sexless marriage and "growing apart" because of insufficient sharing of time and activities together score as close runner-ups. While affairs do not always result in a family break-up, they almost always do create a major marital crisis.

With such serious consequences, why do affairs occur? The answer lies in large part in naiveté about the addictive nature of sexual attraction. Closeness from talking together about personal issues, working together in private places, or physical touching with a new potential partner unleashes a rush of highly addictive "happy chemicals."[73] These potent chemicals of sexual desire can convince you against your better judgment to compulsively pursue an illicit relationship. Awareness of the affair's potential to harm you, your loved ones, and even your affair partner is likely to have little impact once a sexual attraction has become a Stage III addiction.

If you are married or in a committed relationship, you may believe that neither you nor your partner would ever become sexually involved with anyone other than your mate. Not so quick. Affairs, emotional and/or sexual, can tempt anyone given the right combination of naiveté and circumstances.

Like other addictions, affairs increase in likelihood to the extent that there is vulnerability from personal distress such as from marriage problems. At the same time, because of the addictive nature of sexual chemistry with a potential new partner, spouses who enjoy even the best of marriages can be at risk for an extramarital involvement.

What do couples need to know, and preferably to discuss together, to decrease the odds that one partner will stray and betray, addicted to the chemistry of sexual excitement?

Sexual arousal feels good; good feelings tempt you to seek more

Sexual chemistry produces potently pleasurable feelings. Once sexual feelings have been turned on, further time together even without physical contact heightens the intensity of sexual craving. There's probably no news here.

The difficulty lies in the reality that when sexual cravings become strong, they tend to override good judgment. Animal brains, including yours, are programmed to fulfill and repeat any action that brings forth potent messages of *pleasure ahead*. Perhaps sexual connecting is programmed to be super-pleasurable so that living things will sustain their species with procreation.

You also are biologically designed for a potential new partner to arouse more potent sexual intensity than a familiar partner. That's what makes affairs so initially seductive and eventually addictive.

Sexuality researchers have tested the hypothesis that new sexual partners create higher intensity initial attraction than familiar. Here's the experiment. Begin by putting a male and female gerbil together in a cage. What do Mr. and Mrs. Gerbil do? They copulate. Many times. Then over time, familiarity causes the rate of copulation to decrease. Mr. and Mrs. Gerbil then gradually establish a comfortable plateau, that is, a copulation rate at which they can live together happily ever after. While this plateau may lower gradually with age, Mr. and Mrs. Gerbil both appear to be contented with their sexual frequency.

Now put perfectly contented Mr. and Mrs. Gerbil into two separate cages. Add a new Mrs. for him and a new Mr. for her. Boom. The copulation rate zooms up for both of the new couples, rising immediately to the initial copulation rate of the original couple. Then, again, over time the arousal intensity caused by newness gradually declines. The high copulation rate slows and then will plateau.

Separate these gerbil couples and give each individual gerbil yet another new partner. The same pattern repeats. A new partner evokes heightened sexual interest. As the partner becomes familiar, desire to initiate sexual contact gradually wanes. With less intensity of initial arousal, copulation rates slow down.

A new partner does not necessarily increase sexual satisfaction

For humans as well as gerbils, while familiarity may not breed contempt, it does lower a couple's pre-copulation arousal and, therefore, their copulation rates. That decrease generally happens over the years in even the strongest marriages.

Interestingly, while familiarity may bring less sexual excitement prior to physical contact, sexual *satisfaction* does not necessarily decrease with familiarity. To the contrary, sexual satisfaction in the second, third, and fourth phases of sexual connecting for many couples actually increases.

- **Phase I: Initial arousal,** creating desire to initiate sexual activity. Newness increases initial arousal, increasing copulation rates.
- **Phase II: Mutual stimulation,** enhancing arousal. This phase generally becomes more gratifying for sexual partners over time as they learn each other's sexual preferences.
- **Phase III: Orgasm.** Orgasms tend to be produced more consistently with a familiar partner.
- **Phase IV: Post-coital enjoyment.** Post-orgasm positive feelings are especially strong for couples who enjoy friendship in addition to their shared sexual activity. Familiarity enhances affection and attachment.

Pair-bonding matters

Some humans do act like gerbils, happily enjoying new sexual partners whenever possible to enhance the intensity of their initial chemical responses. Most, however, also want to enjoy a phenomenon called pair-bonding. They want a lifelong bond with one mate. If pair-bonding is important to you, beware of naiveté. Awareness of the addictive power of the sexual chemistry of new partners can help you to protect your monogamous relationship from inadvertent violation.

Risk assessment

The five indicators below can warn you that you are heading down a sexual slippery slope. Remember that the first step down a slippery slope often appears neither slippery nor sloped. One more step, though, and . . .

Repeated texts, phone calls, or other contacts

How fun! Or, more realistically, how risky.

Psychologist Shirley Glass identified that the three highest-risk categories for inappropriate sexual connections are old flames, business associates, and chance encounters when traveling alone. The risks increase with the amount of time that you spend in the presence of, or thinking about, these individuals.

> Lane's wife had left him because he had an affair. He later explained to me, "When a woman I'd dated years ago contacted me via LinkedIn, there was a sense of titillation. She then continued to reach out to me."
>
> Be realistic. If you don't want to catch fire, stay far from sparks of titillation. While these sparks initially may feel fun and flattering, they can prove too flammable to be worth the mini-delights of minor sexual excitement.

A fragile or turbulent relationship at home

If your home relationship feels frustrating, painful, or distant, connecting with an alternative loving person can feel all the more appealing. The risks of an infidelity rise further if the new person seems to be kind, provides good company, and appreciates you.

Instead of succumbing to an alternative love source, open a conversation at home. Explore what each of you might do differently to regain the mutual affection you once had. If talking together does not succeed, get help. Find a marriage education course online or in your community. Seek out a couples therapist.

Hiding that you are already taken

When you are communicating with an attractive new someone, if you find yourself refraining from telling them that you already have a committed partner or spouse, you are steadily moving deeper into the danger zone.

As sexual feelings toward the new person grow, the cravings can cause your awareness that you have a loved one at home to fade. Sexual arousal with a familiar versus new partner, as per the gerbils, works this way.

Remember too that higher-intensity feelings of sexual attraction do not necessarily indicate a better life partner. They may only reflect newness.

Enjoying and eventually craving flirtatious talking or texting

Thinking about the new person when the two of you are not together, becoming increasingly flirtatious on the phone or in text messages, craving the next contact: these signs indicate deep trouble.

Sexual cravings indicate third-stage addiction. Review the stages of addiction in Rx 5.2. Now the more you indulge in the habit, the more likely that you will become ever more addicted, abandoning your values and priorities along the way.

Lies

Tempted to claim that you are on a work trip when you are indulging in alone time with a work associate? If so, you are by now fully addicted. You are in serious trouble.

Better come clean immediately. Be honest with yourself, with your affair partner, and potentially also with your loved one. The latter is a judgment call. Some loved ones cannot recuperate from hearing that you have betrayed them sexually. Other partners can react to the disclosure as a first step toward re-establishment of trust. In the latter case, transparency may be best.

Once even minor details of an affair have been exposed, denial and dishonesty radically increase the damage. Full disclosure, full acknowledgment of all the steps in your addictive process, full understanding of how and why you would prevent a subsequent addiction, and a commitment to full transparency in the future accelerate recovery.

To prevent sexual infidelities, discuss guidelines together

Because sexually titillating interactions that feel fun and harmless at the outset can lead to falling off the infidelity cliff, decide together with your spouse how, from this point forward, you both will stay far from the cliff's edge. Establish a proactive plan of action.

The following monogamy protection ground rules all follow the maxim of "better safe than sorry." Which would you want to include in your proactive plan?

❑ **Reserve intimate conversations for your intimate relationship.**
Conversations about personal thoughts and feelings evoke emotional closeness which in turn can evoke impulses toward sexual closeness. Refrain from personal discussions with anyone other than your intimate partner who could turn out to become sexually attractive to you. If you are having problems, personally or in the marriage, that you are unable to discuss with your loved one and are not solving on your own with this or other books, talk with a professional counselor.

Danger signs: "He needed someone to talk with." "I was the only shoulder she had to cry on." "She was so understanding."

❑ **Stay public.**
Spend no time alone in private places with someone who could potentially, in terms of gender, age and appearance, become sexually attractive to you.

Out of bounds: "This restaurant is so crowded—but look, there's a private room in the back that will be quieter." Or, "Let's go to my apartment where it's not noisy so we can talk."

❑ **Observe the open-door rule.**
If you do need to meet alone with a person of the opposite sex in a private place, keep the door open so that at any time someone might walk in. The one exception to this rule may be a consultation with a doctor, lawyer, therapist, or similar professional. In that case, discuss only the topic on which you are seeking professional advice.

❑ **Be especially cautious if there has been any drinking.**
Alcohol potentiates sexual excitement. Alcohol is also "disinhibiting," that is, it decreases the effectiveness of the command and control functions in your brain.

"I wouldn't normally do this, but I'm having such a good time."

❑ **Exit early from potentially risky situations.**
Like a migraine headache, though far more pleasant, sexual arousal is easier to stop the earlier you do something to end it.

"He contacted me to see if I was going to the reunion. I wanted to know what happened to him over the years, so we started talking via Skype."

❏ **Maintain transparency.**

Agree with your spouse that if either of you should begin to experience sexual feelings for someone other than each other, and especially if you are going to have ongoing contact with that person, you will discuss together how to handle the situation. Agree also that in such a case you will respond appreciatively to your partner's revelation.

> "I have something on my mind that I'd like to talk with you about. You remember my high school girlfriend? She's joined the gym where we work out. I see her there several times a week. I'm uncomfortable with how I feel when I see her."
>
> "Thank you for being open with me. I thought I spotted her there the other day. Seeing her made me nervous. I'm so relieved that you brought it up. I would love to figure out a plan of action that we can both feel okay with."
>
> "How would you feel about us switching our membership to the new gym on the other side of town? The programs for children are better there too."

In summary

Naiveté is the single strongest predictor of addictions in general and particularly of infidelities. Become savvy. Agree together on guidelines for keeping your monogamy safe and your love connection strong.

R_X 5.10: CEASE THE FOUR HABITS THAT FEED ENABLING AND CODEPENDENCY.

A husband covers for his wife's late afternoon drinking binges by making up excuses to friends about why he and his wife can't join them for dinner. By hiding the truth, the husband *enables* his wife to continue her addictive habit. A wife who feels increasingly frustrated by her husband's constant watching of TV sports yet pretends that she is fine with it likewise is engaging in enabling behavior. A parent enables bad behavior if he caves in to the desires of a child who shouts to get his way. Waiting to discuss the child's request until the child is talking in normal voice tones, by contrast, would clarify that shouting is out of bounds.

Addiction treatment professionals use the term *codependent* for people who enable others' problematic behaviors. Enablers make it easy for people with alcohol dependency to continue their habit, whence the term *codependent*. This prescription addresses four habits of mind that sustain enabling and codependency. Do any of these habits sound like something you might do?

> Brenda, a personal assistant, fostered her boss Peter's self-defeating, workaholic tendencies by working late several evenings a week to help him catch up. Peter accepted work from too many clients. Brenda's support enabled Peter to keep plunging forward on overload, even though his excessive work hours were ruining his marriage and jeopardizing his health.

What sustains codependency and enabling behaviors?

I have coined terms to clarify four aspects of codependency, that is, of a tendency toward harmful helpfulness: *excessive altruism, appendagitis, wishful thinking*, and *misplaced focus*. If you inadvertently have been enabling self-harming or addictive behaviors of someone in your life, these four phenomena are likely to sound familiar.

Letting go of these mental habits can prove surprisingly difficult. You too may have become addicted, that is, become a codependent, if you compulsively continue to engage in these mistaken habits.

❏ Excessive altruism

Giving feels good. It does good for others. At the same time, excessively helping with too much time, money, or other means can inadvertently encourage others' bad habits.

In healthy ongoing partnerships, altruism is a two-way street. Each partner symmetrically gives and receives. One partner may cook, the other may wash dishes and take out garbage. While the contributions certainly needn't be identical, if they feel subjectively of more or less similar value, goodwill prevails. Excessive altruism, by contrast, involves asymmetrical as well as excessive giving.

> Bonnie gave too much in the form of willingness to work overtime evening hours. As a child in a family of high achievers, Bonnie had grown up

believing that you are not doing enough unless you do over-and-above-the-call-of-duty.

Eventually Bonnie began to question giving up so much of her personal time to support Peter. As she gradually realized that Peter felt entitled to her extra help rather than appreciative, her enthusiasm for working so many evenings waned.

Healthy couples self-correct by discussing their disgruntlements to fix whatever has become askew. In relationships in which no one speaks up when they feel unduly burdened, excessive altruism coupled with excessive taking can continue unchecked, worsening over time. Sometimes, however, one person notices the asymmetry and decides to change.

❏ Appendagitis

Appendagitis is my playful term for ignoring your own life in order to serve as someone else's extra appendage. If you are helping someone else so much that you are losing your own identity, you may have a serious case of appendagitis.

Appendagitis develops if you ignore your own preferences, life goals, and voice, devoting most or all of your energies instead to fostering those of another person's. If the other is a true dependent like a young child, sickly spouse, or aging elder, dedicated helping may be appropriate. If you devote long hours to helping a political candidate whose election is important to you, facilitating your mutual goal can feel invigorating. Helping only becomes appendagitis when giving up on living your life enables another to continue a self-defeating habit. Appendagitis then hurts both of you.

Bonnie had been ignoring her desire to use her evenings to meet other singles her age in order to help Peter continue his workaholic habits. Eventually she began to resent giving up on living her own life. How would she eventually meet a mate if she spent so many after-work hours helping Peter to work excessively?

❏ Wishful thinking

Wishful thinking refers to a mental habit of believing that others will change when there is no realistic basis for this hope. A wife may keep thinking that her husband will stop flirting with other women since each time she gets mad at him he says how sorry he is and that he will change.

> Bonnie wished that her boss would leave the office at five o'clock like other managers and employees in their company. Occasionally Peter would walk out of the office, briefcase in hand, at the end of the normal workday. Bonnie interpreted these rare departures from Peter's late-working norm as confirmation that someday he would change.

Overly optimistic interpretations of occasional better behavior can confirm and intensify wishful thinking.

❑ Misplaced focus

Misplaced focus refers to riveting your attention on what others are doing, feeling, and thinking instead of heeding your own actions, feelings and thoughts. Misplaced focus yields habits of scanning others' faces for clues about what they think and feel and guessing their reactions. Misplaced focus typically leads also to assuming that you can interpret what others think and feel instead of asking.

> Bonnie used to scan Peter's face for signals that there was something further he might want her to do. Hyperfocused on what Peter wanted, she ignored her own preference which was to have time in the evenings for a social life.

Changing habits seldom comes with a Get Out of Jail Free card

If you decide to let go of enabling habits, the person you have been enabling is unlikely to thank you, initially at least, for withdrawing from your helper role. Your change means the person you have been enabling may have to change as well.

> As Bonnie began to cease her enabling habits, Peter expressed annoyance at her unwillingness to continue to work overtime. Bonnie attempted to discuss her concerns with Peter. The discussion proved unproductive, with Peter responding defensively instead of with understanding.

Bonnie concluded that the time had come for her to move on. She heard that a rival firm was looking for someone with her skills. When that firm offered her the position, she accepted it immediately. By focusing on what she herself wanted, rather than exclusively on how she could help Peter, Bonnie ended her era of codependency.

What causes the four enabler mental habits?

People who are at risk for codependent behaviors tend to engage with partners who have an all-about-me perspective, that is, who tend toward narcissism. Narcissistic individuals want to be adored and doted on. They love being the focus of attention and feel entitled to special treatment. When an all-about-me narcissistic individual connects with an all-about-you enabler, the two dovetail beautifully—until the excessive giver's altruism burns out and resentment sets in.

Family of origin can play a strong role in creating templates for enabler-narcissistic partnerships. Both individuals usually have learned these habits subconsciously from observing their parents' marriage interactions. A child learns to speak French by hearing French spoken at home.

At the same time, enabler habits can develop as a way to keep a marriage or other relationship with someone who is narcissistic intact. Hyperfocus on what a partner wants especially emerges if the partner otherwise might get angry and walk out on the marriage.

Gloria had always been successful in her professional work. In her late 30s, when she and her husband began to have children, she became a stay-at-home mother. Focusing so much on her children began to erode her recollections of what she herself enjoyed doing. The larger stimulant for gradually losing her self, however, was her husband Matthew's anger.

For three years, Gloria tiptoed through the marriage ignoring her own preferences, bowing to whatever Matthew wanted, serving as his appendage, and scanning his face for signs that he might become grouchy toward her. Then one day everything changed. Gloria happened to see a message on Matthew's cell phone that said something about a gambling debt. Matthew's irritability and anger outbursts at home had served as cover-up for a major gambling addiction.

Stop the downward spiral

Excessive altruism, appendagitis, wishful thinking, and misplaced focus all feed each other, creating a downward vicious cycle. What can reverse this cycle so that the spin switches upward toward increasingly positive feelings?

- If you tend toward *excessive altruism*, balance your giving with self-care.
- If you are afflicted with *appendagitis,* turn up the volume on your own thoughts and preferences so you can hear your inner drummer. Also, expect bilateral listening and learn win-win decision-making (coming up ahead in Rx 1.1 and Rx 6.6). Make your concerns and also those of your partner count.
- Trade in *wishful thinking* for a reality-based personal guidance system. Make decisions based on what *is* rather than what you wish were true.
- Reverse *misplaced focus* on the other by using starter sentences with the phrases that focus you on yourself, phrases such as "I feel . . ."; "My concern is . . ."; and "I would like to . . ." (see Rx 6.3).

Naming a phenomenon empowers you to recognize it and to change it. Label your moments of excessive altruism, appendagitis, wishful thinking, and misplaced focus.

Support others' strengths instead of their bad habits. Devote your energies to your own as well as to others' concerns. Listen to your thoughts of feelings so you know what you want. Give your own ship a rudder that you can grab onto and steer, fostering more well-being for both of you.

Chapter 6

Well-Being

S o far this book's prescriptions have aimed to help you change directions if you have been heading down routes to depression, anger, anxiety or addictive habits. Healing is good. Still, prevention is preferable. The prescriptions ahead aim to prevent negative emotional states.

The Hand Map from Chapter 1 again will guide us. The Thumb Route on that map, the Route that leads to the realm of well-being, requires ability to find win-win solutions when dilemmas and conflicts present themselves on your life path. Win-win solution-building requires skills for collaborative communication. The prescriptions in this chapter detail these skills.

Why is communication so important? Communication is information-sharing. Dialogue, that is, communication between two people, is like a game of catch. It involves back and forth sharing of information, tossing and catching, then tossing back and catching that toss. For the game of communication to go well, both participants need skills for cooperatively passing and receiving information.

Communication helps you to get to know others more fully, to share perspectives, and to feel a sense of connection. It enables two or more people to do activities in partnership, as a team. When dilemmas and differences arise, talking and listening collaboratively enables you sustain your connection.

Communication is a flow phenomenon, like water in a river, traffic on highways, or money through an economic system. What flows in communication? Information. When talking and listening are collaborative, information flow is smooth, or as they say in physics, laminar. Smooth information flow sustains well-being.

Increases in the quantity or speed of flow can turn laminar flow to turbulence much as too many cars and driving at fast speeds cause traffic accidents. When emotional arousal increases, especially anger, arguments are more likely to erupt. Navigation in turbulence can be dangerous, as it is for rafters who hit whitewater rapids in a river. Blocks in information flow, like blocked water pipes, also bring trouble. Blocks in information flow occur when information is either held onto instead of tossed or else thrown too aggressively, and on the catching end either mistakenly dropped or explicitly rejected.

Use the prescriptions in this chapter to keep your communication flowing smoothly. That's how to stay on the Thumb Road, the collaborative dialogue, win-win problem-solving, laminar flow route to well-being.

R̽ 6.1: NOTE QUICKLY WHEN COLLABORATIVE DIALOGUE BECOMES ADVERSARIAL.

Talking in a friendly way, that is, with laminar rather than turbulent or blocked information flow, enables you to dialogue with others in a mode of camaraderie and partnership. What are the characteristics of this collaborative way of connecting?

- Information flows smoothly with open sharing of thoughts and feelings.
- The tone is relaxed.
- You speak in ways that offer information without criticism or crossovers (telling people what you think they think).
- You both use *bilateral listening,* that is, two-sided listening in which you listen to your own thoughts and listen equally to others'. Bilateral listening in my view is one of the most reliable indicators of emotional maturity.
- Your stance of mutual positive regard conveys, "I like you, and you like me."

- If a dilemma comes up, you aim for a plan of action responsive to the concerns of everyone involved; you aim for a win-win solution.

The alternative to collaborative dialogue is adversarial dialogue. Adversarial conversations feel stressful. Tension builds as voices become insistent, agitated, argumentative, defensive, or aggressive. The listening mode slips from open to critical or dismissive. Instead of bilateral listening there is minimal uptake of others' points. As the information flow becomes turbulent, blocked, or both, participants turn away from the thumb route, heading instead toward anger, depression, anxiety, or addictive escapes.

Up to this point, the examples have been based on actual cases that I have worked with in my clinical practice. In this chapter I will be illustrating communication skills and skill deficits with Tim and Tina, the fictional couple whom I first briefly introduced in Rx 4.9, and Judy and Justin, another fictional couple. What differences do you notice as you listen to how each couple dialogues?

Collaborative:

Justin:	I'd like to leave the party now. We were supposed to stay another hour, but I'm partied out.
Judy:	Yes, I saw you sitting in a corner with a book so I've been getting concerned that your patience with partying was wearing thin. I'd like to help our host with some of the cleanup though. The kitchen is a mess. How about if we stay another ten minutes and then head for home?
Justin:	That would work for me. Thanks for your flexibility.

Adversarial:

Tim:	I'd like to leave the party now. We were supposed to stay another hour, but I'm partied out.
Tina:	No. That's not fair. You promised you'd come here with me. Besides, I want to help clean up the kitchen before we go. I don't want to go yet.
Tim:	This is the last time I'm going to parties with you when I would rather stay home!

Collaborative dialogue feels as if you and the other person are sitting on the same side of the table, combatting a problem rather than each other. With both of you using bilateral listening, you pool your perspectives to build consensus understandings and plans of action.

Adversarial dialogue pits you against the person you are talking with. You compete over whose voice will count, who is right, whose preferences will dominate. Who gets their way is determined by who seems to have more power— or who more readily yields. Thinking becomes either-or. Either I am right or you are. Outcomes are winner-loser, at best, or lose-lose.

Sustaining collaboration is easy if what you are discussing is of minimal import and also if you agree. Chatting to share the events of the day typically flows smoothly. The challenge increases when participants feel substantial concerns about an issue and all the more so if their viewpoints differ.

> Gregory agreed to ride-share with another traveler who also had been waiting in front of their hotel for a taxi to the airport. The two struck up an engaging conversation, discussing their various business projects.
>
> Then as the subject shifted into the political arena Gregory felt his ire rise immediately. The other traveler was locked into views that diametrically opposed his own. Continuing to talk suddenly felt too risky.

How aware are you of emotional tone?

How quickly do you recognize when a conversation has flipped from friendly to an oppositional tug of war? _____

Recognition of a change in tone launches an essential first step toward a return to collaboration. Without recognition that you have been straying into an adversarial dialogue mode, you will feel uncomfortable without knowing why or how to fix it. Without recognition, you risk escalation from tension to argument.

> Jon wanted to put aside savings for future big events.
>
> "I don't want to feel constricted all my life," his new wife, Shana, objected.
>
> "It's irresponsible not to save," Jon insisted.
>
> "I hate feeling like I have to watch every penny we spend," added Shana.
>
> Jon began fuming. "I didn't know that I was marrying someone who would be financially irresponsible!"

The argument escalated quickly, with neither spouse understanding why. The escalation was particularly needless because, in fact, both spouses wanted a similar balance of spending and saving.

Why did this argument occur? Neither spouse recognized the brewing adversarial tone.

You can increase your ability to become aware when you are slipping into adversarial-dialogue mode. In the list below, rate from never (0) to rarely (1) to sometimes (2, 3) or often (4, 5) how frequently you become:

❑ insistent   ❑ defensive
❑ irritated   ❑ critical
❑ heated   ❑ withdrawn
❑ argumentative   ❑ reluctant to speak up
❑ dismissive

Any and all ratings higher than one (rarely) suggest that upgrading your collaborative dialogue awareness will benefit you.

Fortunately, as soon as you recognize that a dialogue has turned adversarial, you have options. A combination of tone control and bilateral listening generally will succeed in flipping the conversation back to collaborative mode.

- Pause to press your emotional reset button.
- Reestablish good humor by switching temporarily to a safer topic.
- Ask about the other's concerns and listen to truly understand them.
- Validate what makes sense in his or her concerns.
- After hearing his or hers, add your concerns in a calm and friendly tone.

As you read the list above, which of these five steps do you regularly take in uncomfortable situations?

_____

Which could you add more often?

_____

When and why do collaborative skills matter?

Close your eyes. Allow an image to come up on your visual screen of an enjoyable conversation with someone you like. Now allow a second scene to come up, this time of an adversarial interaction. What was the same, and what was different, in these two conversations?

Were you discussing a sensitive topic? _____
Did you have differences of opinion? _____
How important was the topic to you? _____
How did you feel toward the person you were speaking with?

Were either of you tired, hungry, over-loaded, or getting ill? _____
What was your relationship to the other person, e.g., parent, employee, friend?

With regard to the last question, relative status can play a surprisingly strong role in what emotional tone you use. Are you more cooperative with your boss or with your children? _____ Odds are that you interact more cooperatively—that is, you are nicer—when you perceive yourself as lower or equal in power or status.

It's unlikely that you speak aggressively or listen dismissively to your boss. More people are at risk for shedding their niceness when they interact with lower-power people like children or employees. This point was mentioned with regard to narcissists in Rx 3.10. Alas, it applies to some extent to many people.

Pause for a moment here to assess the following questions on a scale from 0 (not at all) to 10 (totally). How likely would you be to speak in an irritated voice to your children?_____ To a salesperson? _____To your spouse or other loved one?_____ To friends?_____ To higher-ups at work?_____ To a policeman?_____ What have you discovered?_____

Ideally, you would stay good-natured in all of these interactions. If you do speak irritably to others even occasionally, reviewing the prescriptions for anger might be a good idea. Adversarial interactions sour relationships with remarkable rapidity.

A neighborhood book group had enjoyed meeting together for close to ten years. The members then faced a decision point. One member insisted they should close the group to new members. Others wanted to welcome in several women who had recently moved into the neighborhood.

In the ensuing discussion several group members slipped into an unpleasantly adversarial mode. The outcome: almost half the group stayed away from the next group gathering. One divisive discussion had undermined ten years of group goodwill.

Each communication event—every time you say or hear something—has remarkable potency. Expression of positive emotions like gratitude, appreciation, playfulness, and affection creates a comfortable relationship. Even one unpleasant interchange, by contrast, can cause the whole relationship to feel aversive.

At a recent conference, I chatted during a coffee break with Chad, a handsome young fellow who had just completed an outstanding presentation on music therapy. Chad had mentioned in his presentation that he had two young sons. I lauded Chad on his fun presentation style, adding that his family must love him.

Chad's forehead wrinkled. He looked perplexed. "Don't all dads get irritated with their wife and kids? I'm irritated at home a lot," Chad mused.

How sad. At home Chad had normalized the use of an irritated voice and adversarial dialogue. He would never speak this way to colleagues at work and never to his audiences. Yet, Chad had succumbed to the beliefs that all couples fight and that it is normal for parents to speak in a tone of annoyance to their children.

Rx 6.2: ACTIVATE *WORD PATROL* TO BLOCK WORDS FROM THE *NO-FLY LIST.*

Word Patrol hunts down words and phrases that flip conversations from collaborative to oppositional. Like inadvertent tiny terrorists, they create verbal mayhem. Better to switch to using the words on the *Preferred-Flyer List.*

It is not your job to use *Word Patrol* to challenge others' ways of talking. It is your job to monitor your own. At the same time, understanding the impacts of the *No-Fly List* words can help you realize when and why a conversation is suddenly becoming adversarial.

	Words to Watch | Risky or Safe?	
	No-Fly List	**Preferred-Flyer List**
✈	You	I
✈	We	I
✈	But	And, and at the same time
✈	No, not	Yes...
✈	I would like *you* to...	I would like *to*...
✈	(You) make me feel	I feel
✈	Should	Could, would like to

You

Therapists use the term *I-statements* for statements that begin with the pronoun *I*. Sharing information about your thoughts and feelings enhances connection and intimacy. By contrast, *you* at the beginning of a sentence sounds threatening.

> Justin to Judy: I feel uncomfortable about your leaving on that business trip tomorrow.
>
> Tim to Tina: You feel annoyed at me; I can tell by your frown. You always get irritable before you travel.

How would you react to Justin? _____

And to Tim? _____

Therapists use the term *you-statements* for sentences that start with *you*. These sentences engage in trespassing. In trying to step into another person's head you are likely to step on their toes. By saying what you think someone else thinks, feels, did, or should do, you violate the personal psychological space of the person you are talking with, inviting a defensive response or a counterattack.

I use the term *crossovers* for you-statements. As I explained briefly in Rx 3.8 and in Rx 6.1, crossovers are statements that cross over the boundaries between you and the person you are talking with. When you say what you think the other person thinks, feels, has done, or should do, you are trespassing on that person's territory.

When crossovers cross the boundaries between you and others, they defy a core mantra for healthy dialogue: *You can talk about yourself or ask about the other. No talking about the other.* Each of us owns our own thoughts and feelings. Talking about the other person by saying what you believe that person thinks, feels, or does violates the other person's personal boundaries. Instead, ask.

Judy: How do you feel about my leaving tomorrow?
Justin: What are your thoughts on being away for so long?

You-messages and other crossovers easily invite defensiveness and counterattacks. They are especially likely to flip a conversation from collaborative to adversarial when they imply criticism or tell others what to do.

Tina: You are too controlling. You want me to quit my job so you can
          keep me under your control all the time. You just don't want me
          to have a powerful career. You have to be the only big-shot.

Do you direct critical you-messages to yourself? _____
Tina: You dummy, Tina! Why did you say that?

In the book *Erosion*, psychologist Golan Shahar points out the vicious circle that self-criticism can create. By setting unrealistically high standards for yourself—for instance, that you should be perfect, making no mistakes—and then criticizing yourself when these impossible standards are not met, self-criticism generates distress. The more you become distressed, the more likely you are to make more mistakes and then to respond with more self-criticism.[74]

We

We may be safe when used with actions. *We* went to the movies last night. *We* becomes a problem word when it refers to thoughts or feelings. The problem then is ambiguity. Does *we* mean you, us, or I in the following sentences?

We need to talk. _____

We get grumpy when we get tired. _____

We have to get our homework done—right, Jimmy? _____

When *we* is a *you* in disguise, it goes onto the *No-Fly List* because, even in camouflage, you-statements are crossovers.

But

But provokes antagonism because it dismisses what others have said. Like an eraser, a backspace delete key, or a subtraction sign, *but* removes whatever information came before. No one wants what they have said to be brushed aside, so *but* invites a negative response such as an emotional stiffening or a collapse in the receiver.

Tim:	The sun is shining, and the sky is cloudless. It's a beautiful day.
Tina:	But the weather report says it'll rain this afternoon.

Instead of dismissing what others say with *but*, link with *and* or *and at the same time*. These collaborative dialogue words enable both views to stay on the table.

Judy:	The sun is shining, and the sky is cloudless. It's a beautiful day.
Justin:	I hope so, *and at the same time*, the weather report says it'll rain this afternoon.

No, not, and *n't* (as in *don't like* and *don't want*)

The words *no* and *not*, even when hidden in contraction form—is*n't*, wo*n't*, have*n't*, etc.—make the tone of a conversation feel negative. The more often you say *no*, *not*, or words with *n't*, the more depressing your impact on yourself and on others.

Amy ran in to show her mother, Tina, a snail she just found.

"*Don't* keep it in the house!" Tina replied. "I *don't* like snails. And be sure you *don't* leave dirt on the carpet."

Feeling her enthusiasm dampened, Amy turned to her brother Arthur.

"*No*, that's *not* a snail," Arthur replied. "It's a periwinkle." Another downer. Amy showed her sister Angela.

"Wow, Amy. That's cool! It's the first snail I've seen this spring! Mom likes us to keep pets outside. I'll help you go out and build a house for it."

Amy's spirits revived.

Notice the contrast in tone between the *no* responses from Amy's mom and brother as compared with the positive responses from her sister, Angela. Which would you prefer to hear? Dumb question.

Flip the following *no* and *not* sentences.

I don't believe what you said.	I'm having trouble trusting you.
I don't want to continue this conversation.	I would like to _____
	_____
I'm not cold.	_____
I don't see it that way.	_____

Ideally, you will catch yourself and do the negative-to-positive flip before issuing *not* sentences. If you missed, though, you get a second chance. After hearing yourself say a *not*, add the flip, the positive version. The impacts of the negative will evaporate.

Tim said to Tina, "I don't like listening to your long monologues."

Tina replied tartly, "Well, go find another wife then!" With that, Tina stood up abruptly and left the room for the kitchen, clearly hurt and angry.

Poor Tim and Tina. But hold on! Maybe there is hope for them!

A few minutes later Tim sought out Tina in the kitchen to try again. "I would like to try a new dialogue pattern when you and I sit and talk. Our pattern often has been that we take turns giving lengthy monologues. I'd like to see what would happen if instead I were to adopt a three-sentence rule. I can only say three sentences per talk time, and then the same rule would go for you. How would you feel about trying it, like a game, with me?"

"Interesting idea, Tim," Tina agreed. "Sounds good!"

How often do you express *don't wants* and *don't likes*?

_____

If you have a *don't want/don't like* habit, the hardest part of changing is becoming aware when you do it. You might want to ask a friend or family member to flag you each time they hear a *don't want* so you then can practice doing the positivity flip. Meanwhile, here are some more sentences for practicing:

I don't want to wear warm clothes.	I would like to . . .
I don't want to eat later than seven o'clock tonight.	I _____
I don't like to get places late.	I _____
I don't like to eat overripe bananas.	I _____
I don't like beaches; the sand bothers my skin.	I _____
I don't want potatoes.	I _____

In sum, for a quick route to more well-being, instead of using *no, not,* and *don't want to,* train yourself to say what you *do* want: *"I would like to . . ."*

I would like *you* to . . .

Beware of this *would like to* trap. Which would you prefer to hear?

> Tim: I would like *you to* meet me after work.
>
> Justin: I would like *to* meet you after work.

I would like ***you*** *to. . .* is a crossover. It has the same boundary-violation impacts as you-statements. It tells someone else what to do instead of saying what you yourself would like to do. *I would like you to* is worth eliminating from your vocabulary. What is the better alternative? _____

Practice the *I would like to* form by saying aloud, now, to yourself, three sentences, each starting with *I would like to.* Become the captain of your ship, not a captain who barks out orders to others.

Make me feel (you make me feel . . . or he makes me feel . . .)

Do you sometimes attempt to tell others what you feel and then receive a negative reaction? The problem may be that instead of saying what you feel, you inadvertently are issuing an accusation. The phrase *makes me feel* as in *"You make me feel embarrassed"* is a statement of blame, not a feelings statement.

Blame invites defensiveness and counterattacks from the person you are speaking with.

Tim:	You *make me feel* sad.
Tina:	Well, you *make me* mad!
Tim:	Arguments *make me feel* sad too.

Blaming with *you make me feel* also undermines your sense of personal empowerment. As Rx 2.6 explained, the phrase *makes me feel* turns you into a powerless victim of forces outside yourself. *"I feel,"* by contrast, enhances your sense of personal strength by acknowledging what you feel and at the same time keeping you the owner of your feelings.

| Justin: | I feel sad. |
| Judy: | I'm so sorry. And yet I feel hopeful at the same time. |

Makes me feel is based on a misunderstanding of how emotions work. *Makes me feel* suggests the erroneous idea that your emotional reaction is the only possible one in that situation. In fact, line up four people, give them each the same trigger action or comment, such as, "You idiot! Don't you know that . . .?" Each of the four is likely to react in his or her unique way.

One may laugh. One may take the comment personally and feel hurt. One may react with compassion for the person who spoke so inappropriately. The fourth may deduce that the speaker is too judgmental to be someone desirable as a close friend. What would your reaction be? It could be a fifth and totally different response.

Should

Why is a nice values word like *should* on the *No-Fly List*? Certainly you *should* take good care of your children, and you *should* pay your bills on time. Yet a strange thing happens when you use the word *should*. *Should* undermines you, setting you up to feel dispirited and disempowered. And *should* directed toward others is distinctly off-putting.

Tina: I should call you more often when I'm traveling.

Tim: Yes, you should call me more often.

Muscle testing, also known as muscle kinesiology, is a technique that can access subconscious awareness to assess if a person is in a state of well-being or stress. See Rx 2.10 and Rx 3.2 for more explanations of this helpful procedure. In any case, normally, you would easily be able to hold your arm out straight to your side, parallel to the floor. If I were to push it slightly, just above your wrist, your arm would stay extended. If your emotional state is stressed, however, the slightest pressure that I exert would cause your arm to flop down. A video on prescriptionswithoutpills.com illustrates this phenomenon.

Enter the word *should*. In a muscle-testing workshop, I asked a participant to repeat sentences after me. After each sentence, my colleague Dale Petterson tested her arm. What do you think happened when Dale pushed lightly on her arm after each phrase?

1. "I *would like to* visit my grandmother."
2. "I *could* visit my grandmother."
3. "I *should* visit my grandmother."
4. "I *have to* visit my grandmother."

The workshop participant's muscles stayed rock strong with the first two sentences. With the third, the word *should* made her muscles go limp. Her arm dropped with Dale's slightest touch.

What do you think was the impact of the fourth version of this sentence, the version with *have to*? _____ If you guessed that *have to* would work the same as *should*, rendering the muscles powerless, you guessed right.

What prescription follows from this observation about the impacts of the word *should* and its twin, *have to*? Here it is: Change the letters *sh* to a *c*. "I *should*" then would become "I *could*." Alternatively, change the *sh* in *should* to *w* as in "I *would like to*."

In the same muscle-testing workshop, Tessa, a woman in her early fifties, was frustrated. She said that she had been getting increasingly anxious because she couldn't get herself to complete her tax forms, even with a deadline looming just ahead. She had angrily been telling herself, "I should get those done right now!" Yet, her irate *shoulds* had been totally ineffective. She still had been unable to get herself to sit down at her desk and get started.

I asked Tessa what she felt when she told herself she *should* do her taxes. Tessa responded that *should* for her induced guilt. It created anxiety and stress as well. Sometimes *should* also conveyed to her a sense that someone or something outside herself was trying to control her, telling her what to do, which triggered her rebellious nature. "If I have to, then I won't."

We tested what might happen if Tessa switched her words to "I *could* get those taxes done now." Or, "I *would like to* do them now."

Now Tessa felt motivated. She even sensed that she might be able to go home after our session and finish her taxes one, two, three—which she did!

Should has a similarly negative impact when you use it toward others, e.g., "I think *you should* . . ." or, looking backwards, "*You should have* . . ." *Should* plus *not* is an especially detrimental combination: "*You shouldn't have* . . ."

By the way, did you catch the crossover? _____ You-sentences are crossovers, making *You should* a double whammy.

In the following sentences, convert *should* to *could* or *would like to*:

I should cook dinner now.	_____
She should appreciate me more.	_____
He should talk more quietly.	_____
I should get paid a higher salary.	_____
(Warning: Challenge ahead!)	
You should make these changes.	_____

R̟ₓ 6.3: KEEP SENSITIVE DISCUSSIONS SAFE WITH *SIX SAFE SENTENCE STARTERS.*

Sentence-starters, that is, phrases at the beginning of a sentence, have major impact on whether a conversation will flow in a collaborative mode or will turn adversarial. When initial words in a sentence sound safe, listeners open their ears. If the sentence starter triggers a threat alarm, ears close.

Use the following six safe starter phrases if:

- The topic is sensitive or controversial.
- You feel anxious about bringing up a subject.
- There's been prior tension on the issue, so you feel at risk for an argument.
- A discussion has begun to slip into adversarial mode.

Note that the first four sentence starters initiate talking. The fifth starter initiates a listening response that digests what was heard. The sixth circles you back and re-launches information-sharing, that is, talking.

Starter #1 | *I feel/felt* _____ (a one-word feeling) *when/that* _____ (what it's about).

Justin: *I felt* disappointed last night. The movie has received great reviews and yet *I felt* bored during almost the whole thing.

Feelings are usually expressed in one word: sad, confused, alarmed, etc. "I feel *that*____," by contrast, would express a thought, not a feeling, and generally will not suffice.

Tim: *I feel that* the movie was disappointing. *I felt that* they could have made the plot more interesting.

Expressing feelings enhances closeness between people. Be careful, however, which feelings words you choose. "I feel uncomfortable" is significantly more likely to be received with compassionate listening than "I feel mad." Vulnerable feelings like confused, anxious, concerned, disappointed, or sad will be received empathically and accepted more easily than anger words like mad or annoyed. Pausing to choose a word to express your distress that does not come from the anger family can have positive payoffs.

To clarify the situation associated with your feeling, add a *when you*. The *when you* (or *when I, when we, when they*) can be added at either the beginning or the end of the sentence.

Justin: I *felt* disappointed when you said you'd be home at 6:30 and
            then came in the door at 7:00.

I feel/felt _____ when you _____.
Or
When you _____, I feel/felt _____.

Starter #2 | *My concern is/was* _____.

Justin: *My concern was* that I had prepared a surprise gourmet meal for
            you.

Verbalizing your concerns is essential to help the other person understand
your situation. Expressing concerns is also a key to finding win-win solutions.

Starter #3 | *I would like to* _____.

Justin: *I would like to* enjoy our dinner now, before it's totally overcooked.
            Then later, after I'm not so hungry that I might bite your head
            off, *I'd like to* talk about what happened with your being so late.

Remember (as per Rx 6.2) to avoid "I would like *you* to . . ." Telling
others what to do is a losing strategy, likely to engender resentment. It sounds
controlling, not cooperative. Which sounds better to you? "I would like *you to*
come home at the time you tell me," or "I would like *to* figure out a better system
for communicating about dinnertimes."

Starter #4 | *How* and *what*

The fourth starter, a question word, invites others to share their perspectives.
Symmetry is vital in sensitive conversations.

Justin: *How* do you feel about talking now that we've finished eating?

The question-starter words *how* and *what* invite a broad range of possible
answers. Journalists refer to questions that begin with these words as open-ended
questions. By contrast, "Are you . . .?", "Did you . . .?", "Have you. . .?", and "Do
you . . .?" invite limited yes-no answers.

Starter #5 | *Yes. I agree* (love, appreciate, can see, would like to, etc.) *that* _____.

Starting with *yes* establishes that you are collaborative. As I described earlier, *yes* conveys that you are sitting on the same side of the table, together, against the problem. For uncomfortable or controversial topics, automatically starting with *yes* also buys you time to clarify what you can agree with in what you heard.

> Judy: Yes, I'd like to talk now. And I want to start by telling you that I totally sympathize with what you said before, that my coming home really late for dinner was difficult for you.

Reiterating what makes sense to you about what you heard clarifies which elements you have taken into your information base. It clarifies that you are taking seriously what the other person has said.

Equally helpful, digesting aloud what you have heard may clarify the opposite—that you misunderstood what someone was trying to say. Misunderstandings can be cleared up quickly this way and easily corrected with further information-sharing.

> Judy: I can understand if you were mad at me.
>
> Justin: I wasn't mad. I was concerned. I was worried for my dinner, and also concerned that maybe something bad had happened to you.

Avoid generalities like "I agree with what you said." Generalities sound patronizing. They often convey that you in fact did not really digest what you claim to have heard. By contrast, augmenting with additional information related to what you have heard adds even more to the collaborative tenor of the dialogue.

> Judy: Yes, I can see that you would have been concerned because I usually get home when I say I'll be there. I was watching the clock in my car and feeling increasingly frustrated.

I call these agree-and-add listening responses *digestive listening* because they indicate that you are truly thinking about the information that has been given to you. You are digesting the data to enter it into your information pool much as digesting food involves chewing and swallowing.

Starter #6 | *And, or and at the same time* _____.

Judy:	*And (#6) at the same time,* I was feeling (#1) desperately hungry.
Justin:	(#5) Yes, I can believe that you were very hungry, given that we usually eat at 6:00. *What* (#4) happened that you were so late?
Judy:	There was a huge accident on the highway. The traffic was stuck for so long that people got out of their cars and stood around talking. I tried to phone you and there was no answer. I wonder if your cell phone was in another room.

Beware: If instead of *and* you use the linking word *but*, you will inadvertently delete the prior point that the two of you had just agreed upon. In addition, *but* could convert the dialogue immediately into adversarial mode. Use *and* or *and at the same time*, to keep both viewpoints on the data table.

The *Safe Sentence Starters* create additive dialogue. Each of you safely adds data points to create together a larger picture, co-creating new understandings.

Practice

The six sentence starters above will feel increasingly natural if you practice them. Try the following exercise.

Pick a friend or relative to practice with. Pick a topic. Discuss it using the starter phrases. Here are some tips as you proceed.

- Keep the discussion an interactive dialogue of short chunks, each 3 sentences or less, not sequential monologues.
- Follow the sentence-starter sequence exactly at first; then get more flexible.
- Take turns calling out the number of a starter phrase for the other person to give a sentence. Or call out your own numbers before you start each contribution.

- Memorize the starters so that you have them when you need them.
- Lastly, try using the starter phrases on a controversial topic, like politics, or on an important and sensitive personal issue.

R⨯ 6.4: DISAGREE AGREEABLY WITH *TRIPLE-A.*

From time to time, your viewpoint is bound to differ from someone else's ideas, facts, or preferences. You then have a dilemma. As the prescription on *Word Patrol* explained, the negative words *no*, *not*, and *but* put a damper of negative energy on a discussion. That strategy proves costly.

Tina:	I loved that movie so many people are talking about. It was about the kind of struggles that all teenagers go through.
Tim:	No, they don't. I never had those kinds of problems. I don't believe most kids face them either. I didn't like the movie. It normalized a situation that few kids actually ever have to deal with.
Tina:	No. You're wrong. You just had an unusually privileged childhood.

No and its buddies *never*, *don't*, and *but* flipped this friendly conversation into a tug-of-war about who is right and who is wrong. With the turn toward adversarial came a switch into you-statements. There's danger ahead.

Enter *Triple-A*

The *Triple-A* (AAA) strategy for disagreeing agreeably enables you to express an alternative viewpoint without flipping the dialogue into an oppositional tone.

Agree, starting with the word *yes*, that is, with *Safe Sentence Starter #5* (Rx 6.3).

Justin:	*Yes, I agree* that a lot of people are talking about that movie.

In a highly flammable situation, you may have to listen with concentrated determination to find some aspect of what was said that you can agree with.

Augment, elaborating on the specific word or point you just agreed with.

The Triple-A Strategy

Agree	Augment	Add
"Yes, I agree that..." Specify at least one point that you heard with which you can agree.	*Elaborate* on the point of agreement. You two are now *on the same side of* the table.	*Add* your differing perspective. Link with *and* or *and at the same time.* Do not use *but* or *no.*

Justin: *I agree* that too many teens do have those kinds of problems. The poor girl whose mother kept shouting at her so abusively especially tore my heartstrings. Parents are supposed to help kids, not make their lives painful.

Adding further validating detail enables you to digest what you have heard. At the same time, your augmentation firms up the feeling that the two of you are sitting on the same side of the table vis-à-vis the problem.

Add your alternative perspective. Signal that you are adding information, not subtracting, deleting, or criticizing what you heard, by launching with *and* or *and at the same time.* Absolutely avoid *but*s and *no's.*

Justin: *And at the same time,* it sure is fortunate that most kids grow up in supportive families.

A second example

Discussing another sensitive issue, Tim and Tina again slip into adversarial positioning.

Tim: Participation in politics is essential to being an informed citizen. Let's have some friends over this weekend to talk about the election coming up.

Tina: No way. Not in my house. I hate political discussions.

Tim: But I live here too, and I love talking politics.

Tina: I told you, I hate talking about politics, and I don't want to host political arguments in my house.

Can you hear an argument brewing, with high potential for an angry eruption just ahead? Even if Tim and Tina gracefully exit to separate rooms to prevent further emotional escalation, their disagreement has pitted them against each other.

Justin and Judy utilize *Triple-A* skills for disagreeing agreeably. Notice the emotional tone of their conversation.

Justin: Talking politics is essential to being an informed citizen. Let's have friends over this weekend to talk about the election coming up.

Judy: *Yes* (agreeing), *I agree that* being politically informed probably does make people responsible citizens. It's important (augmenting) for Americans to learn enough about the candidates and what they stand for that they use their vote for someone they truly would want in office. I voted last year for a legislator just because she was a woman, and then it turned out that she voted against the one issue I really cared about.

And at the same time (adding a differing perspective), I get really uncomfortable when political topics come up. People get so adamant that they are right. I prefer calm conversations.

Justin: Yes (agreeing), our friends do get fixed in their political beliefs. They get too certain that they are right to listen to alternative viewpoints (augmenting). Worse, they try to drown alternative views out by getting louder when they talk. I'm sad to admit that I sometimes do that too.

(Adding his alternative perspective) How about if I try to talk politics in a new way, maybe practicing by talking politics with you? I'll aim to stay calm. I'll listen for what could be right in your viewpoints, even when I feel tempted to reject them immediately. If I can pass the test, then how would you feel about having friends over?

Judy: I'm willing to give it a try. Thanks for being so open to my concerns. If we do invite our friends, how about if we tell them that we're going to try to talk politics collaboratively? Make it like a game . . . Call out the numbers of the sentence starters? That could be fun. A lot of our friends could use these skills that we've been learning.

R̽ 6.5: GENERATE GOOD FEELINGS BY *EMANATING POSITIVITY.*

Every time you say anything, you send out both an informational and an emotional message. Sending positive emotional messages is free. You can send as much enthusiasm, warmth, and appreciation as you would like for no charge. What a deal!

Try reading this simple sentence: *The new pot is green.* What did you feel as you read this neutral information? Then read this one: *I'm delighted that the pot is green.* What difference did you experience? While the message is essentially the same in both versions, the second version communicated positive energy along with the neutral information.

Emanating positive energy raises the spirits of the people around you. It adds to your feelings of well-being. It makes you more attractive. It enhances the goodwill in your relationships. A positive emotional tone also increases the likelihood that your input will be received with open ears, especially in sensitive situations.

Of course, overdoing the positivity with excessive gushing, like sunshine that is too intense, can be off-putting. Positive expressions usually need to be interspersed with neutral information exchange. An enthusiastic tone of voice needs to be genuine, not overdone, and appropriate to the task at hand. At the same time, most people err by giving off too little warmth and light.

Elimination of hurtful negativity is a good starting place for becoming a more positive energy source. Negative vibes push people away or even knock them down. Telling people what you don't like, what's wrong with what they have said, and proffering other complaints, criticism, and blame demoralizes the receiver.

A teenager who signs her name as "Penelope Garlic" posted a poignant comment in response to an article I'd written for my psychologytoday.com blog. Her words crystallized for me how sad it is when parents direct negative energy toward their children.

"My stepdad often puts me down. His voice is mad. He tells me again and again, even when I've done everything he's told me he wants me to do, how bad I am. Could that have anything to do with how bad I feel about myself?"

Can a person just make a decision to give forth more positive energy? Yes. Awareness followed by a decision to change can lead to a rapid shift in the tone that you communicate.

Sam, a high school student, realized that his shyness was blocking him from making many friends. He was naturally a quiet person, so initiating conversations was difficult for him. His one close friend, Jared, exemplified the opposite.

What did Jared do, Sam wondered, that made him so popular? Before leaving high school for college, Sam decided to pay close attention to the habits that made his outgoing friend so well liked.

When Sam left home for college, he vowed that he would try the behaviors he had observed Jared doing. Walking on his new campus between classes, he pretended he was Jared. He made eye contact immediately with people he even vaguely knew. He smiled, said warm hellos, and even added each person's name as he greeted them. With genuine interest, he asked, "How are you?" or "What've you been up to?" or "How are your classes going?" Then he would conclude with genuine warmth, "Great to talk with you!"

The upshot? Within days as a university freshman Sam felt embedded in a community with more friends than he had made in all four of his high school years combined.

Judy and Justin send forth good vibes in many ways. Notice their sentence starters, the content of what they say, the tone of voice, and how generously they express agreement, appreciation, affection, gratitude, humor, and interest in each other. Which of the twelve ways of conveying positivity on this checklist might you add to your conversational patterns?

Judy: I'm sweltering. I'm sitting perfectly still, and sweat is dripping down my face. This is the warmest Sunday we've had since I've been here. Could be good for the beach.

❑ **Yes . . .**

Justin: Yes, swimming sounds appealing. Any other exercise would be too much in the heat.

❑ **I agree . . .**

Judy: I agree that it's too hot to do any exercise other than swimming today.

❑ **I appreciate . . .**

Justin: And I appreciate your willingness to go to the beach, even though I know that so much sun sometimes is not your favorite.

❑ **Thank you for . . .**

Judy: Thanks so much, Justin, for recognizing that the sun scares me. I like the bright lights of New York at night, not the kind of bright light that gives me sunburns.

❑ **I like (love, enjoy) . . .**

Justin: I love that new bathing suit! Looks terrific!

❑ **I would love to . . .**

Judy: Thanks. I like it too. I'd be glad to pack a lunch from the leftovers we have in the fridge. I like picnics on the beach.

❑ **That makes sense to me because . . .**

Justin: Bringing lunch definitely makes sense to me. The food there is so expensive.

❑ **How? What? Question words convey that you value the other person's perspective.**

Judy: How would you feel about my calling my parents to join us at the beach?

❑ **Good! (or excellent, great, wow, cool, terrific, brilliant, etc.)**

Justin: Terrific! Your mom loves to swim. And sitting on the beach would be a perfect place for me to talk with your dad about this business idea I've been hatching.

❑ **I'm pleased (happy, delighted) that . . .**

Judy: I'm so glad that you want me to invite my parents. They love hanging out with us, and I love when they do too.

❏ **Positive non-verbals**

Justin: Excellent [with a hug]. Let's raid the refrigerator to pack a quick lunch and hop right in the car. We could call your folks from the cell phone.

❏ **Gratitude**

Judy: I'm so glad we're married so we're lifetime playmates. I love how, even in this immobilizing heat, when you get an idea you right away get moving on it!

Practice *Emanating Positivity*

If you are unaccustomed to expressing many positive emanations, using positive sentence starters will take practice. Try this exercise to begin making them more habitual.

- Think of three people with whom you often interact. The list could include family members, friends, children, a store clerk or anyone.
- Find a private place where you can talk out loud without self-consciousness.
- Close your eyes and picture yourself talking with one of the people on your list.
- Speak out loud to practice using each of the positive energy generators.
- Fill in both sides of the dialogue, speaking both your lines and the replies.
- Repeat the exercise with similar pretend conversations with each of the two additional people on your list.

Three times through on this exercise using all twelve positivity sentence starters with each go-round will give you practice using thirty-six positive-vibe emanations.

Repeating this exercise over several days can further enhance its effectiveness.

In real life, so many positives might be too much. The goal of this exercise though is that, by the end, you will feel a more easy and natural flow of positive expressions of agreement, appreciation, and affection.

Is your inner pool of well-being full enough?

Psychologist Tal Ben-Shahar, whose course at Harvard on happiness attracted record numbers of students, explains in his book *Choose the Life You Want* that happiness is a choice.[75] One mini-choice from Ben-Shahar that I particularly like is to be sure to treat yourself to brief dollops of fun. As he writes, "Taking three minutes to listen to our favorite song even though our inbox is overflowing, spending an hour with a friend despite the looming deadline at work . . . These may be the best things that we can do for ourselves and others."[76] The happier you feel within yourself, the more positive energy you naturally will share with others.

The bottom line

Positivity brightens your life and the lives of all with whom you interact. In addition, the more enjoyment you insert into your everyday life patterns, the more positivity you will be able to emanate to others—and consequently the more positivity you will receive back in return.

R$_x$ 6.6: LEARN THE *WIN-WIN WALTZ*.

Bumps on your life road are inevitable. From time to time, you are bound to encounter troubling situations, tough decisions, and divisive interactions with difficult people. In all of these situations, the three steps that I refer to as the *Win-Win Waltz* can enable you to resolve the dilemma so that you can return to the realm of well-being.

A waltz has three steps. Here are the basic three steps of the *Win-Win Waltz*:

- **Notice** when a problem or conflict is arising.
- **Explore the underlying concerns** on all sides.
- **Find solutions** responsive to all the concerns.

Where does this three-step process come from?

In 1981, authors Roger Fisher and William Ury published a groundbreaking book introducing to the business and political worlds the concept of win-win negotiation. It is said that Mikhail Gorbachev, then head of the Soviet Union, took to carrying this little book in his back pocket. Some say that the book's ideas of win-win as opposed to win-lose or lose-lose conflict resolution led to Gorbachev's listening to the desires of the member states of the Soviet Union and ultimately granting them freedom from the Soviet yoke. The name of this small book that has had such big impacts is *Getting to Yes*.[77]

In *From Conflict to Resolution*, my initial book for therapists, I translated Fisher and Ury's *Getting to Yes* business and political terminology into words suitable for personal situations. Fisher and Ury's advice to understand *the interests that lie behind positions*, which sounds too formal and formidable for talking, for instance, about who is going to fold the laundry, I changed to exploring *underlying concerns*. Fisher and Ury's three steps for dispute resolution in the business world thus became the *Win-Win Waltz* for making decisions in personal, family, friendship, and practical situations.

Step 1 | Notice decision points and express initial solution ideas

Judy phoned Justin from her office before leaving work to say that she wanted to go out for supper. Justin wanted to eat at home.

Judy and Justin need to make a decision about what to do for dinner, a minor decision but a decision nonetheless. Each proposed a different solution. If they then had each insisted on "My way," "No, my way," even this small decision could have turned into an argument.

Step 2 | Explore the underlying concerns

Instead of engaging in a tug-of-war over whose way was better, Justin and Judy shifted from talking about what they would do (solutions) to identifying their underlying concerns.

Judy:	My concern is that I've been working long hours. I'm too exhausted to cook.
Justin:	I can understand that. You left for work at six this morning and now it's past six in the evening.
Judy:	Yes. I am really tired.
Justin:	My main concern is I want to watch the Monday night football game. None of the restaurants we like have a TV screen.

Judy:	Yes, that would be a problem with eating out. Here's the other concern on my end. I'd love a lush green salad with colorful veggies and protein, but our refrigerator is empty.
Justin:	Yes, I noticed too that the fridge is pretty bare. I'd also like healthy, though salad doesn't sound filling enough to be healthy for me. I'm picturing meat and potatoes.

Notice how the *Six Safe Sentence Starters* sustain collaborative dialogue. Justin and Judy both verbalize their feelings (#1), concerns (#2), and would like to's (#3). They both take seriously what the other says, digesting aloud what they have heard (#5) before adding a next thought (#6). These skills keep the dialogue tone friendly.

Step 3 | Find a solution responsive to all the concerns

The ultimate solution will be win-win to the extent that it responds to all the concerns of the parties involved.

Judy:	The sports bar near our house has a large-screen TV. Their meals are okay, not great, but they do have a salad bar for me and a burger and fries for you. If you watch the game there. I'd enjoy watching it with you.
Justin:	Thanks. That could work . . . And here's another option. How about if I go to the grocery store down the street, the one with a big salad bar and also hot foods to go. I could pick up salad for you and meat and potatoes for me. Then we could eat together in front of our TV. I'd be glad to clean up the kitchen after supper if you're still tired. I can see the TV from the sink.
Judy:	I love that idea. Then if I get tired before the game's over I can just go to sleep. It's a deal. See you on the couch!

The plan that Justin and Judy evolved together was responsive to all of both of their criteria, that is, to all of both of their underlying concerns.

The *Win-Win Waltz* worksheet below can guide you so that you too can use win-win patterning for making decisions. The more you practice the three

The Win-Win Waltz Worksheet
Download this worksheet at *prescriptionswithoutpills.com.*

STEP 1 — NOTE A PROBLEM; EXPRESS INITIAL SOLUTION IDEAS

The dilemma:

A's initial solution proposal:

B's initial solution proposal:

STEP 2 — EXPLORE UNDERLYING CONCERNS
Write the concerns of both of you on one list.

❏

❏

❏

❏

❏

STEP 3 — CREATE A WIN-WIN SOLUTION, RESPONSIVE TO ALL THE CONCERNS

❏ Start solution-building by prioritizing your one or two most strongly felt concerns.
❏ Devise a plan of action responsive to these top-priority issues.
❏ Add enhancements to the solution plan until all the concerns are responded to.
❏ Offer what you yourself might be willing to contribute. Unless you have been asked, refrain from suggesting what you think others might do.
❏ Express appreciation of others' offers.
❏ Add additional concerns as they come to mind. Augment the action plan to be sure

it is responsive to these concerns as well.
❏ Aim to build a solution set, that is, a comprehensive plan of action with elements responsive to all of the concerns that have been identified.
❏ Summarize the plan of action aloud to be sure that everyone agrees.
❏ As you approach closure, ask yourself and others: "Are there any little pieces of this that still feel unfinished?" Further modify your plan of action in response to these concerns.
❏ Summarize the full win-win action plan and you're good to go.

steps on dilemmas small or large, within your own thinking or with others, the easier the waltz will become. Eventually you will find that "doing what comes naturally" will mean doing the *Win-Win Waltz.*

R$_x$ 6.7: IDENTIFY CONFLICTS AND DECISIONS THAT NEED THE *WIN-WIN WALTZ.*

Recognizing when a *Win-Win Waltz* moment is in front of you can be the hurdle most likely to block you from using it. Whether the conflict lies within yourself or with someone or something external, pay attention to these indicators:

- A choice, decision, or problem to be solved
- Tension or irritation

The choice point could be a simple one, like whether or not to get out of bed when you first wake up in the morning or which route to take on a trip. The issue may be more complex and with more significant consequences like, with your spouse, whether to buy or rent a place to live, or how, with your siblings, to handle a parent's increasing dementia. In either case, the three steps of the *Win-Win Waltz* will be the same.

Step 1: Note a problem and express initial solution ideas

Judy and Justin felt concerned when they saw that their young son Noah almost every day resisted going to school. Judy wanted to insist he go. Justin felt uncertain, thinking that maybe they shouldn't force him to go to school if he really wanted to stay home.

Step 2: Explore the underlying concerns

Judy and Justin listed, on one shared list, their concerns. Judy worried that Noah resisted so many things including doing homework as well as going to school. She feared that caving in to letting Noah stay home was setting a bad precedent. Would they let him stay home whenever he whined? Besides, with both of them working, who would stay home with him? Justin's main concern was that Noah seemed depressed.

Step 3: Create a win-win solution

Justin and Judy considered their options. They could change Noah's school. That solution, though, would raise a new concern. How would they get him there or back? The school Noah attended now was just across the street from their house, a consideration that they added to their concerns list.

Another option might be to go to the pediatrician. Maybe Noah was physically ill. Or might an antidepressant medication help? They were reluctant (a sign of another concern) to give him a medication, though, without solving the underlying problem.

Maybe they could ask Noah's teacher if she had ideas about what was going on, or if she could offer additional options. They decided on this route and set up an appointment to meet.

Noah's teacher told Judy and Justin that she too had noticed that Noah seemed unhappy at school. "I think the work is too easy for him. Noah is tall as well as smart," she continued. "How would you feel about our moving him up a grade to join the class ahead?"

The next morning Noah began in his new classroom. His school resistance disappeared immediately. He eagerly did his homework. At dinner he chattered happily about what he was learning in his new class. And there were no more morning school departure arguments. Problem solved.

Tension or irritation

Pay attention to negative feelings like anxiety, irritability, or tensions. Emotional perturbations signal the presence of a problem like smoke signals a fire.

In the following example, irritation triggered the realization that a conflict needed resolution.

Judy and Justin often disagreed about parking. Justin didn't want his wife to park in the parking garage downtown. Judy thought Justin was being ridiculous. The parking garage was sometimes her only option for finding a space.

"I'm going to listen to you with the assumption that every concern of yours is a concern of mine," Judy said. Justin agreed to do the same.

Justin said his concern was that the narrow spaces in the parking garage would result in their new car getting scratched or dented by others' car doors. The final straw for him had been when Judy had backed their car into a column, of which there were many in the downtown garage. Ultimately, Justin's concern was money. The damages had been expensive.

What concerned Judy was finding a parking spot. She often cut her timing close, leaving little extra time to circle the downtown streets to find a space when she needed to run errands or go to a doctor appointment. Sometimes, too, there simply were no open outdoor parking spots.

With an understanding of both of their underlying concerns, Judy and Justin launched into brainstorming for a parking plan. They were determined to find one they could both agree on. They also agreed that each of them would think about what they themselves could offer toward a solution instead of, as in the past, Justin telling Judy what he felt she should do.

Justin offered to buy Judy a wide rearview mirror for their car so she would be less likely to bang into poles and columns. He also offered to drive her when she needed to head into town. That would be feasible now since he recently had begun working from home.

Judy offered that she could be more selective about which spaces to choose when she parked in the parking garage. She could drive an extra few minutes to the upper levels where the cars were less crowded than on the lower two levels where she usually parked. She offered to park more carefully in the middle of the space where others' car doors would be less likely to dent hers. She also realized that if she parked in the outdoor lots on the outskirts of downtown where the spaces were both wider and more plentiful, she could count the ten-minute walk as a contribution to the healthier lifestyle she was trying to build for herself.

"I like this way of setting disagreements," Justin answered. "No one has to surrender to the other. I'm delighted. We're coming up with a whole batch of new solution possibilities. And instead of feeling annoyed at you, I'm appreciating you."

"Great," Judy agreed. "How about if we try all of the above solution options? Over time, then, I'll see which work best."

"It's a deal," Justin said, feeling relieved.

By realizing that they were facing a conflict, Judy and Justin were able to use their *Win-Win Waltz* skills. The process was pleasant because they had attacked the problem as if it was on the table, with the two of them sitting side-by-side facing the problem together. They concluded with enhanced affection as well as a mutually agreeable plan of action.

What conflicts, decisions, and/or dilemmas need solving now in your life?

List at least one issue, minor or major, from each of the three conflict arenas: one in which your inner conflicting preferences and concerns make it hard to map a plan of action, one in which you and someone else differ, and at least one struggle against external circumstances such as bad weather, financial limitations, or health issues. You might want to refer back to your list from Rx 1.5.

_____

_____

_____

Let go of the belief that all couples fight

Many couples, and also parents toward their children, normalize irritable interactions. The standards you regard as "what everyone does" affect what you do, so beware of what you believe about conflict. If you believe that all couples have times when one or both partners become adversarial, speaking in annoyed voices or even yelling at each other, that belief will become your reality. If you believe that all parents speak in irritated voice tones daily with their children, that belief will become your reality.

Do all couples (or parents with their children) fight? No! All do sometimes disagree. Fighting, however, is to being a couple or parent what accidents are to driving. All drivers do NOT get into accidents. If you do get into an accident, hopefully the accident is a rare exception for you, not a norm. You can resolve to make arguments a similarly rare exception.

Expectations have powerful impacts. For many years, no one believed that any person would ever be able to run a mile in four minutes. Then, on May 6, 1954, Roger Bannister did it. Once Bannister had accomplished this feat, showing that running a mile within four minutes was possible, many and eventually all serious male runners then discovered that they could accomplish the same.[78]

All conflicts _are_ resolvable without fighting, provided that you choose to talk collaboratively and use the _Win-Win Waltz._

R$_x$ 6.8: RESOLVE INNER CONFLICTS WITH *DO OR BECOME.*

Use this prescription to resolve inner conflicts that have been giving rise to uncomfortable feelings, especially ones that you express with a metaphor, e.g., "I feel like I have a monkey on my back," or "I feel a sense of impending doom." The exercise's effectiveness rests on the belief that your subconscious knows what it needs to do to heal your distress.

In 1989 two British therapists, B.I. Panzer and the late David Grove, published a book and an excellent audiotape illustrating their techniques called *Resolving Traumatic Memories*.[79] I credit Panzer and Grove with the following simple yet surprisingly powerful visualization sequence.

Please refer to the Introduction for suggestions on how to do the visualization prescriptions. See also prescriptionswithoutpills.com for video examples and downloadable worksheets.

The exercise begins with instructions similar to earlier visualizations where you locate and describe the feeling in your body. It then continues with a different set of questions.

- **Localize the feeling:** Close your eyes. Where in your body do you feel the negative emotion? What does it feel like?

  Gina felt overwhelmed. When she closed her eyes, she experienced the overwhelmed feeling as a large burden that she was carrying on her shoulders.

- **Detail the feeling.** What size is it? What shape? What is it made of? Other features? What does it remind you of? What is it doing?

  Gina: It feels like a huge animal with many arms and legs, sitting on both of my shoulders and grabbing at me so I feel I may choke or sink. Or maybe it's lots of animals whose arms and legs are so intertwined that it feels like one animal. And it's very heavy. It's dark and furry, but I can't see its face.

- **Repeat what you have heard and then ask the *Do or Become* question:** "As you focus on that _____ (fill in the exact words from the physical description, using all of them), what would a _____ like that want to *Do or Become?*"

Dr. H: And as you focus on that heavy, dark, furry, huge animal, with so many intertwined arms and legs that it feels like one animal that's grabbing at you so you may choke or sink, what would an animal like that want to *Do or Become*?

- **Detail this image. Ask, "What else do you notice about a   ? "** Find out how it looks, and what it is doing, feeling and thinking.

Gina: It wants to find help. It's very needy and wants me to take care of it. It wants to become a little baby in a crib so I'll take care of it.

- **Ask the *Do or Become* question again:** "And what could a _____ (use the full description each time, including all of the visualization's features) like that want to *Do or Become?*"

Dr. H: And what could a needy little baby in a crib like that, a needy baby who wants you to take care of it, want to *Do or Become*?

Gina: It would want to go look for another caretaker because I don't want to take care of it anymore. I walk in the other direction, away from it. Now it's all alone and crying. It wants a caretaker, but there isn't one. So it cries until it becomes a pool of tears.

- **Repeat the *Do or Become* question, followed by asking for more details as needed,** until the image is a fully positive one.

Dr. H: And what would a pool of tears like that want to *Do or Become*?

Gina: It would want to become a lake.

Dr. H: Tell me more about the lake.

Gina: It started out as just a pool of tears, and then it got big enough to be a small pond, and then it became a big lake.

Dr. H: What kind of a lake?

Gina: It's a big lake, with lots of trees and flowers around it. It's not agitated anymore, not like before. Now it looks calm. And the lake provides water for all the fish who live in it and the flowers and trees that grow around it.

Dr. H: And as you see that lake with the fish and the flowers and trees, what feeling comes up within you?

- **Check for closure** by asking how you feel. Keep asking more *Do or Become* question sequences until you feel fully positive.

Gina: I feel peaceful and much happier, like I can go on now and live my life without feeling overwhelmed.

Continue the questioning until the image and the feeling that the image creates within you are fully positive. If remnants of aggressive actions or negative feelings still remain, return to asking and requesting details of more *Do or Become* questions.

After the visualization has finished, open your eyes and think about or discuss what you saw. You are likely to feel relieved that the metaphor has brought you to a comfortable state.

You now may want to discuss the issues in your life that the metaphor helped you to resolve. Alternatively, you may feel a sense of closure without desire to discuss it further, which is fine.

> Gina had no desire to discuss the metaphor. She was very pleased that the visualization had relieved the sense of overwhelming weight she had carried for so long on her shoulders. She did, though, feel eager to discuss what the new feeling of relief would mean for her current life.
>
> Gina: I have had so many people hanging on me and asking me to do things for them. Actually, a lot of the time they don't ask; when I see them suffering, I look for what I might do to help them out. The trouble is that we belong to a large church, and I am trying to help too many people there. Can I really stop helping all of them?
>
> Dr. H: Let's look at who specifically you have been carrying on your shoulders and which, if any, of them, you would still want to carry.
>
> Gina: I feel an immediate answer in my gut. I've given too much for too long. I just want to be free of all of it.
>
> The remainder of the session focused on how to bring a positive closure to her helping role in a way that would be sensitive also to the feelings of the people she had been helping. Her focus then shifted to what she would like to do with her energies now that she would be free to live her life instead of giving all her energies over to helping others.
>
> Gina: I want to paint! I'm going to fix up our barn into a big studio. I can't wait to get started painting again. That's my real life work!

As I mentioned in the Introduction, the key to using this and the other visualizations is to trust that your inner subconscious knows what it needs to do to heal. Trust whatever images come up for you. Your images may not make logical sense. The subconscious mind sometimes makes strange connections. That's fine. You can still trust them.

R͓x 6.9: HEAL TOGETHER AFTER UPSETTING INCIDENTS.

This prescription builds on the prescription presented earlier in Rx 3.9. That prescription offered multiple strategies for enabling healing to replace harboring upset feelings about past painful incidents. The focus now is on joint recovery, for shared healing when an upset has occurred between you and someone else.

In ongoing intimate relationships, the ability to heal together after upsetting incidents has high payoffs. If you and the other person both are open to reflecting back on upsetting incidents in a non-blaming, growth-inducing way, your relationship over time will get better and better. Without effective healing routines, rifts can yield canyons of distance and distrust.

The formula for being able to heal together after upsets has four steps:

- **Put together the puzzle pieces of what happened.**
- **Find the miss.**
- **Devise a better system for the future.**
- **Apologize.**

Step 1 | Put together the puzzle pieces of what happened

Think of the upsetting event as a puzzle with many pieces. To put together the puzzle pieces of what happened, you are responsible for adding only the blue pieces. Your partner adds the red pieces. The blue pieces describe what you thought, felt, did, and said in the incident. The red pieces describe what your partner thought, felt, did, and said. By each of you verbalizing your own thoughts, feelings and actions, you together will gradually be able to see the whole puzzle picture of what happened.

Strictly observe the rule that no one gets to offer crossovers, speaking about what the other person said, felt, thought, or did. Crossover comments trespass over the boundary between the two of you, invading the other's territory. The job for each of you is only to share about yourself. This rule prevents attacking and defending, fostering collaborative dialogue instead.

> Judy felt both hurt and angry when Justin came home from work empty-handed. Justin had forgotten to pick up the dry-cleaning on his way home from work, even though Judy had called to remind him. Now Judy had no appropriate dress to wear to the fund-raising dinner that evening. She felt furious.
>
> Several days later, Judy decided that it would be better to heal than to harbor resentment, so she invited Justin to sit down to talk.
>
> Judy: When you came home without having picked up my black dress, my first feeling was panic. I was counting on wearing it to the dinner. I didn't have any other options.
>
> Justin: I felt like a total idiot as soon as I saw the panic on your face. I had reminded myself to stop at the cleaners when I picked up my briefcase to leave the office. Then driving home, I spaced out. I was preoccupied trying to solve a computer problem and drove right by the cleaners.
>
> Judy: I know how focused you get when you are thinking about a work problem, so I can picture that. When I panicked, though, my panic quickly flipped into fury. I went instantly from zero to one hundred on the anger speedometer. I felt like I was vomiting anger.
>
> Justin: And when I saw your anger coming, my teenage gang years kicked into gear. I haven't shouted like that in a long time. At least I had enough sense to walk out of the apartment. If I hadn't gone out for a walk, even though it made us late for the dinner, I might have pummeled you like I used to pummel kids who'd jump me on the street.

Step 2 | Find the miss

Once enough puzzle pieces have been put in place that you can see the full picture of what happened in the upsetting incident, the next step is for each of you to find your *miss*. What did you *mis*understand? Was there a *mis*conception? A *mis*communication? A *mis*take?

Judy: I can see that I *mis*estimated how likely it would be that you might forget. I also made a *mis*take by asking you to pick up the dress without having a backup plan. It's not like you've never forgotten things before. Then what stoked my fury was *mis*interpreting you. When you came home without having stopped at the cleaners, I immediately thought, "He doesn't love me. He doesn't care about me enough to remember to do the things he's said he'll do."

My fury was like the rage I used to feel when my alcoholic dad would let me down. He'd say he was going to pick me up or take me to something, then he'd almost never show. As a kid, I would feel terrible when that happened, which was often. I assumed that his forgetting about me happened because he didn't love me. Now I see that in a way I was right. He didn't love me, or at least not as much as he loved to drink.

I'm surprised that I'm not so angry thinking about it now as I was when I was a kid. Now I feel sorry for my dad. He was clueless about how alcohol was destroying him—and us. My dad was just repeating what his dad, and probably his dad's dad, had done. It was all so sad.

Justin: Thank heavens I'm not an alcoholic. Still, I am like your dad in that when I go into problem-solving mode, I totally forget everything else going on around me. I can see that my version of ADD, that total hyper-focus I go into, may be helpful at work, but it causes me to let you down. My *miss* is that I repeatedly *mis*estimate how much my ADD results in my disappointing you.

As to my anger when I first heard you getting mad, I'm just glad I didn't make the *mis*take of staying in the house. I could have hit you. As soon as I saw you getting mad, I knew my anger could explode. I turned and walked out of the house to cool down. I feel totally grateful to that anger management class—and to you for insisting that I go to it. If I had stayed, I could have physically hurt you. It frightens me to think about it.

Judy:	Thank you for leaving. And I'm glad that instead of going into a full "see how much you've hurt me" boiling-over mode, after you left I calmed down enough that I could focus on the practical problem of what I might wear for the party. We both did some things right, for which I feel very grateful.
Justin:	Yes! We were lucky, too, that the dry cleaning store was along our route to the dinner party. I loved that you had the spunk to change clothes in the car. Yay, Jude!

Step 3 | Devise a better system

Create a better system for handling this kind of situation to prevent future recurrences. You are not the problem; neither is the other person. The problem is a glitch in the system. Fix it.

Judy:	Next time I'm tempted to ask you to do something for me, I'm going to ask myself, "Is this something that I'll be upset about if Justin forgets?" If it is, I'll find another solution instead of relying on you. Like this time, I could have worn the dress as it was, ignoring the one small stain that really didn't show that much anyways, and waited to ask you to bring it to the dry cleaners until after the dinner party. Then if you forgot to pick it up on the way home, no problem. You could have just tried again the next day to remember.
Justin:	Thanks, Judy. That plan would help a lot to prevent my letting you down when it really counts. At the same time, I can see that I need to teach myself to listen to my "little voices." When you asked me about the cleaners, a little voice in my head had said, "Sometimes you forget to do things on the way home." If I'd listened and spoken up, we could have made a decision together about if the risk of my forgetting was worth it. I think in the future, too, if I do say I'll pick up something on the way home, I'll use a tech solution. When I'm leaving my office, I'll set a reminder on my cell phone that will ding me when I'm to do what I said I'd do. Tech solutions do help me.

Judy:

My main change though is that I'm going to go back to that doctor who told me about ADD medicine. I wanted to handle the ADD without meds but the costs to our relationship are too high. I'll give the medication a try. Will you help me to remember to call the doctor for an appointment?

Judy: (laughing): Yes, for sure. And the day of the appointment I'll phone you when it's time to leave. I hugely appreciate your giving the meds a try. I do hope they make a difference!

Step 4 | Apologize

Apologize for your part, summarizing what you will do differently in the future.

Apologies work best when they include:

- Regret for what you did that caused harm: "I'm so sorry that I . . ."
- Non-intentionality: "I didn't mean to . . ."
- Learning: "I see now that my miss was to . . . In the future, I'll . . ."

Judy: So, I'm sorry, Justin, that I set you up by asking you to remember to do something so essential. I didn't do it on purpose. I can see that I hadn't learned sufficiently from other times when this has happened. And I'm especially sorry that I blew up at you. I don't want to pop off in anger like that anymore. I want to learn to exit like you do, to step back or out of the situation as soon as I feel anger welling up.

Justin: Thanks, Judy. I totally appreciate that you didn't do any of those mistakes on purpose. As for me, I'm so sorry for forgetting to stop at the cleaners. I feel terrible that I let you down yet again. I sure didn't do it on purpose. At the same time, I'm excited now to try the ADD medication. I hope it helps!

The bottom line is that life is like a river. It keeps moving downstream. If you hold on to painful events and errors from the past, you will miss out on enjoying the surprises ahead. Better to find ways, together, to go with the flow.

R℞ 6.10: HOLD ON TO YOUR CIRCLE OF SKILLS.

The following graphic clarifies the four main skill areas that together sustain well-being.

The Circle of Skills

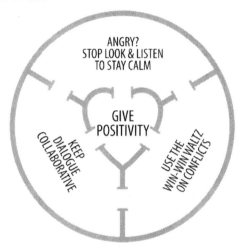

Prescriptions in earlier chapters for each of these four skill arenas have included the following. Which do you need to review?

- **Anger management:** Stop, Look, and Listen. Take early exits when you or others are getting heated. Remove old angers, let go of resentments, Put Your Past in the Past, heal by learning from your mistakes, and stay in the calm zone.

- **Collaborative dialogue:** Become aware of shifts from collaboration to opposition and take action right away to resume goodwill. Use *Word Patrol* and the *Six Safe Sentence Starters* to launch and sustain a collaborative mode. Use *Triple-A* to express disagreement agreeably. Use the two listening sentence starters *Yes* and *And at the same time* to rescue a conversation that has slipped into oppositional mode.

- **Win-win conflict resolution:** Within your own thoughts and also between you and others or external circumstances, solve problems with the *Win-Win Waltz*. Be sure your solutions are responsive to all the relevant underlying concerns.

- **Positivity:** Sprinkle goodwill liberally via affection, humor, appreciation, and lots more.

Use the leakage between the chambers to your advantage

Note the openings between the *Circle of Skills'* chambers. These openings enable each skill set to influence others. When you are effective in one arena, positive energy flows into the other areas and raises your level in those skills as well. Downgrade any one of the four factors and you become at risk for spiraling downward in all four arenas.

Jonas and Alison's marriage had been strong for years after learning the skills in this chapter. During a period of overwhelmingly difficult life circumstances, however, their relationship had again deteriorated. Now they were on the verge of divorce.

Because several years of mild depression self-medicated with alcohol had kept Jonas relatively self-absorbed, Alison built a separate life with the children and her community work. The alcohol now was gone. Jonas had stopped drinking, but neither Jonas nor Alison seemed able to reconnect.

In their first session back in therapy, I asked Jonas and Alison to try an experiment. They were to take turns sharing positive comments with their partner. The receiver was to respond by taking in the positive message such as, "I appreciate . . ."; "I enjoyed . . ."; "Thanks for . . ."; or "I agree that . . ." The receiver then would add yet another dollop of positivity.

"I loved the way you handled little Jake's upset about the chocolate cake last night," Jonas began.

"Oh, I'm glad! I was amazed too how quickly he recovered. And I appreciated your help in . . ."

Jonas and Alison both now had begun smiling. Sharing positives led to remembering and sharing funny in-jokes from their fifteen years of being together. With the smiles and laughter came surprising surges of affection. Jonas reached out, putting his hand on Alison's knee.

Sharing positivity had pressed the reset button.

"Forget the lawyers and divorce," Jonas said. "Let's go back to enjoying each other."

Alison added, "I'd like to do this exercise for a few minutes every day."

"Yes," Jonas responded. "When I remember to appreciate you, I feel affection for you again. And my skills for healthy communicating seem magically to fall back into place."

Even just one bad incident or episode can temporarily obscure what each spouse likes about the other. Remembering the rest of the picture, the positives, can restore goodwill and with it the full *Circle of Skills*.

And the moral of the story is . . .

The four skill sets in the *Circle of Skills* together create a formidable bulwark against negative emotions. These so-called "people skills" also rank at the top of factors that predict career success. Use them to secure peaceful and enduring relationships. Use them to raise emotionally healthy children. Use them to enhance your well-being and, in the process, build a better world.

Chapter 7

Look Back
and Look Ahead

From the yellow armchairs in my sunny office, I generally close each therapy session by reviewing what we've done. I share what stood out for me in the session. I ask my clients what stood out for them, what is their take-home. Then we may also, together, look ahead at where to go next.

Summarizing plus next-step planning significantly enhances the potency of a therapy session. These are the goals of this brief final chapter.

Rₓ 7.1: REVIEW THE HAND MAP AND ITS BASIC ASSUMPTIONS.

What most stands out for me is the Hand Map way of understanding emotional distress from Rx 2.1. Here's a short review of the understandings that the Hand Map illustrates, understandings that constitute the main theoretical underpinnings of this book.

- **Problems always present themselves.** Life inevitably will put life bumps in front of you, that is, problematic situations for which you will need to choose a pathway, a plan of action for moving forward. Bumps on the road go by many names, e.g., difficult situations, issues, disagreements, arguments, dilemmas, frustrations, problems, or conflicts. All bumps, though, are choice points.

244

- **There are five potential routes.** Any time that you face a challenging situation, there are pretty much always five potential pathways.

- **Proceeding down Fight, Fold, Freeze, and Flee pathways is costly.** These routes may settle the issue for the time being. At the same time, they charge both you and others an emotional toll.

- **Each route consistently leads to the same emotional outcome.** Which route you choose will determine whether you, and also the others involved in the situation, will emerge feeling depressed, angry, anxious, addicted, or enjoying well-being.

- **Choosing to find win-win solutions sustains well-being.** Win-win solutions enhance both personal well-being and collective goodwill.

- **If you find yourself on one of the routes to negative emotional outcomes, return to the problem situation and readdress your difficulty.** Clarifying the underlying concerns in the conflict and then finding win-win solutions re-establishes well-being.

- **Develop your skills in all four realms of the Circle of Skills.** Keep anger out. Keep dialogue collaborative. Use bilateral listening by taking both your own and others' concerns seriously. When difficulties and differences arise, find win-win solutions responsive to all the participants' concerns. Sprinkle positivity generously around your life space.

- **With the Hand Map plus your Circle of Skills, enjoy a life of well-being.** As you do face inevitable disappointments, suffering, and adversities, address the triggering issues with your prescriptions and return as soon as possible to thriving.

R̽ 7.2: WRITE OUT YOUR ACTION PLAN.

To make optimal use of the prescriptions in this book, more steps lie ahead.

- **Review.** Look back over the prescriptions to select which are most likely to benefit you. What stands out for you as you review what you have read?

_____

_____

_____

_____

- **Remind yourself that your only option is success.** There will always be new challenges to face. There will be times when you backslide into old habits. There is, however, no such thing as failure. *Mistakes are for learning.* Learning keeps you on the road to success.

R_x 7.3: ENJOY WELL-BEING.

Living happily ever after cannot be guaranteed. We each repeatedly are dealt hands that include both blessings and challenges, advantages and adversities. At the same time, the prescriptions in this book can enable you to minimize the time that you might otherwise spend in depression, anger, anxiety, or addictive habits. May you thereby maximize the time you spend enjoying well-being. And may you season all the days of your life with positivity, generosity, and gratitude.

Thumbs up for staying on the thumb route to well-being!

Which is the right path for man to choose for himself? Whatever is harmonious for the one who does it, and harmonious for mankind.

Judah HaNassi [135-219 AD]

Further Learning Resources from Dr. Heitler

BOOKS

From Conflict to Resolution offers a conceptual map and techniques for integrative therapists by bringing understandings of win-win conflict resolution from the world of business into the psychological literature. *Contemporary Psychiatry* says, "This book exemplifies the best of therapy."

The Power of Two: Secrets to a Strong & Loving Marriage clarifies for both the general public and for therapists the collaborative dialogue, conflict resolution, and emotion management skills essential for relationship success. Published in six foreign language editions and adapted for online marriage education as poweroftwomarriage.com.

The Power of Two Workbook, coauthored with Abigail Heitler Hirsch, PhD, provides exercises to advance you from understanding Power of Two skills to utilizing them. Therapists are welcome to duplicate the exercises as therapy homework handouts.

David Decides about Thumb-sucking, with photographs by Paula Singer, motivates young children to end thumb-sucking habits and guides parents on how to help.

Forthcoming: Co-authored with Naomi Grunditz, a book of client handouts for therapists who use the techniques in *Prescriptions Without Pills*.

ARTICLES
See TherapyHelp.com for articles on narcissism, terrorism, conflict resolution, and more.

AUDIO PROGRAMS
For therapists:
> *Working with Couples in Conflict*

For the general public and therapists:
> *Conflict Resolution for Couples*
> *Depression: A Disorder of Power*
> *Anxiety: Friend or Foe?*

VIDEOS
The Win-Win Waltz, a video with co-author Abigail Heitler Hirsch, Ph.D., teaches the skills couples need to be able to talk about sensitive subjects and deal with their differences without fighting. For couples, therapists, and marriage educators.

The Angry Couple: Conflict-Focused Treatment, a video available on psychotherapy.net, illustrates Dr. Heitler's therapy methods. Produced as part of a master therapist series, this video is utilized worldwide in marriage therapist training programs. Interesting for couples as well as for therapists.

The Angry Couple Manual (an ebook, available in online bookstores) summarizes the theory and techniques taught in the video.

ONLINE
Prescriptionswithoutpills.com augments the information in this book. Use the videos and worksheets there to help you implement the prescriptions in this book. Check often for updates and blogposts to add to your understandings.

TherapyHelp.com describes Dr. Heitler's clinical practice. It also serves as a gateway to her articles and her blog posts. To select posts on specific topics, use the topic index called "Dr. H's Blogposts."

PsychologyToday.com is where Dr. Heitler's blog *Resolution, Not Conflict* has received over seven million clicks. Dr. Heitler also blogs for GoodTherapy.org, for YourTango.com, and for HuffingtonPost.com.

PowerOfTwoMarriage.com offers a fun interactive online version of the *Power of Two* book and workbook. Check out the free trial of quizzes, videos, PDFs, and exercises to help you learn the skills for marriage success.

To sign up for Dr. Heitler's email list and to receive notices of her blogposts, please fill in the Contact Us form on prescriptionswithoutpills.com or therapyhelp.com.

Appendix B:

How to Choose a Therapist

While the prescriptions in this book primarily offer a do-it-yourself approach, for persisting emotional problems do consider getting professional help as well.

If you do decide that you would like to work with a psychotherapy professional, you could easily get overwhelmed by the alphabet soup of therapy modes: CBT, IPT, DBT, EMDR, etc. Fortunately, research on the efficacy of these various methods has concluded that, for the most part, virtually all of them work, most of the time. The bottom line is that when people feel distressed, those who avail themselves of help from a mental health professional of almost any type generally end up feeling better, and sooner, than those who do not.[80]

Interestingly, more than specific methods, what does predict therapy outcomes is the quality of the therapist. Therapy researcher Bruce Wampold writes the following:

> In clinical trials as well as in practice, some therapists consistently achieve better outcomes than others, regardless of the treatment approach used. For example, whether the therapist delivers cognitive behavioral treatment (CBT) or interpersonal psychotherapy (IPT) for depression matters not at all. On the other hand, some CBT therapists (in our study) were more effective than other CBT therapists, and some IPT therapists were more effective than other IPT therapists, even though the therapists in this clinical trial were all

experts, received training and supervision, and were required to adhere to the treatment manual.[81]

So how can you evaluate which therapy and therapist are likely to be a good fit for you? Here are five key research-based factors to keep in mind:

- **Mutual agreement** about the method. Ask your therapist to explain how the treatment you are receiving is supposed to help you.
- **Therapist activity level**. Therapists who ask good questions, offer useful information, and structure interventions such as visualizations get best results.
- **Accurate empathy.** Perceiving your therapist as attuned and accurately understanding you predicts positive therapy outcomes.
- **Apparent helpfulness**. The effectiveness of your particular therapist's approach is likely to be apparent within the first several sessions.[82]
- **Preservation of your family**. If you are married, explore couples therapy.

The bottom line? Pick a therapist. If the match doesn't feel right, pick again. If you are not feeling improvement soon, change therapists. Therapists are not parents. You are always free to leave and pick another.

Endnotes

1   J. A. Chiles, M. J. Lambert, and A. L. Hatch, "Medical Cost Offset: A Review of the Impact of Psychological Interventions on Medical Utilization over the Past Three Decades," in *The Impact of Medical Cost Offset on Practice and Research*, eds. N. A. Cummings, W. T. O'Donohue, and K. E. Ferguson (Reno: Context Press, 2002).

2   N. N. Jacobs, "Bibliotherapy Using CBT," in *General Principles and Empirically Supported Techniques of Cognitive Behavior Therapy*, eds. W. T. O'Donohue and J.E. Fisher (Hoboken: John Wiley & Sons, 2009), 158–165.

3   P. C. Gotzsche, "Why I Think Antidepressants Cause More Harm than Good," *Lancet Psychiatry* 1 (2014): 104–6.

4   "Recognition of Psychotherapy Effectiveness," *American Psychological Association*, August 2012, http://www.apa.org/about/policy/resolution-psychotherapy.aspx.

5   "Recognition of Psychotherapy Effectiveness," http://www.apa.org/about/policy/resolution-psychotherapy.aspx.

6   S. Hollon, M. Stewart, and D. Strunk, " Enduring Effects for Cognitive Behavior Therapy in the Treatment of Depression and Anxiety," *Annual Review of Psychology* 57 (2006): 285–315.

7   J. Kelley, "Antidepressants: Do They 'Work' or Don't They?" *Scientific American* (2010), http://www.scientificamerican.com/article/antidepressants-do-they-work-or-dont-they/.

8   C. Illiades, "7 Antidepressant Side Effects," *Everyday Health*, July 23 2015, http://www.everydayhealth.com/depression/drug-side-effects.aspx.

9   C. H. Warner, W. Bobo, C. Warner, S. Reid, and J. Rachal, "Antidepressant Discontinuation Syndrome," *American Family Physician* 74, no. 3 (2006):449-456.

10 Margarita Tartakovsky, "SSRI Discontinuation or Withdrawal Syndrome," *PsychCentral,* January 3, 2011, http://psychcentral.com/lib/ssri-discontinuation-or-withdrawal-syndrome/.

11 H. Ashton, "The Diagnosis and Treatment of Benzodiazepine Dependence," *Current Opinion in Psychiatry* (2005).

12 N. Byatt, K. M. Deligiannidis, and M. P. Freeman, "Antidepressant Use in Pregnancy: A Critical Review Focused on Risks and Controversies," *Acta Psychiatrica Scandinavica* 127, no. 2 (2012): 94–114, doi: 10.1111/acps.12042.

13 J. Reefhuis, O. Devine, J. M. Friedman, C. Louik, and M. A. Honein, on behalf of the National Birth Defects Prevention Study, "Specific SSRIs and Birth Defects: Bayesian Analysis to Interpret New Data in the Context of Previous Reports," *The BMJ* 351 (2015), http://dx.doi.org/10.1136/bmj.h3190: BMJ 2015;351:h3190.

14 P. Wehrwein, "Astounding Increase in Antidepressant Use by Americans," *Harvard Health Publications*, October 20, 2011, http://www.health.harvard.edu/blog/astounding-increase-in-antidepressant-use-by-americans-201110203624.

15 N. A. Shcharansky (Sharansky), *Fear No Evil* (New York: Random House, 1988).

16 T. Bernhard, *How to Wake Up: A Buddhist-inspired Guide to Navigating Joy and Sorrow* (Boston: Wisdom Publications, 2013).

17 S. Arieti, *American Handbook of Psychiatry*, 2nd ed. (New York: Basic Books, 1974).

18 Aaron T. Beck, A. John Rush, Brian F. Shaw, and Gary Emery, *Cognitive Therapy of Depression* (New York: The Guilford Press), p. 11.

19 M. E. P. Seligman, *"Learned Helplessness," Annual Review of Medicine 23, no. 1 (1972): 407–412,* doi:10.1146/annurev.me.23.020172.002203.

20 M. E. Seligman, L. Y. Abramson, A. Semmel, and Carl von Baeyer, "Depressive Attributional Style," *Journal of Abnormal Psychology* 88, no. 3 (1979): 242–247, http://dx.doi.org/10.1037/0021-843X.88.3.242.

21 J. K. Kiecolt-Glaser and R. Glaser, "Depression and Immune Function: Central Pathways to Morbidity and Mortality," *Journal of Psychosomatic Research* 53, no. 4 (2002): 873–876, http://dx.doi.org/10.1016/S0022-3999[02]00309-4. 2013]. 013): HEge of Cardiology, how Washington, DC and 1974 fit with this entry.]on? I could not verify online.]info was availa

22 E. Broadbent, K. Petrie, P. Alley, and R. Booth, "Psychological Stress Impairs Early Wound Repair Following Surgery," *Psychosomatic Medicine* 65, no. 5 (September/October 2003): 865–869.

23 L. Breuning, *Meet Your Happy Chemicals* (Oakland, CA: System Integrity Press, 2012).

24 J. Alpert and M. Alpert, "Music Influences on Mood and Purchase Intentions," *Psychology and Marketing Psychology* (2006): 109–133, DOI: 10.1002/mar.4220070204.

25 "Step 4: Resentment," March 1, 2015, *Big Book Step Study*, http://www.bigbookstepstudy.org/step-4/step-4-resentment/.

26 Brandi C. Fink and Alyson F. Shapiro, "Coping Mediates the Association between Marital Instability and Depression, but Not Marital Satisfaction and Depression," *Couple Family Psychology* 2, no. 1 (March 2013): 1–13, doi: 10.1037/a0031763.

27 Mikaela Conley, "New Study: Happy Wife, Happy Life," March 7, 2012, *ABC News*, http://abcnews.go.com/blogs/health/2012/03/07/new-study-happy-wife-happy-life/.

28 E. Kubler-Ross and D. Kessler, *On Grief and Grieving: Finding the Meaning of Grief through the Five Stages of Loss* (New York: Scribner, 2014, reprint edition).

29 E. Goldberg, *The Wisdom Paradox: How Your Mind Can Grow Stronger as Your Brain Grows Older* (New York: Gotham Books, 2005).

30 R. A. DiGiuseppe and R. C. Tafrate, *Understanding Anger Disorders* (Oxford: Oxford University Press, 2007).

31 S. Tagliareni, *Hitler's Priest* (Dallas: Brown Books Publishing Group, 2012).

32 K. Lawler-Row, J. Karremans, C. Scott, M. Edlis-Matityahou, and L. Edwards, "Forgiveness, Physiological Reactivity and Health: The Role of Anger," *International Journal of Psychophysiology* 68, no. 1 (April 2008): 51–58.

33 "Anger—How It Affects People," *Better Health Channel*, http://www. betterhealth.vic.gov.au/bhcv2/bhcarticles.nsf/pages/Anger_how_it_affects_ people.

34 D. Collins, "The Deadly Effects of Anger on Your Health and Mind," *Underground Health Reporter*, http://undergroundhealthreporter.com/ effects-of-anger-dangerous-to-health-and-mind/Rx ixzz3U0qQ2hMQ.

35 A. Park, "Are You a Type D Personality? Your Heart May Be at Risk," *Time*, Sept. 14, 2010, http://healthland.time.com/2010/09/14/a-new-risk-factor-for-heart-disease-type-d-personality/.

36 K. C. van den Broek, H. Versteeg, R. A. M. Erdman, and S. S. Pedersen, "The Distressed [Type D] Personality in Both Patients and Partners Enhances the Risk of Emotional Distress in Patients with an Implantable Cardioverter Defibrillator," *Journal of Affective Disorders* 130, no. 3 (May 2011): 447–453, http://dx.doi.org/10.1016/j.jad.2010.10.044.

37 J. Liao, *American Journal of Epidemiology* (October 22, 2014), quoted in K. Doyle, "Stressful Relationships Tied to Mental Decline," *Reuters*, November 19, 2014, http://www.reuters.com/article/2014/11/19/us-mental-decline-relationships-idUSKCN0J322N20141119.

38 R. Axelrod, *The Evolution of Cooperation* (New York: Basic Books, 1984).

39 S. Pappas, "How Mom and Dad's Fights Could Stunt Kids' Brains," *Live Science*, March 28, 2013, http://www.livescience.com/28284-marital-conflict-child-development.html.

40 L. Walker, *The Battered Woman* (New York: HarperCollins, 2009, reprint edition).

41 R. Fisher, and W. Ury, *Getting to Yes: Negotiating Agreement without Giving In,* 2nd ed. (New York: Penguin Books, 1991).

42 H. Ginott, *Between Parent and Child* (New York: Macmillan, 1961).

43 D. Kahneman, *Thinking, Fast and Slow* (New York: Farrar, Straus, & Giroux, 2013).

44 J. Feinstein, R. Adolphs, A. Damasio, and D. Tranel, "The Human Amygdala and the Induction and Experience of Fear," *Current Biology* 21, no. 1 (2011): 34–38, http://dx.doi.org/10.1016/j.cub.2010.11.042.

45 S. Heitler, PhD, *The Power of Two* (Oakland: New Harbinger Publications, 1997).

46 S. Diamond, *Anger, Madness, and the Daimonic: The Psychological Genesis of Violence, Evil, and Creativity* (New York: SUNY Press, 1996).

47 "Quotes about Moving On," *Goodreads*, http://www.goodreads.com/quotes/tag/moving-on.

48 Ibid.

49 S. Heitler, "Narcissism: A Redefinition and Case Study" (blog), *Therapy Help*, August 28, 2014, http://www.therapyhelp.com/blog/.

50 S. Heitler, "Borderline Personality Disorder: The Sufferer's Experience" (blog), *Psychology Today*, March 28, 2014, https://www.psychologytoday.com/blog/resolution-not-conflict/201403/borderline-personality-disorder-the-sufferers-experience.

51 T. Bernhard, *How to Wake Up*.

52 S. Heitler, "When Your Mother Has a Borderline Personality" (blog), *Psychology Today*, October 31, 2012, https://www.psychologytoday.com/blog/resolution-not-conflict/201210/when-your-mother-has-borderline-personality.

53 C. Streeter, T. Whitfield, L. Owen, T. Rein, S. Karri, A. Yakhkind, and J. Jensen, "Effects of Yoga Versus Walking on Mood, Anxiety, and Brain GABA Levels: A Randomized Controlled MRS Study," *Journal of Alternative and Complementary Medicine* 16, no. 11 (2010): 1145–1152.

54 J. A. Astin, "Stress Reduction through Mindfulness Meditation," *Psychotherapy and Psychosomatics* 66 (1997):97–106, doi:10.1159/000289116.

55 R. McCraty, B. Barrios-Choplin, M. Atkinson, and D. Tomasino, "The Effects of Different Types of Music on Mood, Tension and Mental Clarity," *Alternative Therapies in Health and Medicine* 4, no. 1 (1998): 75–84.

56 D. E. Bowler, L. M. Buyung-Ali, T. M. Knight, and A. S. Pullin, "A Systematic Review of Evidence for the Added Benefits to Health of Exposure to Natural Environments," *BMC Public Health*, 10 (2010): 456.

57 E. Largo-Wight, W. W. Chen, V. Dodd, and R. Weiler, "Healthy Workplaces: The Effects of Nature Contact at Work on Employee Stress and Health," *Public Health Reports* 126, suppl. 1 (2011): 124–130; T. Bringslimark, G. Patil, and T. Hartig, "The Association between Indoor Plants, Stress, Productivity and Sick Leave in Office Workers," *Acta Horticulturae* 775 (2008): 117–121, doi: 10.17660/ActaHortic.2008.775.13.

58 R. S. Ulrich, "View through a Window May Influence Recovery from Surgery," *Science,* 224 (April 27, 1984): 420–421.

59 S. Park and R. Mattson, R. "Ornamental Indoor Plants in Hospital Rooms Enhanced Health Outcomes of Patients Recovering from Surgery," *Journal of Alternative & Complementary Medicine* 15, no. 9 (2009): 975–980.

60 J. R. Lim, "How Hiking Leads to Happiness," *Men's Journal,* July 27, 2015, http://www.mensjournal.com/health-fitness/health/how-hiking-leads-to-happiness-20150727.

61 E. Stamatakis, "Screen-Based Entertainment Time, All-Cause Mortality, and Cardiovascular Events: Population-Based Study with Ongoing Mortality and Hospital Events Follow-Up," *Journal of the American College of Cardiology* 57, no. 3 (2011): 292–299.

62 A. Meyer-lindenberg, "Urban Living Raises the Risk of Emotional Disorders," *Scientific American Mind* 24 (2013): 1, http://www.scientificamerican.com/article/urban-living-raises-risk-of-emotional-disorders/.

63 D. Feinstein, "Acupoint Stimulation in Treating Psychological Disorders: Evidence of Efficacy," *Review of General Psychology* 16 (2012): 364–380, doi:10.1037/a0028602.

64 L. Breuning, *Meet Your Happy Chemicals.*

65 C. Nakken, *The Addictive Personality: Understanding the Addictive Process and Compulsive Behavior,* 2nd ed. (Center City, MN: Hazelden, 1996).

66 Y. S. Nikolova, A. R. Knodt, S. R. Radtke, and A. R. Hariri, "Divergent Responses of the Amygdala and Ventral Striatum Predict Stress-Related Problem Drinking in Young Adults: Possible Differential Markers of Affective and Impulsive Pathways of Risk for Alcohol Use Disorder," *Molecular Psychiatry,* June 30, 2015, https://today.duke.edu/2015/07/sexalcohol, doi:10.1038/mp.2015.85.

67 A. Sulovari, H. Kranzler, L. Farrer, J. Gelernter, and D. Li, "Eye Color: A Potential Indicator of Alcohol Dependence Risk in European Americans," *American Journal of Medical Genetics Part B: Neuropsychiatric Genetics* (2015): 347–353.

68 E. Goldson, unpublished manuscript, available from Dr. Goldson at Children's Hospital, Denver (1980).

69 G. C. Anderson, "Pacifiers: The Positive Side," *Maternal and Child Nursing*, March/April 1986, 122–124.

70 N. Eyal, *Hooked: How to Build Habit-Forming Products* (CreateSpace, 2013).

71 The White House Office of the National Drug Control Policy, "Teens Using Marijuana at Younger Ages," 2010, https://www.whitehouse.gov/ondcp/news-releases-remarks/teens-using-marijuana-at-younger-ages.

72 L. D. Johnston, P. M. O'Malley, R. A. Miech, J. G. Bachman, and J. E. Schulenberg, "Monitoring the Future National Results on Drug Use: 1975–2014: Overview, Key Findings on Adolescent Drug Use," Ann Arbor, MI: Institute for Social Research, The University of Michigan (2014).

73 L. Breuning, *Meet Your Happy Chemicals*.

74 G. Shahar, *Erosion: The Psychopathology of Self-Criticism* (London: Oxford University Press, 2015).

75 T. Ben-Shahar, *Choose the Life You Want* (New York: The Experiment, 2012).

76 Ibid., p. 124.

77 R. Fisher and W. Ury, *Getting to Yes*.

78 Wikipedia contributors, "Four Minute Mile," *Wikipedia, the Free Encyclopedia,* accessed 2015, http://en.wikipedia.org/wiki/Four-minute_mile.

79 D. Grove and B. I. Panzer, *Resolving Traumatic Memories: Metaphors and Symbols in Psychotherapy* (New York: Irvington Publishers, Inc., 1989).

80 L. F. Campbell, J. C. Norcross, M. J. T. Vasquez, and N. J. Kaslow, "Recognition of Psychotherapy Effectiveness: The APA Resolution," *Psychotherapy* 50 (2013): 98–101.